The $5 Dinner Mom
Breakfast and Lunch
Cookbook

The $5 Dinner Mom Breakfast and Lunch Cookbook

OVER 200 QUICK, DELICIOUS, AND NOURISHING

MEALS THAT ARE EASY ON THE BUDGET AND

A SNAP TO PREPARE

ERIN CHASE

ST. MARTIN'S GRIFFIN ⚜ NEW YORK

www.stmartins.com

Book design by Jessica Shatan Heslin/Studio Shatan, Inc.

ISBN 978-0-312-60734-0

First Edition: January 2011

10 9 8 7 6 5 4 3 2 1

To Grammy Goodman~
For sharing with me a love for cooking and
for teaching me the importance of connecting as a family
around the dinner table

CONTENTS

Acknowledgments ix

Introduction 1

PART I *Breakfast — At Home and On-the-Go 7*

ONE *Breakfast Cereals — Oatmeals, Granolas,
Rice Puddings, and More 29*

TWO *Egg Dishes — Frittatas, Breakfast Casseroles,
French Toast Bakes, and More 53*

THREE *Breakfast Breads — Waffles, Pancakes,
Muffins, and More 85*

FOUR *Breakfast Tacos and Breakfast Sandwiches 126*

PART II *Lunches — At Home and On-the-Go 137*

FIVE *Sandwiches, Wraps, Quesadillas, and More 157*

SIX *Soups and Other Hot Lunches 198*

SEVEN *Pasta Salads and Garden Salads 219*

EIGHT *Side Salads and Side Dishes for Lunch 241*

PART III *Snacks — Tasty Between-Meal Treats that Fill You Up and Keep You on Your Budget* 257

NINE *Morning, Afternoon, and Midnight Snack Recipes* 265

Afterword: A Practical Look — Putting It All Together 299

Appendix A: Pantry Staples List 303

Appendix B: Essential Kitchen Gadgets 310

Appendix C: Online Resources 312

Index 314

ACKNOWLEDGMENTS

To my dearest family and friends, thanks for the encouragement as I worked these past few months on getting this book together. I am so appreciative of all the cheerful words and kind deeds!

I am forever grateful to Mary Sanford and Stephanie O'Dea for seeing the cookbook potential of $5 Dinners, for connecting me with the right people and pushing me towards pursuing this dream. To Stephanie, thanks for your guidance and listening ear these past few years. It's wonderful to have you as a friend.

To the $5 Dinner Mom's team at St. Martin's Press, I continue to be amazed at your dedication and passion for helping me share this concept with so many people. I am so grateful for your hard work and enthusiasm for this book. And to my editor, Michael Flamini, for talking sense into my ear when I needed it and for being committed to the ideal of helping others eat well without spending more.

Finally, to my supportive and loving husband Steve. I could not have accomplished so much without your support and passion for my work. I appreciate all the feedback and your honest critiques of my recipe creations. And to my three adorable little men, for being the taste-testers for all the other little people out there. Thanks for trying all sorts of foods and for letting me know, in a not so subtle way, whether or not you approve or disapprove of the meal. I love each of you boys dearly.

INTRODUCTION

Is it really possible to feed a family of four for just $5 . . . for the entire dinner meal? What about the costs of breakfast and lunch too? Can I make an entire family breakfast for less than $2 or even a dollar? And lunch for $3 to 4, is that really feasible? Could I pull off a $10 per day food budget, even after tossing snacks into the mix?

In the summer of 2008 and in the midst of the $4 per gallon gasoline crisis, I set out to spend less of my husband's hard-earned money and keep our family out of debt. Being a stay at home mom, I was limited in what I could do to contribute to the family income. It didn't take me long to figure out that I could "contribute" by spending less of our income at the grocery store.

I needed a challenge. I needed a goal. I needed some accountability. My goal came to me in a lightbulb moment while doing the dishes one hot August evening in 2008. I would make dinner meals for my young family of four for just $5. Total. For the entire meal.

Shortly after beginning my quest to make $5 Dinners every night, I found that I could make breakfasts for as little as a buck, and lunches for $3 to 4 for the entire family. And we're not talking mac 'n cheese with hot dogs for lunch every day either. We're talking wholesome, hearty meals and snacks; meals that will give your family the energy and the fuel they need to not only get going in the morning, but to keep going all day long.

As I started this great adventure of spending less money at the grocery store, I really thought I'd only be able to come up with a month's worth of meals. But I was wrong and have found so much joy in feeding my family creative meals, without spending a fortune. Let's revisit the strategies for shopping, couponing, and meal planning from *The $5 Dinner Mom Cookbook,* and how they can bring down the costs for all the meals in each day.

Strategic Grocery Shopping

- Avoiding Temptations and Spending Pits in the Grocery Store. Do not succumb to the marketing strategies of the stores and the manufacturers to get you to buy their products at top dollar. We are after rock-bottom prices!

- Using the Store Circulars To Make Your Grocery List. Look at the store circulars *before* you go into the store and make your grocery list based on all the products listed on sale.

- Ditching the Plastic and Use Only Cold, Hard Cash at the Checkout. Cash, cash, cash is key to staying within your budget. After all, you can't show up at the checkout with $84 worth of products and $80 in cash. $4 worth has to go back on the shelves.

- Landing on that Magic Grocery Store Budget Number. Track your grocery spending and come up with that magical dollar amount that works for your family. The number should be a challenge to reach each week, but still a reasonable amount to get the products and ingredients you need each week.

Strategic Couponing

- Stockpiling. By making it a habit to use coupons only when the product is on sale, you'll be able to build a nice stockpile of foods for your pantry and freezer while spending as little money as possible. The goal of paying the rock-bottom price for products by matching a coupon with a sale price can even score you a free lunch.

    1. Whoever said there was no such thing as a FREE LUNCH. We all know the expression well. *"There's no such thing as a free lunch."*

        Well, there might . . . there *just* might be such a thing as a free lunch—or at least a nearly free lunch. With some clever combinations from free ingredients, you might just be able to come up with a free lunch.

        Here is a quick example of a nearly free lunch based on ingredients that I regularly get for free by combining sale prices with coupons. Products purchased for free, with sale price and coupon included: 6 ounce cans of tuna, an 8-ounce container of cottage cheese, a name-brand sandwich bread loaf, small container of mayonnaise, and canned fruit in juice—lunch Tuna Salad Sandwiches with a side of cottage cheese and canned fruit.

        With the power of coupons, combined with sale prices, it is possible to have a free lunch!

    2. "Never-pay-more-than-" prices for Fresh Meats and Produce. In the Frugal Fact notes following each recipe, I'll share with you some examples of my "never-pay-more-than" prices for common ingredients used in breakfast, lunches, and snacks.

- Coupon Organization. Keeping those coupons organized is essential to maximizing your savings and spending as little as possible on your favorite products each week. Remember, coupons are "free money."

Strategic Meal Planning

- Benefits. Having a meal plan each week will keep you out of the drive-through line and out of debt, too.

- Phases of Meal Planning. Meal planning happens in three phases, from beginner to professional, depending on how long you have been meal planning and whether or not you plan on a weekly or monthly basis, and whether you plan your meals and then shop, or shop from the store's circular and then plan your meals around what you have on hand.

- Batch Cooking. An essential to being prepared when it comes to breakfasts and lunches is the concept of batch cooking. It's not a day you set aside to prepare all the food for the month, but it's the concept that you make extra of whatever is on the stove or in the oven. And that while you have the oven on, you might as well make some muffins or an egg casserole for the following day's breakfast or to stash in the freezer for when you need a quick on-the-go breakfast or snack. There will be more discussion on batch cooking in upcoming chapters.

- Leftovers. Having a plan for those dinner leftovers is essential, especially since many times lunch is when leftovers are eaten. With just one ingredient mix-in and some reheating, leftovers can easily be repurposed and enjoyed a second time.

Over the past few years, I have found that it is possible to save even more on the commonly used ingredients for breakfasts and lunches, like bread, tortillas, rolled oats, cold cereal, eggs, deli meats, etc. using coupons and having a meal plan in place based on the store's sale for the week.

In this cookbook, I will teach you more money- and time-saving tips to get your family the food they need to fuel their busy lives. In today's fast-paced society, it's difficult to slow down and get your act together for the week. But if you don't, you'll find yourself wasting all sorts of time and energy later in the week. I'll help you see the importance of taking an hour or two at some point during the week to prepare some snacks or get your lunches ready for the week.

If you choose not to use that one hour of prep time, let me quickly show you how else you could use up the minutes in that "getting-food-ready" hour.

- Monday: 14 minutes waiting in the drive-through at 12:30 A.M. for lunch (I see plenty of drive-through lines wrapped once or twice around the building at lunch time!)

- Tuesday: 4 minutes on the phone complaining to a friend about how you don't have any time to make breakfast or lunch for your family

- Wednesday: 7 minutes waiting in line at Starbucks

- Thursday: 11 minutes complaining and arguing with your spouse about how you don't have time to do anything, and how you are spending too much money, or about how many times you found yourself in the drive-through line so far that week

- Friday: 6 minutes to gather dinner requests and to call in a take-out order, followed by a 10 minute round-trip drive to the restaurant and 5 minutes waiting for your order to be ready (And in those 20 minutes, you could have made a simple dinner and started a batch of muffins or assembled an egg casserole)

- Saturday: 3 minutes opening and closing the refrigerator hoping a delicious lunch will magically appear!

Time's up. There's your hour! Let's use those precious minutes to make some healthy, hearty food instead of waiting in line, arguing and complaining, and sitting at the curb waiting for your food.

Whether you eat most meals at home or you are on-the-go from the wee hours of the morning, I've got some meal and snack ideas that are sure to fit into your busy life. With a little planning ahead and an hour of food preparation time each week, you won't find yourself frustrated over the money spent at the drive-through, or the time you spent arguing with your spouse.

Also, included in this cookbook are over 200 recipes, complete with cost breakdowns and frugal facts. Please note these recipes are written for a family with 2 adults and 2 children, but most of the recipes will feed 4 adults. Larger families and/or families with teenagers will need to double or triple the recipes, depending on family size and the number of bottomless stomach pits at the table.

The prices associated with each ingredient are more or less standard throughout the book. Some prices may vary, especially on fresh produce or fresh meats, as produce prices fluctuate widely throughout the seasons. Prices are accurate and reflect the lowest sale prices that I paid for the products, during the years 2009 and early 2010. Living in the Midwest, I find that prices tend to be lower than other parts of the country. Please do not expect to find these exact same prices in your stores. However, I will teach you what to look for and how to find the rock-bottom prices on your favorite products from the grocery stores in your area.

The $5 Dinner Mom's Recipe for Being Successful with Breakfast and Lunch Preparation

- 1 cup shopping strategies

- 1 cup couponing strategies

- 2 cups meal-planning strategies

- 1 tablespoon self-discipline to prepare for your shopping trip

- 1 tablespoon self-control when in the grocery store

- 1 hour batch-cooking prep time per week

This recipe has helped get our food budget under control, while keeping our tummies full and happy.

I hope you catch on to my vision and the method to my madness. Let's make it a priority to feed your family healthy, well-balanced meals for less!

PART I

Breakfast—
At Home and On-the-Go

Snooze button. Snooze button. Yawn. Stretch. Yawn. Pull the covers back up. Yawn.

The alarm didn't go off in time, or the snooze button was more irresistible than on most other mornings. Perhaps the baby woke up four times with teething pain, or the potty-training toddler woke up in a puddle at 2 A.M. Or maybe you were up late worrying about the whereabouts of your teenager who recently got his driver's license. How do you start the day with a hearty, nutritious, and balanced breakfast when you are always running out the door in a frenzy?

It would certainly be easier to just forget about breakfast entirely and rush out the door to work or school. But breakfast is a necessity. *Don't skip breakfast. You'll wish you'd slowed down at least for a bowl of cereal.* That's your mother's voice in the back of your head.

But you are running so fast out the door that you risk leaving behind the jump drive that holds the files for your quarterly presentation, or the paperwork you need to have the doctor sign for your child's school enrollment. You don't even have a second to think about breakfast, much less make it. But you'll think again when the hunger pangs hit as soon as you get to the doctor's waiting room or the conference room where you'll give your presentation.

If I had just grabbed a muffin or two from the freezer . . . That's your inner voice talking this time. *I just wish I hadn't hit the snooze button that last time.*

Morning Routines

Because our sleep is cut short for many different reasons and we often find ourselves running around like headless chickens, it's crucial to have a solid morning routine, a plan for breakfast, and at least be prepared with some "grab-and-go" homemade convenience foods in the freezer.

The furthest thing from my mind when I wake for a peaceful slumber: making breakfast. My brain cannot put together a coherent thought in the early morning, much less think about what we'll be having for breakfast. If I had to pull a breakfast plan through the cobwebs of my sleepy brain at 7 A.M., we would never eat breakfast.

Morning routines look different for each of us. There are working families, in which both mom and dad work and the kids go to school or day care. And there are families with one parent going to work and another staying home to care for the children. And there are others in which one or both parents work from home. It doesn't matter what the situation, what time you have to get out of bed, what time you have to get out the door, or what day of the week it is, you *must* have a plan and a routine for each morning that includes a hearty, nutritious breakfast that will jump-start your day.

For those families with both parents working or with an early bus pick-up time for school, plan to alternate a quick bowl of cereal with an "on-the-go breakfast" during the weekday. Even if it means bites in between helping tie the kids' shoes or wrap their scarves around their necks on a brisk morning. You'll be glad you took those few seconds during shoelace duty to fill your tummy, especially when you get to your client meeting or when you sit down at your desk and start on the daunting task of responding to the overnight e-mails.

For the families with a stay-at-home parent and little ones (who don't get on the bus at the crack of dawn) don't forget to eat, yourself. It's all too easy to fix their breakfast, clean up the dishes, then feed the baby while wiping off the counters and get started on the day. By 10 A.M., the hunger pangs hit and oops, you forgot breakfast again. (I am speaking from personal experience here.) Slow down for just a few minutes and you might be able to eat breakfast as a family, to connect and talk about what you'll be facing that day. That might not be as far-fetched as you might think. Try it one week and see if it makes a difference!

Morning People versus Night Owls

Once upon a time I was a morning person. I used to be able to put a coherent thought together at 6 A.M. I was chipper in the morning and could open the fridge and figure out what to make for breakfast. *Then I had kids, and turned into a night owl!*

If you enjoy being up early in the morning, put an egg casserole (which you assembled during last night's dinner prep and let sit in the refrigerator overnight) into the oven and then go about your morning routine. If time allows, make some muffins and serve them warm out of the oven to your family. (And if there are any leftovers, could you bring them by my house on your way to work or school?!)

For my fellow night owls, bake a batch or two of muffins in the evening while you are enjoying a bowl of ice cream, or your favorite reality TV show. Here's what it looks like (not that I do this every week):

- Commercial break #1: Preheat the oven and pull out the ingredients from the fridge or cabinet, and prepare the muffin tin.

- Commercial break #2: Make the muffin batter.

- Commercial break #3: Finish the batter and pour into the muffin tin and put in the oven. Set the timer. Put away the baking ingredients.

- Commercial break #4, or Whenever the Timer Goes off: Check the goodies and pull them out to cool down.

- End of the Show: Put the cooled muffins into plastic storage bags and place in the freezer.

- Clean-up the kitchen.

While it's certainly easier to space out during your favorite TV episodes and sit on the couch the entire time, reality is that you have a family to feed and if you're going to a start each day out with a wholesome, hearty breakfast, you've got to do a little work. So you might as well squeeze it in during the commercial breaks. If you were to peek in my living room window, you'd likely see me folding laundry while a show was on and running in and out of the kitchen during the commercial breaks. Such is the life of a busy mom who wants to feed her family wholesome, healthy meals!

Can I be so bold as to suggest that hearty breakfasts be mandatory? If you want to give your body the right fuel it needs to start the day, then yes, having a plan and a routine are not optional. Listen to the voice in your mother's head and start to figure out the best way to squeeze a hearty, balanced breakfast into your busy morning routine. Setting up a weekday breakfast routine is essential for reducing frustration during the morning rush.

Weekend Breakfasts

For the slower, leisurely weekend breakfasts, take the time to enjoy them as a family. Unless you have 8 A.M. soccer games on Saturday mornings, take the time to try a new recipe or have the kids help make the waffle batter. And while you're at it, make a few extra breakfast tacos or breakfast sandwiches for the freezer. Bake an extra batch of muffins while you have the oven on, or whip up more waffle batter and make them when you're cleaning up from your unrushed weekend breakfast. You'll be glad to have those muffins or egg-wiches in the freezer on Wednesday morning when you're flying out the front door, at what feels like the speed of light.

Meal Planning

Now that we've settled on the fact that having a breakfast plan in place is vital to having a successful morning routine and saving what few shreds of sanity you may have left, let's talk about some options and meal plans.

THE "DAYS OF THE WEEK" BREAKFAST PLAN

Give each day of the week a general breakfast type, and then vary by week what you actually have for breakfast.

- Monday: Scrambled Eggs Day

- Tuesday: Cold Cereal Day

- Wednesday: Pancakes Day

- Thursday: Hot Cereal Day

- Friday: Muffins/Biscuit Day

- Saturday: Omelet Day

- Sunday: Pancakes/Waffles Day

On Scrambled Eggs Day, mix it up and make the Sausage, Egg, and Cheese Breakfast Tacos (page 128). Or try a new pancake batter and make the Ginger Maple Pancakes (page 96) on Wednesday. Try the Pumpkin Spice Oatmeal (page 32) or Vanilla Brown Rice Pudding (page 47) on Thursday for Hot Cereal Day, using leftover brown rice from dinner.

This will keep the breakfast routine interesting, and the kids (or your spouse) from complaining about having the "same old thing" every morning.

THE "GRAB-AND-GO" BREAKFAST PLAN

This type of plan works well for families with multiple members rushing out the door at different times of the morning.

- Monday: Southwest Sausage Muffins (page 112)

- Tuesday: Homemade Instant Oatmeal Packets (page 37)

- Wednesday: Bacon, Egg, and Cheese Bagel Melts (page 136)

- Thursday: Slow Cooker "Cran-ola" (page 44)

- Friday: Raspberry Cereal Bars (page 50)

- Saturday: Raspberry French Toast (page 70)

- Sunday: Sour Cream and Chive Drop Biscuits (page 103)

Each of the above foods is freezer-friendly. Keep a variety of homemade frozen convenience foods, and then set out the ones you'll need in the refrigerator the night before. And if you forget, you can always pop them in the microwave or toaster oven to thaw. The entire family can all enjoy a breakfast treat, even if you can't slow down long enough to sit at the table to eat together.

THE "NO-COLD-CEREAL CHALLENGE WEEK" BREAKFAST PLAN

Skip the cereal aisle and spend one week exploring other breakfast foods and get out of the cold cereal rut!

- Monday: Huevos Rancheros (page 54)

- Tuesday: Hawaiian Ham-wiches (page 135)

- Wednesday: Eggs in a Nest with Avocado Circle Sandwiches (page 83)

- Thursday: Maple Pecan Oatmeal (page 37)

- Friday: Whole Wheat Apple Waffles (page 89)

- Saturday: Berry Breakfast Bread Pudding (page 59)

- Sunday: Zucchini-Tomato Frittata (page 64)

Cereal boxes can be expensive; especially if you have a child (specifically, a teenage boy) who can eat an entire box at one sitting. Planning a "No Cold Cereal Challenge Week" is also perfect for when your boxed cereal stockpile dwindles, or while you wait for the next sale on your favorite cereals.

A quick note about cereal prices . . . my "never-pay-more-than" price for a medium-size box of cereal (14 to 18 ounces) is $1. For specialty cereals, organic cereals, and gluten-free cereals, my "never-pay-more-than" price is $2.

THE "EAT-AT-HOME" BREAKFAST PLAN

This plan would work well for those early morning risers who don't have to rush out the door and can bake or cook something on the stovetop in the mornings.

- Monday: Baked Oatmeal with Pecans (page 39). Prep the night before, bake in the morning.

- Tuesday: Sausage, Apple, and Egg Casserole (page 72). Prep the night before, bake in the morning.

- Wednesday: Baked Apple Brown Rice Pudding (page 48). Use leftover brown rice from the night before.

- Thursday: Baked Walnut French Toast (page 71). Prep the night before, bake in the morning.

- Friday: Bacon-Spinach Frittata (page 65)

- Saturday: Spinach and Swiss Omelet (page 80)

- Sunday: Chocolate Chip Raspberry Pancakes (page 97). Double up and make a batch for the freezer.

With one of these plans and all the right ingredients, actually preparing breakfast doesn't have to be a chore. Work in the time necessary each morning to scramble or assemble or thaw or microwave or toast your favorite goodies and you'll be having the hearty breakfast that you and your family need and deserve. And once you have the routine in place, the kids won't be guessing what's for breakfast, and hopefully won't be complaining either. I get very few complaints from the little people sitting at the breakfast table with the structure and predictability that comes from having a breakfast meal plan in place.

Breakfast Ingredients

Whether you are grabbing muffins from the freezer or going to whip up an omelet for a weekend breakfast, you'll want to have the right ingredients on hand to make your favorite breakfast.

Have these ingredients on hand, and the breakfast possibilities are endless:

- Eggs

- Bacon: turkey or pork

- Sausage: pork or chorizo

- Shredded cheese

- Tortillas, bagels, English muffins, breads

- Rolled oats: quick-cooking and old-fashioned; steel cut

- Baking ingredients: flours, baking powder and baking soda, sugars, spices, milk

- Baking nuts and dried fruits

- Butter, jam, or jelly; syrups

- Vegetables; zucchini, tomatoes, onions

- Variety of fresh fruits

For even more essential ingredients to have in your pantry, visit the complete Pantry Staples List in Appendix A (page 303).

Coffee

We've all heard about "The Latte Factor," and how much money we could earn if we invested that $3 to $4 a day spent on the necessary stimulants to get us going. But that doesn't help the fact that we (and I mean you, because I don't drink coffee often) still NEED our (your) coffee. If you must have coffee before you can start your day, invest in getting the supplies and machines you need to become your own barista! Invest in your coffee.

Let's do a quick cost analysis, shall we?

For one $3.45 Grande Nonfat Latte:

- Weekly Cost $24.15

- Monthly Cost $96.60

- Yearly Cost $1,255.80

For a simple espresso machine and for the coffee and milk:

- Espresso Machine $100, one-time cost

- Coffee and Supplies $20 per month

Looking at these figures we can see that the espresso machine will pay for itself in just over one month. So if you must have a latte to jump-start your brain each morning, then buy a simple espresso machine and learn to make them yourself. While the convenience of a drive-through Starbucks is a nice treat every now and then, the wise way to budget for your regular morning coffee, latte, or frappuccino is to make it yourself. It's a worthy investment that will help keep the caffeine flowing without burning a hole in your pocketbook, or your retirement fund.

When it comes to buying coffee from the store, the different coffee manufacturers regularly release coupons for their products, including coffee beans, ground coffee, and all the coffee flavorings and accessories. Use those coupons with sale prices to get the most java for your dollar.

Buy coffee in bulk, or buy the whole beans and grind them yourself. And, dare I say it, don't be brand-particular. But if you must be brand-specific, at least stock up when it's on special.

Now go grab a cup of coffee and snuggle up. It's time to learn the ins and outs of batch cooking.

Batch Cooking and Stocking your Freezer

So I keep talking about grabbing something from the freezer. I'm not referring to boxed waffles or breakfast sandwiches from the freezer section of the grocery store. I'm talking about Pumpkin Nut Muffins (page 116), Ginger Maple Pancakes (page 96), Pumpkin Chocolate Chip Waffles (page 90), or Hawaiian Ham-wiches (page 135), which you have made from scratch during a weekly prep hour, or the night before while you were making dinner.

Batch cooking is making your own convenience foods. The key is that you get to eat the foods you love without the additives and preservatives often found in frozen convenience foods.

Batch cooking can be structured or unstructured. It can be an hour that you set aside and devote only to making breakfast or lunch goodies for the freezer. It can be 10 minutes here and there when you prepare the food while you are already making other meals in the kitchen. It can be when you double the recipe for a favorite meal and stash the uneaten portion in the freezer for lunch the following week. It can set up so that you double every dinner that week and you end up with several meals worth in the freezer, to eat the rest of the month. The purpose of batch cooking is to maximize your time and efficiency in the kitchen, cooking your favorite foods from scratch, without the burden of cooking for an entire day.

I typically add a list of the food and ingredients that I need to batch cook each week to my weekly meal plan. This keeps my freezer stocked with homemade convenience foods, and also helps me stay on budget.

Money-Saving Benefits of Batch Cooking

The cost-savings benefits of batch cooking are twofold. Not only will you save money because you are not paying more for either convenience food or fast food, but the savings are multiplied when you make your plan for what you'd like to batch cook around the different sale prices, and use coupons for the different ingredients you'll need.

For example, when you see milk marked down on special, grab that reduced-price carton and come home and whip up a few batches of waffles or biscuits. Waffle and biscuit recipes generally call for at least a cup or two of milk, and by making a few batches, you'll be able to use up that "reduced-for-quick-sale" milk before it goes bad, and stock your freezer in the meantime. Kills two birds with one stone!

This also works for all-natural sausage. With the right coupon matchup and sale price, packages of pork and turkey bacon, and a 1-pound roll of sausage can be purchased for as little as $1.49 to $1.99. When I see these prices, I grab two or three packages and then use them up that week in some batch cooking. I will brown the entire pound of sausage and then make some Southwest Sausage Muffins (page 112) using half of the sausage, and then Cheesy Sausage Muffins (page 113) with the other half pound. With the next roll, I'll slice and cook the sausage for the Sausage Eggwiches (page 134) and use the last pound of sausage to make Sausage, Egg, and Cheese Breakfast Tacos (page 128). Same concept applies to a package of bacon that's on sale or has a coupon matchup.

Perhaps you have a few high-value coupons for tortillas, and you end up buying 4 packages of 20 soft, taco-size tortillas, or 4 packages of 10 burrito-size tortillas. The best way to batch cook those tortillas is to prepare a few meals worth of breakfast tacos. They can be frozen in "individual" bags with 2 tacos each, or in "family" bags with 6 or 8 tacos. I prefer to wrap the tacos in aluminum foil and then place them into the plastic freezer bags. I have found that breakfast tacos reheat best in the oven. Let them thaw in the refrigerator overnight, then place the foil-wrapped breakfast tacos in the oven for a few minutes to reheat in the morning.

By taking advantages of store circulars and making your batch-cooking plan around the sales of your favorite ingredients, batch cooking will not only save you time later in the week, but lots of "green" as well.

Make-Ahead Mixes

When it comes to batch cooking and batch baking, another option for streamlining the overall process and spending less time in the kitchen is to make up mixes of the dry ingredients from your favorite baked goods recipes. If you like to enjoy your muffins or pancakes fresh from the oven or griddle each morning, then preparing your baking mixes ahead of time will help you save time in the kitchen because you won't have to get the baking ingredients and measuring cups out every time you want to bake some goodies.

MAKE-AHEAD BAKING MIXES

The process is simple. Place all the baking ingredients, like all-purpose flour, whole wheat flour, granulated and/or brown sugar, baking soda, baking powder, salt, and any other dry ingredients the recipe may call for and set up an assembly line. Line up a few large plastic ziplock bags and add the correct amount of each ingredient to each bag. Once all the dry ingredients are in the bag, seal and mix together. Then, label each bag with the name of each recipe, the wet ingredients that each mix will need to prepare the batter, and the baking temperature and time.

Once the mix has been used, the plastic bags can be rinsed and reused when they are completely dry. To effectively dry a plastic bag, turn it inside out and press it against a smooth wall upside down. The wetness will help the bag stick to the wall, and the moisture can drop out of the bag. When completely dry, reuse the plastic bag for the same baking mix. The baking mixes should be stored in a cool, dry place or in the freezer. Make-ahead baking mixes work well for pancakes, waffles, loaf breads, muffins, and biscuit recipes.

Every so often I'll come across a fantastic deal on an essential baking ingredient. Two times in early 2010, I purchased a 5-pound bag of a name-brand flour for just $.49 using a high-value coupon. As soon as I finished unloading the groceries from that shopping trip, I got out my plastic bags, set up the make-ahead mixes assembly line, and put that $.49 flour to work. At just $.03 per cup of flour, we enjoyed some pretty inexpensive pancakes and waffles for over a month.

MAKE-AHEAD OATMEAL PACKETS

This same concept of make-ahead baking mixes can also be applied to oatmeal mixes. Make-ahead oatmeal packets can be made for individuals or for the whole family.

For the individual packets, use a snack-size plastic bags or a ziplock sandwich bag. For family packets, use a quart-size ziplock plastic bag. Set up the assembly line, just as you would for the make-ahead baking mixes, and start adding the ingredients.

In just 5 minutes, you can have at least 2 weeks' worth of oatmeal packets made, or even more if you have a helper working alongside you. Also, be sure to label each bag with how much liquid will be needed to make the oatmeal. Make-Ahead Oatmeal Packets can be stored in a cool, dry place or in the freezer.

Every so often, with the right sale price and the right coupon, a smaller container of oats will come up free. Rather than let the container sit on the back of the shelf (because you're not up for measuring and reading recipes while it's still dark outside), set up an assembly line and get some oatmeal packets made.

Being the not-so-chipper-in-the-morning person that I am, the idea of being able to drop a homemade oatmeal mix into a saucepan, or even straight into a bowl with boiling water . . . it just makes me giddy. Not having to think and measure and actually pay attention in the morning is my ideal way to prepare breakfast. Dump, and stir . . . works for me!

Recipes for Make-Ahead Oatmeal Packets can be found on page 37.

Batch Cooking Single Ingredients for the Freezer

I don't know about your family, but ours does not need an entire package of bacon for one meal. When the boys are teenagers that might be another story, but for now we only use a third or a half of a package of bacon. The easy thing to do would be to toss the uncooked bacon back into the refrigerator. But chances are, I'll forget about it and by the time I'm ready to make bacon again for another meal, it will have gone bad. Since letting food go to waste makes me cringe, I just cook it all at once while I have the package out on the counter and don't let it go to waste.

Bacon can be batch cooked, and the cooked slices or crumbled bacon can be frozen to use for future meals. To quickly batch cook bacon, place a piece of aluminum foil on a rimmed baking sheet and lay the bacon slices on the foil, with no overlapping. Bake the bacon at 350 degrees for about 20 minutes. The cooking time may vary depending on the thickness of the bacon piece. Place the cooked bacon on paper towels to drain excess fat. Crumble or place the whole slices into a plastic freezer bag or freezer container. Another "no-mess" way to cook bacon is to place 4 to 6 slices on a microwave-safe plate lined with 2 paper towels. Cover with another paper towel. Microwave on high for 3 to 5 minutes, or until crisp.

Also, an entire roll of sausage can be browned in crumbles, or cooked in slices and then frozen. An entire package of sausage links can be cooked, and what is not eaten for breakfast that morning can be frozen for a future breakfast. The cooked sausage patties could also be used for breakfast sandwiches and breakfast tacos, and then frozen all together as a homemade breakfast sandwich.

Freezer-friendly Foods

I wanted to include a list of freezer-friendly breakfast foods, along with a few methods for freezing and thawing your breakfasts.

The following foods do well in the freezer: muffins, pancakes, waffles, biscuits, raw and cooked bacon, raw and cooked sausages, shredded cheese, tortillas, breads for casseroles, as well as bagels, English muffins, and sandwich bread.

Eggs and milk are both ingredients that can be frozen "raw," but I don't recommend it. Purchasing them at the store each week, rather than trying to stockpile them, is the best way to use milk and eggs. Of course, you can buy extra cartons when on sale and use to make waffles, biscuits, or pancakes for a baking day, as I mentioned above.

Quick freezing is a method used for freezing fresh fruit and cookie or biscuit dough. It can also be used to freeze other foods like gnocchi, pesto sauce, and dumplings. To quick freeze fruit, cut the fruit away from the pit and peel off the skin, if necessary. Place the cut fruit onto a piece of wax paper on a rimmed baking sheet. Place the baking sheet in the freezer for 10 to 15 minutes, then transfer the fruit to a space saving plastic freezer bag. If you forget about the fruit on the baking sheet, that's okay. Simply transfer the frozen fruit into the freezer bag when you remember. By quick-freezing the fruit, individual pieces will not stick to each other in the plastic bag and you will be able to easily remove what fruit you need for smoothies or baking. I recommend using frozen fresh fruit for smoothies and for baking because most fruits will lose their same texture and crunch after thawing.

When it comes to quick freezing cookie and biscuit dough, simply prepare the dough as directed in the recipe, and then scoop it out onto the rimmed baking sheet. Because you won't be baking the dough, you can place the dough balls close to, but not touching each other. Just as with the fruit, place the baking sheet in the freezer for 10 to 15 minutes, then transfer the dough balls to a space-saving plastic freezer bag. Use a straw to suck out any air, and place the bag with the dough balls back into the freezer.

To bake the dough balls from frozen, add 2 to 3 extra minutes to the baking time called for in the recipe for the biscuits, cookies, etc. If you prefer to bake them according to the recipe, place the frozen dough onto the prepared baking sheet and let it thaw to room temperature before baking.

Remember to clearly mark all freezer bags or containers before you put them in the freezer. If you forget and try to add tape or a label to the container after it is frozen, it won't stick. (Not that I speak from personal experience here!)

Sample Batch Cooking Plans

You might be thinking . . . *Well this all sounds good on paper, but what does it actually look like in the kitchen?* Below you will find a few different sample, batch-cooking plans for what you could get accomplished in a 1-hour cooking prep session for breakfast foods, or while you are already in the kitchen working on dinner. Each of these plans below will require 2 oven racks.

ONE-HOUR PREP: PLAN A

1. Preheat the oven and prepare the batter for Lemon Coconut Mini Loaves (page 284), and begin baking—10 minutes prep, 20 to 25 minutes baking.

2. Batch cook bacon in the oven (page 20)—5 minutes prep, 20 minutes baking.

3. Prepare Make-ahead Baking Mixes for Apple Cinnamon Pancakes (page 93), Banana Nut Waffles (page 88), and Cranberry-Raisin Loaf Bread

(page 105) while muffins and bacon are in the oven—10 minutes to make, seal, mix, and store bags

4. Remove muffins and bacon from the oven and let cool. Pat the bacon slices dry—5 minutes.

5. Scramble 8 to 10 eggs and get out the other breakfast taco ingredients—10 minutes.

6. Chop fruits for the freezer and/or veggies for wraps, salads or pasta salads, slice tomato for sandwiches—while the eggs are scrambling plus 5 minutes.

7. Assemble Salsa Breakfast Tacos (page 129) and place in freezer bags; 5 minutes.

8. Clean up and put all the food into the freezer—5 minutes.

End Results: Lemon Coconut Mini Loaves, Cooked Bacon, Make-Ahead Mixes for Apple Cinnamon Pancakes, Banana Nut Waffles, and Cranberry-Raisin Loaf Bread, Salsa Breakfast Tacos, Chopped Fruit and Veggies for the week's breakfast, lunches, or smoothies

ONE-HOUR PREP: PLAN B

1. Brown a pound of all-natural sausage—10 minutes.

2. Preheat the oven and prepare the batter for a double batch of Southwest Sausage Muffins (page 112)—while sausage is browning.

3. Finish the muffins and begin baking—5 minutes, 20 to 25 minutes baking.

4. Slice a pound of all-natural sausage and brown the patties in the same skillet—10 minutes.

5. Get out the ingredients and label bags for Make-ahead Oatmeal Mixes (page 37) while the sausage patties are cooking.

6. Assemble the Make-ahead Oatmeal Mixes and set the sausage patties aside to cool—10 minutes.

7. Remove the muffins from the oven and let cool, Get out the remaining ingredients for Sausage Eggwiches (page 134).

8. Fry 6 eggs in the same sausage skillet—10 minutes.

9. Chop fruits for the freezer and/or veggies for wraps, salads, or pasta salads. Slice tomatoes for sandwiches—while the eggs are frying and the muffins are cooling.

10. Assemble the Sausage Eggwiches with fried eggs and sausage patties—5 minutes.

11. Clean up and put all the food into the freezer—5 minutes.

12. Start the Overnight Green Chile Grits (page 46) in the slow cooker—5 minutes (in the late evening)

End Results: Double Batch Southwest Sausage Muffins, Make-Ahead Oatmeal Mixes, Sausage Eggwiches, Overnight Green Chile Grits in the slow cooker, and chopped fruit and veggies for the week's breakfasts, lunches, or smoothies.

ONE-HOUR PREP: PLAN C

1. In a medium saucepan, boil the 12 eggs for 12 minutes and then remove from the heat. Let sit for 10 minutes, and then drain the hot water. Place the eggs into a bowl of cold water for 15 to 20 minutes.

2. Preheat the oven and prepare the Baked Oatmeal with Pecans (page 39) batter—10 minutes prep, 25 to 30 minutes baking.

3. Make the batter for a triple batch of the Maple Pecan Pancakes (page 94) batter—5 minutes prep, 20 to 30 minutes of flipping pancakes.

4. Assemble the Cranberry-Apple Breakfast Casserole (page 76), cover, and place in the refrigerator to bake the next morning (or bake and reheat in the morning)—10 minutes while flipping pancakes.

5. Chop fruits for the freezer and/or veggies for wraps, salads, or pasta salads. Slice tomatoes for sandwiches—while flipping pancakes.

6. Start the Overnight Spiced Granola (page 43) in the slow cooker; in the morning let cool and then place in plastic freezer bag in the freezer—5 minutes.

7. Clean up and put all the food into the freezer—5 minutes.

End Results: One dozen hard-boiled Eggs, Baked Oatmeal with Pecans, triple batch of Maple Pecan Pancakes, Cranberry-Apple Breakfast Casserole, Overnight Spiced Granola, and chopped fruit and veggies for the week's breakfasts, lunches, or smoothies.

WHILE PREPPING DINNER: PLAN A

1. Preheat the oven and make the Raspberry Cereal Bars (page 50)—15 minutes prep, 25 to 30 minutes baking while you eat dinner.

2. Make the Sour Cream and Chive Drop Biscuits (page 103)—5 minutes prep, 8 to 10 minutes baking while you eat dinner.

3. Cut fruit or veggies for next day's breakfast and lunch and refrigerate.

4. Clean up with the dinner dishes, put the cooled cereal bars and biscuits into the freezer.

5. Assemble lunch boxes.

End Results: Raspberry Cereal Bars, Sour Cream and Chive Biscuits, cut fruit and veggies, assembled lunch boxes.

WHILE PREPPING DINNER: PLAN B

1. Preheat the oven and make Banana Blueberry Loaf Bread (page 107) and bake while eating dinner. Let cool and then slice before freezing.

2. Make a double batch of batter for Banana Nut Waffles (page 88) and cook them while eating dinner and cleaning up, let cool before freezing.

3. Cut fruits or veggies for the next day's lunches and refrigerate.

4. Clean up with the dinner dishes, put the cooled cereal bars and biscuits into the freezer.

5. Assembles lunch boxes.

End Results: Banana Blueberry Loaf Bread, Double Batch Banana Nut Waffles, cut fruits and veggies, assembled lunch boxes

By either spending just an hour in the kitchen or preparing food for the next day while you make dinner, you'll find yourself cruising through the week, rather than stressing about the meal plan or feeling guilty about another stop at the drive-through.

Once you get into the routine of making your own convenience food and realize the peace that it can bring to your frazzled week, you'll never look back. The key is having the plan, executing the plan, and staying one step ahead of yourself in the kitchen.

Tips for Freezing and Thawing Foods

FREEZER CONTAINERS

If packaged correctly, your homemade convenience breakfast foods will keep well in the freezer. The ideal would be to use a vacuum-type system to remove all the air from the plastic bags used. Removing all the air will reduce the chances of freezer burn. If you don't wish to pay for a vacuum-seal system, you can create one yourself using a straw. Place the cooled items you wish to freeze into a plastic freezer bag. Press out as much air as you can without squishing the food and seal the bag, leaving just enough room for a straw. Use your fingers to hold the straw tightly inside the opening in the bag. Suck out any remaining air and seal the bag quickly. You have just vacuum-sealed your food and it's now ready for the freezer.

Another way to reduce the amount of freezer burn is to completely cool the baked goods, pancakes, or waffles before adding them to the plastic freezer bags. This will prevent condensation within the bag and fewer ice crystals will form inside the freezer bag and on your food.

A double batch of pancakes that you plan to eat later in that week can be stored in a recycled sandwich bread bag. Sandwich bread bags are the perfect size for 3- to 4-inch pancakes. Cool the pancakes completely on a cooling rack before adding to the sandwich bag. Freeze and enjoy later in the week.

If you will be storing your baked goods for longer periods of time, I recommend double-bagging them, or using a combination of aluminum foil or disposable foil containers and plastic freezer bags. This will seal and preserve the food better.

LENGTH OF TIME FOR FREEZING

The length of time recommended for freezing varies with the food and with the freezer. Foods in a deep freezer can stay in longer than foods in a refrigerator freezer. My rule of thumb is to keep foods in the freezer for less than 3 months or in the deep freezer for 6 months. Keep an inventory list on the outside of your freezer that you update every time you add to or pull from the freezer. Every 2 or 3 months take stock of your freezer's contents and rewrite your inventory list. By rotating your freezer foods and not allowing them to overstay their welcome, you will not waste money on those foods that would otherwise get lost in the depths of the freezer.

THAWING OPTIONS

- In the fridge: The ideal for thawing your homemade convenience foods is placing them in the refrigerator the night before, then reheating them in the microwave or toaster oven just before breakfast time.

- In the microwave: Since it's easy to forget to pull your breakfast from the freezer the night before, most breakfast foods thaw and reheat easily in the microwave.

- In the toaster: Pancakes and waffles can be quickly warmed in the toaster or toaster oven. They are less soggy than if you were to reheat them in the microwave. My experience has been that it takes 2 "cycles" in the toaster on the medium-heat level to reheat them from frozen and 1 "cycle" on the medium-heat level if they are coming out of the refrigerator. Reheating times and cycles will vary by toaster oven. If trying this for the first time, watch them closely—burned waffles for breakfast are not a great way to start the day.

Moving on to the Recipes

Whether its waffles or pancakes or fruit for a smoothie and some frozen muffins, having some homemade convenience food in the freezer will help save you a few shreds of sanity come the middle of the week. Now that you have a few new tricks to help squeeze a quick and nutritious breakfast into your busy morning routine, let's move on.

I leave you now with a collection of easy breakfast recipes that will give you the energy you need to start your day on the right foot.

ONE

Breakfast Cereals—
Oatmeals, Granolas,
Rice Puddings, and More

Apple Cinnamon Oatmeal

1 large Honeycrisp apple, cored
 and diced ($1)
1 teaspoon lemon juice ($.02)
½ teaspoon ground cinnamon ($.02)
¼ cup firmly packed brown sugar ($.06)

1 teaspoon salt
4 cups water
2 cups quick-cooking, rolled oats ($.24)
Milk, cream, or yogurt for serving
 ($.25)

4 hard-boiled eggs ($.40)

In a small mixing bowl, combine the diced apples and lemon juice. Toss with cinnamon, brown sugar, and salt. Set aside.

In a medium saucepan, bring the water to a boil and then stir in the oats; return to a boil and let cook for 1 minute. After 1 minute, stir in the sweet, apple-cinnamon mixture and then remove the pan from the heat. Cover and let stand for 4 to 5 minutes.

Serve warm Apple Cinnamon Oatmeal with Milk, Cream, or Yogurt and Hard-boiled Eggs.

Makes 4 breakfast servings

Cost $1.99

FRUGAL FACT: *If you see a bag of reduced-price apples, or like to stock up during their low-price season, then dice a few of the apples and freeze them. Because the apples will be cooked in the oatmeal, using diced apples from the freezer is a great way to keep costs down on this recipe.*

Maple Pecan Oatmeal

4 cups water
2 cups quick-cooking, rolled oats
  ($.24)
1 teaspoon salt

⅓ cup maple syrup ($.75)
1 cup pecans, chopped ($.75)
Milk, cream, or yogurt for serving
  ($.25)

Blueberry Smoothies (page 275) ($1.89)

In a medium saucepan, bring the water to a boil and stir in the oats and salt; return to a boil and let cook for 1 minute. After 1 minute, stir in the maple syrup and chopped pecans and then remove the pan from the heat. Cover and let stand for 4 to 5 minutes.

Serve warm Maple Pecan Oatmeal with Milk, Cream, or Yogurt and Blueberry Smoothies.

Makes 4 breakfast servings

Cost $3.88

FRUGAL FACT: *Store pecans in the freezer to preserve their freshess and flavor.*

Pumpkin Spice Oatmeal

4 cups water
2 cups quick-cooking, rolled oats ($.24)
1 teaspoon salt
1 cup canned pumpkin pie filling ($.67)

2 teaspoons brown sugar ($.02)
1/2 cup chopped pecans ($.37)
Milk, cream, or yogurt for serving
  ($.25)

Fresh fruit ($.50)

In a medium saucepan, bring the water to a boil and stir in the oats and salt; return to a boil and let cook for 1 minute. After 1 minute, stir in the canned pumpkin pie filling and brown sugar, then remove the pan from the heat. Cover and let stand for 4 to 5 minutes. Sprinkle with the chopped pecans just before serving.

Serve warm Pumpkin Spice Oatmeal with Milk, Cream, or Yogurt, and Fresh Fruit.

Makes 4 breakfast servings

Cost $2.05

FRUGAL FACT: *If using canned, 100 percent pure pumpkin, add 1/4 cup sugar, 1 teaspoon ground cinnamon, 1/2 teaspoon ground ginger, and 1/2 teaspoon ground cloves to the pumpkin puree.*

Banana Nut Oatmeal

2 ripe bananas ($.40)
⅓ cup firmly packed brown sugar
   ($.08)
1 teaspoon ground cinnamon ($.05)
4 cups water

2 cups quick-cooking, rolled oats ($.24)
1 teaspoon salt
½ cup chopped walnuts ($.37)
Milk, cream, or yogurt for serving
   ($.25)

4 hard-boiled eggs ($.40)

On a dinner plate, mash the bananas with a fork until mushy. Stir in the brown sugar and cinnamon. Set aside.

In a medium saucepan, bring the water to a boil and then stir in the oats and salt; return to a boil and let cook for 1 minute. After 1 minute, stir in the mashed bananas and the chopped walnuts and remove the pan the from heat. Cover and let stand for 4 to 5 minutes.

Serve warm Banana Nut Oatmeal with Milk, Cream, or Yogurt and Hard-boiled Eggs.

Makes 4 breakfast servings

Cost $1.79

FRUGAL FACT: *A kid-favorite breakfast around our house.*

Peaches 'n Cream Oatmeal

4 cups water

2 cups quick-cooking, rolled oats ($.24)

1 teaspoon salt

2 peaches, pitted and diced ($.50)

3 tablespoons sugar ($.06)

Cream or yogurt for serving ($.25)

Mango-Raspberry Smoothies (page 274) ($2.04)

In a medium saucepan, bring the water to a boil and then stir in the oats and salt; return to a boil and let cook for 1 minute. After 1 minute, stir in the diced peaches and sugar. Remove the pan from the heat. Cover and let stand for 4 to 5 minutes.

Serve warm Peaches 'n Cream Oatmeal with Cream or Yogurt and Mango-Raspberry Smoothies.

Makes 4 breakfast servings

Cost $3.09

FRUGAL FACT: *Grab an extra bag or two of peaches when you see them on sale for 3 pounds for $1.50 or less. Slice and freeze the slices on a rimmed, baking sheet and then place them into a plastic freezer bag once frozen. Frozen peaches are great for this oatmeal and for smoothies (pages 273–278).*

Cinnamon Swirl Oatmeal

....

1 tablespoon ground cinnamon ($.15)

1 teaspoon ground nutmeg ($.05)

½ teaspoon ground ginger ($.03)

¼ cup firmly packed brown sugar ($.06)

4 cups water

2 cups quick-cooking, rolled oats ($.24)

1 teaspoon salt

Milk, cream, or yogurt for serving ($.25)

Fresh fruit ($.50)

In a small mixing bowl, combine the cinnamon, nutmeg, ginger, and brown sugar.

In a medium saucepan, bring the water to a boil and then stir in the oats and salt; return to a boil and let cook for 1 minute. Stir in the spice mixture and remove the pan from the heat. Cover and let stand for 4 to 5 minutes.

Serve warm Cinnamon Swirl Oatmeal with Milk, Cream, or Yogurt and Fresh Fruit.

Makes 4 breakfast servings

Cost $1.28

FRUGAL FACT: *Toss a few spices into a basic oatmeal recipe for a yummy and frugal breakfast treat.*

Slow Cooker Raisin Oatmeal

....

2 cups steel-cut oats ($1.50)
⅓ cup firmly packed brown sugar
  ($.08)
1 tablespoon ground cinnamon ($.15)
1 teaspoon salt
8 cups hot water

1 teaspoon vanilla extract ($.05)
1 cup raisins ($.75)
½ cup chopped walnuts ($.37)
Milk, cream, or yogurt for serving
  ($.25)

Fresh fruit ($.50)

Toss together the steel-cut oats, brown sugar, cinnamon, and salt in the base of a slow cooker. Stir in the hot water and vanilla.

Set the slow cooker on low and cook the oats for 9 to 10 hours, or overnight for 8 to 10 hours. Stir in the raisins and chopped walnuts just before serving.

Serve Slow Cooker Raisin Oatmeal with Milk, Cream, or Yogurt and Fresh Fruit.

Makes 4 breakfast servings

Cost $3.65

FRUGAL FACT: *Keep an eye out for newspaper and Internet coupons for steel-cut oats.*

Make-Ahead Oatmeal Packets

Want to make your own oatmeal packets for much less than buying them in the store?

Cranberry Oatmeal

½ cup quick-cooking, rolled oats ($.06)
3 tablespoons dried cranberries ($.25)
1 teaspoon nonfat milk powder ($.02)

1 teaspoon brown sugar ($.01)
½ teaspoon ground cinnamon ($.02)
Pinch of salt

Cinnamon Raisin Oatmeal

½ cup quick-cooking oats ($.06)
3 tablespoons raisins ($.15)
1 teaspoon nonfat milk powder ($.02)

2 teaspoons brown sugar ($.01)
1 teaspoon ground cinnamon ($.02)
Pinch of salt

Blueberries and Cream Oatmeal

½ cup quick-cooking, rolled oats ($.06)
¼ cup dried blueberries ($.40)

2 teaspoons nonfat milk powder ($.02)
1 teaspoon brown sugar ($.01)
Pinch of salt

In addition to the directions below, stir in ¼ cup milk, cream, or yogurt after adding the water.

Maple Pecan Oatmeal

½ cup quick-cooking, rolled oats ($.06)
2 tablespoons chopped pecans ($.20)
1 teaspoon nonfat milk powder ($.02)

1 teaspoon brown sugar ($.01)
½ teaspoon ground cinnamon ($.02)
Pinch of salt

In addition to the directions below, stir in 2 tablespoons maple syrup after adding the water.

DIRECTIONS FOR EACH PACKET

Each set of ingredients make an individual, single-serving packet. Simply mix the ingredients in a small plastic container or in a plastic sandwich-size storage bag with a zipper seal. To use, add in 1 to 1¼ cups boiling hot water, and stir vigorously for 20 to 30 seconds. (Note any additional ingredients to be added after the water—see recipes above.) Store homemade packets in an airtight container for up to 4 weeks.

Cost $.25 to $.50 per individual packet

FRUGAL FACT: *Set up an assembly line with 20 to 30 plastic ziplock bags and a large box of quick-cooking, rolled oats to save time in preparing the packets. Label the bags, then clean and reuse them again after using the contents.*

Baked Oatmeal with Pecans

2 large eggs ($.20)
½ cup applesauce ($.12)
½ cup granulated sugar ($.05)
1½ cups milk ($.15)
3 cups quick-cooking, rolled oats ($.36)
⅓ cup whole wheat flour ($.09)

1 tablespoon baking powder ($.15)
1 teaspoon salt
½ cup chopped pecans ($.37)
3 tablespoons brown sugar ($.03)
1 teaspoon ground cinnamon ($.05)
Milk, cream, or yogurt for serving ($.25)

Fresh fruit ($.50)

Preheat the oven to 350 degrees. Lightly coat a 9 × 13-inch glass baking dish with nonstick cooking spray.

In a large mixing bowl, whisk together the eggs, applesauce, granulated sugar, and milk. Stir in the oats, whole wheat flour, baking powder, and salt until a batter forms. Fold in the chopped pecans. Pour the batter into the prepared baking dish.

In a small mixing bowl, stir together the brown sugar and cinnamon. Sprinkle the brown sugar–cinnamon mixture over the top of the batter in the baking dish.

Bake the oatmeal in the preheated oven for 25 to 30 minutes, or until a toothpick inserted in the middle comes out clean. Let cool on a wire rack a few minutes before slicing.

Serve Baked Oatmeal with Pecans and Milk, Cream, or Yogurt and Fresh Fruit.

Makes 8 breakfast servings

Cost $2.32

FRUGAL FACT: *Slice the baked oatmeal and cool completely before freezing the slices in a plastic freezer bag.*

FREEZER FRIENDLY

Blueberry Baked Oatmeal

2 large eggs ($.20)
½ cup applesauce ($.12)
½ cup granulated sugar ($.08)
1½ cups milk ($.15)
3 cups quick-cooking, rolled oats ($.36)
1 tablespoon baking powder ($.05)

1 teaspoon salt
2 cups fresh blueberries ($1)
2 tablespoons brown sugar ($.05)
1 teaspoon ground cinnamon ($.05)
Milk, cream, or yogurt for serving
   ($.25)

4 hard-boiled eggs ($.40)

Preheat the oven to 350 degrees. Lightly coat a 9 × 13-inch glass baking dish with nonstick cooking spray.

In a large mixing bowl, whisk together the eggs, applesauce, granulated sugar, and milk. Stir in the oats, baking powder, and salt until a batter forms. Fold in the fresh blueberries. Pour the batter into the prepared baking dish.

In a small mixing bowl, stir together the brown sugar and cinnamon. Sprinkle the brown sugar–cinnamon mixture over the top of the batter in the baking dish.

Bake the oatmeal in the preheated oven for 25 to 30 minutes, or until a toothpick inserted in the middle comes out clean. Let cool on a wire rack a few minutes before slicing.

Serve Blueberry Baked Oatmeal with Milk, Cream, or Yogurt and Hard-boiled eggs.

Makes 8 breakfast servings

Cost $2.71

FRUGAL FACT: *Substitute fresh raspberries, strawberries, or dried cranberries or cherries for the blueberries. To prepare this recipe with dried fruit, soak the dried fruit in a large bowl with hot water for 5 to 10 minutes. Drain and pat dry before folding into the batter.*

FREEZER FRIENDLY

Tropical Granola

½ cup honey ($.80)

1 can (15 ounces) sliced pineapple with juice ($1)

6 tablespoons butter or margarine ($.60)

1 teaspoon salt

5½ cups rolled oats, old-fashioned or quick-cooking ($.66)

1 cup sweetened coconut flakes ($1)

Milk, cream, or yogurt ($.25)

Preheat the oven to 325 degrees.

In a large saucepan, heat the honey, pineapple juice, butter or margarine, and salt until the mixture starts to bubble. Remove the pan from the heat and stir in the oats and sweetened coconut flakes. Toss until evenly coated.

Spread the mixture evenly in a thin, single layer on 2 ungreased, rimmed, baking sheets.

Bake in the preheated oven for 30 to 45 minutes, or until the granola is crisp and golden brown, turning the granola every 10 to 15 minutes to prevent burning around the edges. Let cool before eating.

Serve Tropical Granola with Milk, Cream, or Yogurt and Sliced Pineapple.

Makes 4 breakfast servings

Cost $4.31

FRUGAL FACT: *This is a great way to use up the extra pineapple juice from canned pineapple. If you don't plan to use the juice right away, don't pour it down the sink. You can also freeze the juice in ice cube trays and use them to sweeten up your favorite smoothies.*

Overnight Honey Nut Granola

....

½ cup canola or vegetable oil ($.20)
⅔ cup honey ($1.10)
1 teaspoon vanilla extract ($.05)
1 tablespoon ground cinnamon ($.15)
5 cups rolled oats, quick-cooking or
    old-fashioned ($.60)

1 cup sliced almonds ($.75)
1 cup chopped pecans ($.75)
Milk, cream, or yogurt for serving
    ($.25)

Fresh fruit ($.50)

Preheat the oven to 300 degrees.

In a small bowl, whisk together the oil, honey, vanilla, and cinnamon.

In a large bowl, combine the rolled oats, sliced almonds, and chopped pecans. Pour the honey mixture over the oat mixture. Toss until evenly coated.

Spread the mixture evenly in a thin, single layer on 2 ungreased, rimmed, baking sheets.

Bake in the preheated oven for 10 minutes. Turn off the oven and leave the granola in the oven overnight.

In the morning, remove the granola from the oven and serve.

Serve Overnight Honey Nut Granola with Milk, Cream, or Yogurt and Fresh Fruit.

Makes 4 breakfast servings

Cost $4.35

FRUGAL FACT: *Be sure to match up the coupons for rolled oats and other oatmeal products with a sale price to get the very best deal.*

Overnight Spiced Granola

½ cup butter or margarine, melted ($.80)

½ cup honey ($.80)

1 tablespoon ground cinnamon ($.15)

1 teaspoon ground nutmeg ($.05)

3 cups old-fashioned, rolled oats ($.36)

3 cups quick-cooking, rolled oats ($.36)

Milk, cream, or yogurt ($.25)

Fresh fruit ($.50)

Preheat the oven to 300 degrees.

In a small bowl, whisk together the melted butter, honey, cinnamon, and nutmeg.

Add the oats to a large bowl and pour in the honey mixture. Toss until coated evenly.

Spread the mixture evenly in a thin, single layer on 2 ungreased, rimmed, baking sheets.

Bake in the preheated oven for 10 minutes. Turn off the oven and leave the granola in the oven overnight.

In the morning, remove the granola from the oven and serve.

Serve Overnight Spiced Granola with Milk, Cream, or Yogurt and Fresh Fruit.

Makes 4 breakfast servings

Cost $3.27

FRUGAL FACT: *Granola will "clump" better if you use a half-and-half combination of old-fashioned, rolled oats and quick-cooking rolled oats.*

Slow Cooker "Cran-ola"

½ cup firmly brown sugar ($.12)
½ cup butter or margarine ($.80)
3 cups old-fashioned, rolled oats ($.36)
3 cups quick-cooking, rolled oats ($.36)

1 tablespoon ground cinnamon ($.15)
1 cup dried cranberries ($.75)
Milk, cream, or yogurt ($.25)

Strawberry-Banana Smoothies (page 273) ($1.74)

In a small, microwave-safe bowl, cook the brown sugar and butter or margarine in the microwave on high for 1 to 1½ minutes, or until the butter has melted. Whisk briskly just before pouring over the oats.

Add the oats and cinnamon into the base of a slow cooker and stir together. Pour the brown sugar–butter mixture over the oats and toss until evenly coated. Stir in the dried cranberries.

Set the slow cooker on high and cook the granola for 3 to 4 hours. When placing the lid on the slow cooker before cooking, place it at a slight angle, leaving a small vent for the steam to escape. Stir the mixture every 45 minutes to an hour. Failure to stir can result in burning the cranberries.

Once the granola clumps have formed, turn off the slow cooker and let cool before serving.

Serve Slow Cooker "Cran-ola" with Milk, Cream, or Yogurt and Strawberry-Banana Smoothies.

Makes 4 breakfast servings

Cost $4.53

FRUGAL FACT: *Start this Slow Cooker "Cran-ola" just as you are finishing up dinner. Keep an eye on it throughout the evening, stirring as indicated. Leave it in the slow cooker overnight and serve for breakfast the next morning.*

Peanut Butter–Chocolate Cream of Wheat

4 cups water

1 teaspoon salt

¾ cup Cream of Wheat ($.99)

Pinch of salt

¼ cup firmly packed brown sugar ($.06)

2 tablespoons natural peanut butter ($.20)

½ cup semisweet chocolate chips ($.37)

Milk or cream for serving ($.25)

Fresh fruit ($.50)

In a saucepan, bring the water to a boil and add the 1 teaspoon salt. When the water is boiling, slowly pour in the Cream of Wheat, whisking continuously until all of it has been added. Add a pinch of salt. Whisk until the mixture returns to a boil. Let boil for about 2 minutes, then whisk in the brown sugar, peanut butter, and chocolate chips. Stir continuously for 30 seconds, then remove from heat. Let cool a few minutes before serving.

Serve Peanut Butter Chocolate Cream of Wheat with Fresh Fruit.

Makes 4 breakfast servings

Cost $2.27

FRUGAL FACT: *Since there are rarely coupons for name-brand Cream of Wheat, consider buying the store brand and stock up when the store brand goes on sale.*

Overnight Green Chile Grits

1 tablespoon canola or vegetable oil ($.02)
8 cups boiling water
2 cups old-fashioned grits ($1.99)
2 teaspoons salt

1 can (4 ounces) green chilies, chopped ($.59)
1 cup shredded Monterey Jack or Mexican blend cheese ($.75)

4 eggs, hard-boiled, poached, or fried ($.40)

Add the oil to the base of a slow cooker. Pour in the 8 cups of boiling water. Whisk in the grits and the salt. Stir in the green chilies. Set the slow cooker on low and cook the grits for 8 to 9 hours. Just before serving, stir in the shredded cheese and let it melt.

The grits can also be prepared in a large saucepan on the stovetop. Bring the water and oil to a boil, then whisk in the grits and salt. Reduce the heat and simmer for 15 to 20 minutes, stirring frequently. Once the grits begin to thicken, add the green chilies and the shredded cheese. Let cool slightly before serving.

Prepare the eggs as you prefer, hard-boiled, poached, or fried.

Serve Overnight Green Chile Grits with your favorite style of Eggs.

Makes 4 breakfast servings

Cost $3.75

FRUGAL FACT: *Start these grits in the slow cooker in the late evening and they'll be ready just in time for breakfast in the morning.*

Vanilla Brown Rice Pudding

....

4 cups cooked brown rice ($.60)
2 cups milk ($.20)
¼ cup sugar ($.03)
1 tablespoon vanilla extract ($.15)

1½ teaspoons ground cinnamon ($.07)
1 teaspoon ground nutmeg ($.05)
1 large egg white ($.10)
¼ cup milk ($.02)

Pumpkin Smoothies (page 276) ($1.25)

In a large saucepan, stir together the cooked brown rice, milk, sugar, vanilla, cinnamon, and nutmeg. Bring to a boil and let cook at a rolling boil for 5 to 7 minutes.

In a small bowl, whisk together the egg white and milk. Stir the mixture into the cooking rice pudding. Reduce the heat and let simmer for 15 to 20 minutes. Let cool slightly before serving.

Serve Vanilla Brown Rice Pudding with Pumpkin Smoothies.

Makes 4 breakfast servings

Cost $2.47

FRUGAL FACT: *When writing your meal plan, make extra brown rice for dinner, and use the leftover rice to prepare this for breakfast.*

Baked Apple Brown Rice Pudding

2 small Granny Smith apples, peeled, cored, and diced ($.50)

1 teaspoon lemon juice ($.02)

¼ cup firmly packed brown sugar ($.02)

1 egg ($.10)

1 tablespoon ground cinnamon ($.15)

1½ cups cooked brown rice ($.30)

2½ cups milk ($.25)

1 teaspoon vanilla extract ($.05)

Spinach ("Green") Smoothies (page 277) ($1.20)

Preheat the oven to 350 degrees. Lightly coat an 8 × 8-inch glass baking dish with nonstick cooking spray.

In a medium mixing bowl, toss the diced apples with the lemon juice. Add the brown sugar and cinnamon and toss. Pour the apple mixture into the prepared baking dish.

In the same bowl, stir together the cooked rice, milk, eggs, and vanilla. Pour the rice mixture over the top of the apples in the baking dish.

Bake the pudding in the preheated oven for 1 hour 15 minutes to 1 hour 30 minutes. Let cool on a wire rack before serving.

Serve Baked Apple Brown Rice Pudding with Spinach ("Green") Smoothies.

Makes 4 1-cup servings

Cost $2.59

FRUGAL FACT: *Be sure to coat the apples with the lemon juice to prevent the apples from browning.*

Protein-Packed Cereal Bars

....

1 cup natural peanut butter ($.56)
½ cup firmly packed brown sugar ($.12)
½ cup milk ($.05)
1 teaspoon vanilla extract ($.05)

3 cups quick-cooking, rolled oats ($.36)
½ cup slivered or sliced almonds ($.37)
1 teaspoon ground cinnamon ($.05)
½ cup raisins or dried cranberries ($.37)

Fresh fruit ($.50)

Preheat the oven to 350 degrees. Lightly coat an 8 × 8-inch glass baking dish with nonstick cooking spray.

In a mixing bowl, stir together the peanut butter, brown sugar, milk, and vanilla. Stir in the oats, almonds, cinnamon, and raisins; the batter will be thick. Press the batter into the prepared baking dish using the bottom of a measuring cup or the back of a large serving spoon.

Bake in the preheated oven for 15 to 20 minutes. Let cool on a wire rack before slicing. Slice into 4 rows on one side, and then one slice down the middle on the other side, making 8 bars.

Serve Protein-Packed Cereal Bars with Fresh Fruit.

Makes 8 breakfast bars

Cost $2.43

FRUGAL FACT: *The perfect quick, filling, and nutritious on-the-go breakfast.*

Raspberry Cereal Bars

CEREAL CRUST

1½ cups whole wheat flour ($.49)
2 cups rolled oats, old-fashioned
  or quick cooking ($.24)
½ cup firmly packed brown sugar ($.12)
1 teaspoon ground cinnamon ($.05)

½ teaspoon baking soda ($.01)
¼ teaspoon salt
1 cup butter or margarine, softened
  ($1.60)

RASPBERRY FILLING

1 cup fresh raspberries ($1)
⅓ cup sugar ($.03)

1 teaspoon vanilla extract ($.05)

4 hard-boiled eggs ($.40)

Preheat the oven to 350 degrees. Lightly coat a 9 × 13-inch glass baking dish with nonstick cooking spray.

In a large mixing bowl, combine the flour, oats, brown sugar, cinnamon, baking soda, and salt. Cut the softened butter into the dry ingredients using a pastry blender or serving fork.

Prepare the raspberry filling. Add the raspberries, sugar, and vanilla to a blender or food processor and puree.

Add about one-half of the oat-flour mixture to the prepared baking dish. Press the crust into the bottom of the dish, using the bottom of a measuring cup or the back of a large serving spoon. Pour over the raspberry filling and spread evenly to cover the crust. Add the remaining oat-flour mixture on top of the raspberry filling. Press lightly using the measuring cup or large serving spoon, to form a top crust.

Bake in the preheated oven for 25 to 30 minutes, or until the top begins to turn golden brown. Let cool on a wire rack before slicing.

Serve Raspberry Cereal Bars with Hard-boiled Eggs.

Makes 12 to 16 cereal bars

Cost $3.99

FRUGAL FACT: *Substitute a cup of strawberries, blueberries, or apples for the cup of raspberries to create a new flavor of homemade cereal bar.*

Peach-Raspberry Breakfast Parfait

2 cups store-bought plain or vanilla
   yogurt ($1)
2 cups Overnight Spiced Granola
   (page 43) ($.90)

1 cup raspberries ($.99)
1 cup peaches, pitted and
   diced ($1)
¼ cup honey ($.40)

Assemble 4 tall glasses on the countertop. Add 2 tablespoons of the yogurt, 2 tablespoons of the granola, and a few raspberries and diced peaches to each glass. Drizzle honey over the fruit. Then repeat the layering of yogurt, granola, fruit, and honey in each glass.

Serve Peach-Raspberry Breakfast Parfait.

Makes 4 breakfast servings

Cost $4.29

FRUGAL FACT: *This parfait is an excellent choice for when the granola stash is running low. This recipe can stretch the last of the granola to feed the whole family.*

TWO

Egg Dishes — Frittatas, Breakfast Casseroles, French Toast Bakes, and More

Huevos Rancheros

1 tablespoon plus 2 teaspoons butter ($.30)
½ onion, chopped ($.15)
1 can (10 ounces) diced tomatoes with green chilies, drained ($.59)

1 teaspoon ground cumin ($.05)
4 corn tortillas ($.30)
6 large eggs ($.60)
¼ cup milk ($.03)
Salt and pepper

Fresh fruit ($.50)

In a saucepan, melt 1 tablespoon of the butter, add the chopped onions, and sauté for 4 to 6 minutes, or until they begin to turn opaque. Add the drained diced tomatoes with green chilies and the cumin.

Set the salsa aside.

In a skillet, melt the remaining 2 teaspoons of butter and warm the corn tortillas one at a time on each side, until the tortilla puffs up slightly.

Beat the eggs with the milk and scramble in the same skillet. Season to taste with salt and pepper.

To serve the Huevos Rancheros, place each warmed tortilla on a plate and top with the scrambled eggs and then the tomato salsa.

Serve Huevos Rancheros with Fresh Fruit.

Makes 4 breakfast servings

Cost $2.52

FRUGAL FACT: *Stock up when the price for canned tomatoes is $.59 or less. They can often be found for as little as $.19/can with a sale price, store promotion discount, and a coupon matchup.*

Bacon and Egg Quesadillas

6 bacon slices ($.50)
8 large eggs, beaten ($.80)
8 burrito-size flour tortillas ($1.09)

2 cups shredded Monterey Jack cheese ($1.50)
½ cup homemade (page 255) or store-bought salsa for dipping ($.25)

Fresh fruit ($.50)

Preheat the oven to 300 degrees.

In a medium skillet, cook the slices of bacon until brown and crisp. Remove the bacon from the pan and place on paper towels to absorb excess fat. Let cool. Pour most of the fat from the pan into a grease jar (and save for use another time), leaving just enough in the pan to scramble the eggs. Crumble the cooled bacon.

Scramble the eggs in the same skillet, with the remaining bacon fat.

Place 4 tortillas on a baking sheet and top each tortilla with the scrambled eggs, crumbled bacon, and about ½ cup shredded Monterey Jack cheese. Top each with another tortilla and press down firmly.

Bake the quesadillas in the preheated oven for 10 minutes, until the cheese melts and the tortillas are slightly crispy. Remove from the oven and slice into quarters.

Serve Bacon and Egg Quesadillas with Salsa and Fresh Fruit.

Makes 4 breakfast servings

Cost $4.64

FRUGAL FACT: *Use corn tortillas for a gluten-free breakfast alternative.*

Egg Tortilla Casserole

6 soft, taco-size flour tortillas ($.75)
1 plum tomato, seeded and diced ($.55)
½ yellow onion, chopped ($.30)
6 large eggs ($.60)
¼ cup milk ($.03)

½ cup homemade (page 255) or
   store-bought salsa ($.25)
1 cup shredded cheddar cheese ($.40)
Salt and pepper to taste

Blueberry Smoothies (page 275) ($1.89)

Preheat the oven to 325 degrees. Lightly coat an 8 × 8-inch glass baking dish with nonstick cooking spray.

Tear the tortillas into 1-inch pieces and place them in the prepared baking dish. Add the diced tomatoes and chopped onions to the torn tortillas and toss gently.

In a mixing bowl, whisk together the eggs, milk, and salsa. Pour the egg mixture over the torn tortillas, tomatoes, and onions. Sprinkle the top with the shredded cheddar cheese. Season with salt and pepper to taste.

Bake the casserole in the preheated oven for 25 to 30 minutes, or until the egg mixture has cooked through and it begins to golden on top. Let cool before slicing and serving.

Serve Egg Tortilla Casserole with Blueberry Smoothies.

Makes 4 breakfast servings

Cost $4.77

FRUGAL FACT: *Substitute a well-drained, 15-ounce can of diced tomatoes from your stockpile for the diced plum tomato. Since diced tomatoes can sometimes be purchased for less than $.20 per can, this meal would cost around $2.50 with the substitution.*

Dutch Baby with Berry Syrup

PANCAKE

6 large eggs ($.60)
2 cups milk ($.20)
2 cups all-purpose flour ($.40)
¼ cup sugar ($.02)

1 teaspoon vanilla extract ($.05)
½ teaspoon ground cinnamon ($.02)
1 teaspoon salt
½ cup butter, melted ($.80)

BERRY SYRUP

2 cups fresh or frozen blueberries,
strawberries, blackberries,
or raspberries ($1)

3 tablespoons honey ($.30)

Fresh fruit ($.50)

Preheat the oven to 400 degrees. Lightly coat a 9 × 13-inch glass baking dish with nonstick cooking spray.

In a mixing bowl, whisk together the eggs until frothy, and then add the milk, flour, sugar, vanilla, cinnamon, and salt. Whisk until the batter becomes smooth. Pour the melted butter into the prepared baking dish and then pour the batter over it.

Bake the pancake in the preheated oven for 20 to 25 minutes, or until it puffs up and turns golden. Let cool a few minutes before serving.

Prepare the syrup by placing the berries and honey into a blender or food processor. Puree, streaming in 2 to 3 tablespoons of water until it reaches the desired consistency.

Serve Dutch Baby with Berry Syrup with Fresh Fruit.

Makes 4 to 6 breakfast servings

Cost $2.89

FRUGAL FACT: *Alternative toppings for Dutch Baby includes berries, honey, confectioners' sugar with a squeeze of lemon juice, and cinnamon.*

Berry Breakfast Bread Pudding

2 cups milk ($.20)
2 large eggs ($.20)
¼ cup firmly packed brown sugar ($.06)
1 teaspoon vanilla extract ($.05)
¼ teaspoon ground allspice ($.03)

½ teaspoon salt
6 slices whole wheat bread, torn ($.30)
2 cups fresh or frozen berries ($1)
1 teaspoon ground cinnamon for sprinkling ($.05)

Fresh fruit ($.50)

Preheat the oven to 350 degrees. Lightly coat an 8 × 8-inch glass baking dish with nonstick cooking spray.

In a mixing bowl, whisk together the milk, eggs, brown sugar, vanilla, allspice, and salt.

Place the torn bread pieces and berries in the prepared baking dish. Pour the milk and egg mixture over the top and let soak for at least 30 minutes. To soak overnight, cover the baking dish with plastic wrap and place in the refrigerator.

Bake the bread pudding in the preheated oven for 50 to 60 minutes, or until the egg mixture has cooked through and the top begins to turn golden.

Serve Berry Breakfast Bread Pudding with Fresh Fruit.

Makes 4 breakfast servings

Cost $2.39

FRUGAL FACT: *My stockpile price for a pint of berries is $1. When berries hit this price, I grab 10 or more pints to quick freeze. I then have fresh frozen bluberries to use in recipes like this one.*

Tomato-Basil Quiche

CRUST

½ cup all-purpose flour ($.10)
½ cup whole wheat flour ($.14)
½ teaspoon salt

⅓ cup solid vegetable shortening or
   butter ($.25)
3 to 4 tablespoons cold water

FILLING

1 small onion, finely chopped ($.30)
2 garlic cloves, crushed ($.10)
2 medium tomatoes, seeded and
   diced ($1)
5 to 6 fresh basil leaves, chopped ($.75)

6 large eggs ($.60)
1½ cups milk ($.15)
1 cup shredded, sharp cheddar
   cheese ($.75)
salt and pepper

Fresh fruit ($.50)

Preheat the oven to 350 degrees. Lightly coat a 9-inch pie plate with nonstick cooking spray.

Prepare the quiche crust by combining the all-purpose flour, whole wheat flour, and salt in a mixing bowl. Using a pastry blender, cut in the shortening or butter until it is the size of small peas. Add the cold water 1 tablespoon at a time, whisking with a fork and then kneading gently with your hands as the dough forms. Form the dough into a ball and then roll it out into a circle a few inches larger in diameter than your pie plate, on a clean and floured surface. Fold the dough in half and then in quarters to make it easier to transfer it to the pie plate. Unfold the crust dough and press it into the pie plate and form a border.

Place the chopped onion, crushed garlic, diced tomatoes, and chopped basil leaves into the quiche crust.

In a mixing bowl, whisk together the eggs, milk, and shredded cheese and season with salt and pepper. Beat until well combined and pour the egg mixture over the onions and tomatoes in the pie plate.

Bake the quiche in the preheated oven for 35 to 45 minutes, or until it is set in the middle and golden brown on top.

Serve Tomato-Basil Quiche with Fresh Fruit.

Makes 4 breakfast servings

Cost $4.64

FRUGAL FACT: *Shave $.75 off this meal by growing your own basil, as opposed to buying it from the grocery store.*

Mini Sausage Quiches

CRUST

1 cup all-purpose flour ($.20)
1 cup whole wheat flour ($.28)
1 teaspoon salt

⅔ cup solid vegetable shortening
   or butter ($.50)
6 to 8 tablespoons cold water

FILLING

½ pound all-natural pork
   sausage ($1)
6 large eggs ($.20)
½ cup milk ($.05)

½ teaspoon crushed red pepper
   flakes ($.03) (optional)
salt and pepper
1 cup shredded cheddar cheese ($.75)

Fresh fruit ($.50)

Preheat the oven to 400 degrees. Lightly coat 24 wells of a regular-size muffin pan with nonstick cooking spray.

Prepare the quiche crust by combining the all-purpose flour, whole wheat flour, and salt in a mixing bowl. Using a pastry blender, cut in the shortening or butter until it is the size of small peas. Add the cold water 1 tablespoon at a time, whisking with a fork and then kneading gently with your hands as the dough forms. Form the dough into a ball and then roll it out on a clean and floured surface. Cut the dough into 2-inch circles and gently press the dough circles into the prepared muffin cups.

In a large skillet, brown the sausage, crumbling it as you cook it, and drain on paper towels to absorb excess fat.

In a small mixing bowl, whisk together the eggs, milk, crushed red pepper flakes, if using, and season with salt and black pepper.

Place about ¼ cup of the browned sausage into each of the muffin wells. Add about 3 tablespoons of the egg-milk mixture and top with a pinch of the cheese.

Bake the mini quiches in the preheated oven for 16 to 18 minutes, or until set in the middle and golden on top. Let cool on a wire rack, then remove from pans.

Serve Mini Sausage Quiches with Fresh Fruit.

Makes 24 mini quiches

Cost $3.51

FRUGAL FACT: *Double this recipe and stash the extra quiches in the freezer for a quick breakfast "on the go." Let thaw in the refrigerator overnight and microwave for 15 to 20 seconds per quiche to reheat. If reheating from frozen, defrost the quiches in the microwave and then reheat for 15 to 20 seconds.*

Zucchini-Tomato Frittata

1 tablespoon extra-virgin olive oil ($.10)

1 zucchini, thinly sliced ($.79)

¼ red onion, sliced ($.50)

2 garlic cloves, crushed ($.10)

salt and pepper

10 large eggs ($1)

¼ cup milk ($.03)

2 plum tomatoes, sliced ($1)

1 teaspoon dried basil ($.05)

Spinach ("Green") Smoothies (page 277) ($1.20)

Preheat the oven to 400 degrees.

In a large ovenproof or cast-iron skillet, warm the olive oil over medium heat. Add the zucchini slices, red onion slices, and crushed garlic cloves and sauté for 4 to 6 minutes, or until the zucchini begins to turn translucent. Season to taste with salt and pepper.

In a mixing bowl, whisk together the eggs and milk. Once the zucchini has turned translucent, pour the eggs into the skillet and cook over high heat for 4 to 5 minutes, or until the egg sets along the inside edge of the skillet. Gently float the tomato slices in the eggs and sprinkle the basil on top.

Place the skillet into the preheated oven and bake the frittata for 12 to 15 minutes, or until eggs have cooked through and are set in the middle. Carefully remove the pan from the oven, as the handle will be hot. Let the frittata cool before slicing and serving.

Serve Zucchini-Tomato Frittata with Spinach ("Green") Smoothies.

Makes 4 breakfast servings

Cost $4.77

FRUGAL FACT: *Ask your local farmers' market if they offer discounts on zucchini that needs to be sold quickly.*

Bacon-Spinach Frittata

4 cooked bacon slices, crumbled ($.50)
½ yellow onion, thinly sliced into circles
($.15)
About 2 cups baby spinach ($1)
salt and pepper

10 large eggs ($1)
¼ cup milk ($.03)
1 cup shredded cheddar cheese ($.75)
1 tablespoon olive oil ($.10)

Fresh fruit ($.50)

Preheat the oven to 400 degrees.

Cook the bacon slices in a skillet, or in the microwave. To cook in the microwave, place the bacon slices on a microwave-safe plate covered with 2 paper towels. Cover the bacon slices with another paper towel to prevent splattering. Cook the bacon on high for 3 minutes or longer until crisp. Transfer to clean paper towel and let cool. Crumble the cooled bacon.

In a large ovenproof or cast-iron skillet warm the olive oil over medium heat. Add the the onion slices and baby spinach and sauté for 4 to 6 minutes, or until the spinach wilts and the onions begin to turn translucent. Season to taste with salt and pepper.

In a mixing bowl, whisk together the eggs and milk. Once the onions have turned translucent pour the eggs into the skillet and cook over high heat for 4 to 5 minutes, or until the egg sets along the inside edge of the skillet. Gently add the crumbled bacon and the shredded cheddar cheese on top.

Place the skillet into the preheated oven and bake the frittata for 12 to 15 minutes, or until the eggs have cooked through and are set in the middle. For a brown and bubbly top, run the frittata under the broiler for a few minutes. Carefully remove the pan from the oven, as the handle will be hot. Let the frittata cool before slicing and serving.

Serve Bacon-Spinach Frittata with Fresh Fruit.

Makes 4 breakfast servings

Cost $4.03

FRUGAL FACT: *Fresh spinach can be frozen and used in recipes where the spinach will be cooked, such as this one. So grab a few extra bags of spinach when it's on special and freeze it to use in this kind of meal.*

Italian Herb Frittata

1 tablespoon extra-virgin olive oil ($.10)
1 cup chopped red onion ($.50)
2 garlic cloves, crushed ($.10)
1 can (15 ounces) diced tomatoes, drained ($.59)

2 teaspoons fresh or dried basil ($.10)
½ teaspoon each fresh or dried oregano, thyme, and rosemary ($.08)
salt and pepper
10 large eggs ($1)
¼ cup milk ($.03)

Peach-Strawberry Smoothies (page 278) ($2.24)

Preheat the oven to 400 degrees.

In a large ovenproof or cast-iron skillet, warm the olive oil over medium heat. Add the chopped red onion, crushed garlic cloves, diced tomatoes, the basil, oregano, thyme, and rosemary and sauté for 4 to 6 minutes, or until the onions turn translucent. Season to taste with salt and pepper.

In a mixing bowl, whisk together the eggs and milk. Once the onions have turned translucent, pour the eggs into the skillet and cook over high heat for 4 to 5 minutes, or until the egg sets along the inside edge of the skillet.

Place the skillet into the preheated oven and bake the frittata for 12 to 15 minutes, or until the eggs have cooked through and are set in the middle. Carefully remove the pan from the oven, as the handle will be hot. Let the frittata cool before slicing and serving.

Serve Italian Herb Frittata with Peach-Strawberry Smoothies.

Makes 4 breakfast servings

Cost $4.74

FRUGAL FACT: *In a large patio planter, grow fresh herbs like basil, oregano, thyme, and rosemary to use in all your favorite Italian meals.*

Ham and Swiss Frittata

....

1 tablespoon extra-virgin olive oil
($.10)
1 large potato, peeled and diced ($.15)
½ yellow onion, sliced into half-moons
($.15)

salt and pepper
10 large eggs ($1)
¼ cup milk ($.03)
2 cups diced ham ($1)
1 cup shredded Swiss cheese ($.75)

Fresh fruit ($.50)

Preheat the oven to 400 degrees.

In a large ovenproof or cast-iron skillet, warm the olive oil over medium heat. Add the diced potatoes and onions and sauté for 6 to 8 minutes, or until the potatoes are brown and the onions begin to turn translucent. Season to taste with salt and pepper.

In a mixing bowl, whisk together the eggs and milk. Pour the eggs into the skillet and cook over high heat for 4 to 5 minutes, or until the eggs set along the inside edge of the skillet. Gently add the diced ham and sprinkle the shredded Swiss cheese on top.

Place the skillet into the preheated oven and bake the frittata for 12 to 15 minutes, or until the eggs have cooked through and are set in the middle. For a brown and bubbly top, run the frittata under the broiler for a few minutes. Carefully remove the pan from the oven, as the handle will be hot. Let the frittata cool before slicing and serving.

Serve Ham and Swiss Frittata with Fresh Fruit.

Makes 4 breakfast servings

Cost $3.68

FRUGAL FACT: *If you have hash brown potatoes on hand in your freezer, you can use about 1½ cups in place of the diced potato.*

Vanilla Almond French Toast

5 large eggs ($.50)
⅔ cup milk ($.07)
1 tablespoon maple syrup ($.10)
1 tablespoon vanilla extract ($.10)
⅓ cup slivered or sliced almonds,
   ground ($.50)

12 slices sandwich bread ($.90)
Butter, maple syrup, or confectioners'
   sugar ($.25)

Fresh fruit ($.50)

Preheat an electric griddle to 300 degrees, or warm a skillet over medium-high heat on the stovetop. Lightly coat with nonstick cooking spray.

In a mixing bowl, whisk together the eggs, milk, maple syrup, and vanilla. Stir in the ground almonds.

Dip both sides of each slice of bread into the bowl with the egg mixture. Transfer to the preheated griddle or skillet and cook on each side. Stir the egg mixture before dipping each slice bread, to ensure that the almonds coat the bread. Repeat until all the bread has been used.

Serve Vanilla Almond French Toast with Butter and Maple Syrup or Confectioners' Sugar and Fresh Fruit.

Makes 12 pieces of French toast

Cost $2.92

FRUGAL FACT: *Use your coffee grinder or blender to grind the almonds into a loose almond powder.*

Raspberry French Toast

1 cup fresh raspberries ($.50)
5 large eggs ($.50)
½ cup milk ($.05)
2 teaspoons vanilla extract ($.20)

12 slices whole wheat bread ($.90)
Butter and confectioners' sugar
    for serving ($.20)

Mango-Raspberry Smoothies (page 274) ($2.04)

On a plate, mash the raspberries with a fork. Set aside.

Preheat an electric griddle to 300 degrees, or warm a skillet over medium-high heat on the stovetop. Lightly coat with nonstick cooking spray.

In a mixing bowl, whisk together the eggs, milk, and vanilla. Stir in the mashed raspberries and any raspberry juices.

Dip both sides of each slice bread into the bowl with the egg mixture. Transfer to the preheated griddle or skillet and cook on each side. Stir the egg mixture before dipping each slice of bread, to ensure that the mashed raspberries coat the bread too. Repeat until all the bread has been used.

Serve Raspberry French Toast with Butter and Confectioners' sugar and Mango-Raspberry Smoothies.

Makes 12 pieces of French toast

Cost $4.39

FRUGAL FACT: *Just the same as with all other fresh berries, buy extra pints of raspberries when they are on sale for around $1 and freeze those you won't use right away on a rimmed baking sheet. Then transfer the frozen raspberries to a plastic freezer bag. Let frozen raspberries thaw before mashing.*

Baked Walnut French Toast

6 large eggs ($.60)
1 cup milk ($.10)
¼ cup maple syrup ($.50)

6 slices whole wheat bread, torn ($.45)
1 cup chopped walnuts ($.50)
Maple syrup for serving ($.10)

Fresh fruit ($.50)

Preheat the oven to 350 degrees. Lightly coat an 8×8-inch glass baking dish with nonstick cooking spray.

In a mixing bowl, whisk together the eggs, milk, and maple syrup.

Place the torn bread pieces and the chopped walnuts into the bottom of the prepared baking dish. Pour the egg-milk mixture over the top. Refrigerate at least 30 minutes. For best results, cover the baking dish with plastic wrap and refrigerate overnight.

Bake the casserole in the preheated oven for 35 to 45 minutes, or until the eggs have cooked through and the top is golden brown. Let cool before slicing and serving.

Serve Baked Walnut French Toast with Maple Syrup and Fresh Fruit.

Makes 4 breakfast servings

Cost $2.75

FRUGAL FACT: *Be sure to look at online grocery retailers for better prices on maple syrup than you'll find in your grocery store and even your farmers' market.*

Sausage, Apple, and Egg Casserole

6 slices whole wheat bread ($.25)
1 pound all-natural pork sausage roll
   ($1.99)
1 small yellow onion, chopped ($.30)
1 Granny Smith apple, peeled and
   chopped ($.25)

8 large eggs ($.80)
½ cup milk ($.05)
salt and pepper

Spinach ("Green") Smoothies (page 277) ($1.20)

Preheat the oven to 350 degrees. Lightly coat a 9 × 13-inch glass baking dish with nonstick cooking spray.

Tear the whole wheat bread into pieces and place into the prepared baking dish.

Brown the pork sausage, crumbling it as you cook it, and drain. Add the cooked sausage, the chopped onion, and the chopped apples to the prepared baking dish with the bread. Toss lightly.

In a mixing bowl, whisk together the eggs, milk, and salt and pepper to taste. Pour the mixture over the bread, sausage, and apples in the baking dish. Refrigerate at least 30 minutes. For best results, cover the baking dish with plastic wrap and refrigerate overnight.

Bake the casserole in the preheated oven for 45 to 55 minutes, or until the eggs have cooked through and are set in the middle. Let cool before cutting and serving.

Serve Sausage, Apple, and Egg Casserole with Spinach ("Green") Smoothies.

Makes 6 to 8 breakfast servings

Cost $4.84

FRUGAL FACT: *Batch cook twice as much sausage as you need for this recipe, and freeze the cooked, crumbled sausage in a plastic freezer bag.*

Blueberry Breakfast Bake

6 slices stale French bread (about 1 inch thick) ($.50)
1 cup fresh or frozen blueberries ($1)
8 large eggs ($.80)
½ cup milk ($.05)

½ cup sugar ($.05)
½ teaspoon ground cinnamon ($.03)
½ teaspoon ground allspice ($.03)
Syrup or confectioners' sugar for serving ($.10)

Strawberry-Banana Smoothies (page 273) ($1.74)

Preheat the oven to 350 degrees. Lightly coat an 8 × 8-inch glass baking dish with nonstick cooking spray.

Place the slices of stale bread into the prepared baking dish. Sprinkle the blueberries around and on top of the bread slices.

In a mixing bowl, whisk the eggs, milk, sugar, cinnamon, and allspice. Pour the mixture over the bread and blueberries in the baking dish. Refrigerate at least 30 minutes. For best results, cover the baking dish with plastic wrap and refrigerate overnight.

Bake the casserole in the preheated oven for 35 to 45 minutes, or until the eggs have cooked through and the top is golden. Let cool before cutting and serving.

Serve Blueberry Breakfast Bake with Syrup or Confectioners' Sugar and Strawberry-Banana Smoothies.

Makes 4 breakfast servings

Cost $4.30

FRUGAL FACT: *Don't throw out that loaf of stale French bread. The bread can be saved by soaking it in the egg-milk mixture.*

Fiesta Breakfast Casserole

6 large eggs ($.60)
¼ cup milk ($.03)
½ teaspoon salt
½ teaspoon pepper
1 can (4 ounce) green chilies, drained
($.59)

1 red bell pepper, seeded and
diced ($1)
1 cup shredded Mexican blend cheese
($.75)

Fresh fruit ($.50)

Preheat the oven to 350 degrees. Lightly coat an 8×8-inch glass baking dish with nonstick cooking spray.

In a mixing bowl, whisk together the eggs, milk, and salt and pepper. Stir in the drained green chilies.

Place the diced bell pepper and the shredded Mexican cheese blend in the bottom of the prepared baking dish. Pour the egg mixture over the top.

Bake the casserole in the preheated oven for 25 to 30 minutes, or until the eggs have cooked through and are set in the middle and the top golden. Let cool before cutting and serving.

Serve Fiesta Breakfast Casserole with Fresh Fruit.

Makes 4 breakfast servings

Cost $3.47

FRUGAL FACT: *Because the red bell pepper is cooked, this is the perfect recipe to use up that stockpile of frozen diced, red bell pepper from the freezer.*

Cream Cheese–Stuffed French Toast

10 large eggs ($1)
1 cup milk ($.10)
3 tablespoons syrup ($.15)
½ teaspoon ground cinnamon ($.03)

2 ripe bananas ($.40)
4 ounces cream cheese, softened ($.50)
8 slices whole wheat bread ($.60)
Syrup for serving ($.10)

Fresh fruit ($.50)

Preheat the oven to 350 degrees. Lightly coat a 9 × 13-inch glass baking dish with nonstick cooking spray.

In a mixing bowl, whisk together the eggs, milk, syrup, and cinnamon.

In another mixing bowl, mash together the bananas and softened cream cheese.

Arrange 4 slices of the whole wheat bread so they cover the bottom of the prepared baking dish. Spread the banana–cream cheese mixture over the top of the bread. Then place the other 4 slices of whole wheat bread on top of the banana–cream cheese mixture. Pour the egg-milk mixture over the bread. Refrigerate at least 30 minutes. For best results, cover with plastic wrap and refrigerate overnight.

Bake the stuffed French toast in the preheated oven for 35 to 45 minutes, or until the eggs have cooked through and the top has turned golden. Let cool before cutting and serving.

Serve Cream Cheese–Stuffed French Toast with Syrup and Fresh Fruit.

Makes 6 to 8 breakfast servings

Cost $3.38

FRUGAL FACT: *My "never-pay-more-than" price for 8 ounces of cream cheese is $1, although it can be found for $.50 with the right sale and coupon matchup.*

Cranberry-Apple Breakfast Casserole

½ cup firmly packed brown sugar ($.13)

1 teaspoon ground cinnamon ($.03)

½ cup butter or margarine, melted ($.40)

3 Granny Smith apples, peeled, cored, and diced ($.75)

1 cup dried cranberries ($.75)

8 slices whole wheat bread, torn ($.60)

6 large eggs ($.60)

1½ cups milk ($.15)

1 tablespoon vanilla extract ($.15)

2 teaspoons ground cinnamon ($.10)

Syrup for serving ($.10)

Fresh fruit ($.50)

Preheat the oven to 375 degrees. Lightly coat a 9×13-inch glass baking dish with nonstick cooking spray.

In a mixing bowl, toss together the brown sugar, cinnamon, melted butter or margarine, diced apples, and dried cranberries. Spread the fruit over the bottom of the prepared baking dish. Arrange the torn bread pieces over the top of the apples and cranberries. Toss lightly.

In a mixing bowl, whisk together the eggs, milk, vanilla, and ground cinnamon. Pour the egg mixture over the bread, apples, and cranberries. Refrigerate at least 30 minutes. For best results, cover the casserole with plastic wrap and refrigerate overnight.

Bake the casserole in the preheated oven for 35 to 45 minutes, or until the eggs have cooked through and the top is golden. Let cool before cutting and serving.

Serve Cranberry-Apple Breakfast Casserole with Syrup and Fresh Fruit.

Makes 6 to 8 breakfast servings

Cost $4.26

FRUGAL FACT: *Keep an eye out for $1 sale prices on dried cranberries at the national drugstores.*

Caramel Apple Breakfast Casserole

6 large eggs ($.60)
1 cup milk ($.10)
2 teaspoons ground cinnamon ($.10)
¼ teaspoon ground nutmeg ($.02)
4 medium apples, peeled, cored,
  and diced ($1)

¼ cup butter or margarine, melted
  ($.40)
¼ cup firmly packed brown sugar ($.20)
6 slices of whole wheat bread,
  torn ($.45)

Fresh fruit ($.50)

Preheat the oven to 350 degrees. Lightly coat an 8 × 8-inch glass baking dish with nonstick cooking spray.

In a mixing bowl, whisk together the eggs, milk, 1 teaspoon of the cinnamon, and the nutmeg.

In another mixing bowl, toss the diced apples with the melted butter, brown sugar and the remaining teaspoon cinnamon. Pour them into the bottom of the prepared baking dish. Add the torn bread pieces and toss lightly. Pour the egg mixture over the top. Refrigerate at least 30 minutes. For best results, cover the casserole with plastic wrap and refrigerate overnight.

Bake the casserole in the preheated oven for 30 minutes covered with aluminum foil. Uncover the baking dish and bake for another 15 to 20 minutes, or until the eggs have cooked through and the top is golden. Let cool before slicing and serving.

Serve Caramel Apple Breakfast Casserole with Fresh Fruit.

Makes 4 breakfast servings

Cost $3.37

FRUGAL FACT: *This recipe can easily be doubled and baked in a 9 × 13-inch glass baking dish—perfect for a brunch or weekend breakfast with houseguests.*

Bacon and Tomato Omelet

....

4 bacon slices ($.50)
12 large eggs ($1.20)
4 tablespoons milk ($.03)
salt and pepper

2 plum tomatoes, seeded and
   diced ($1)
1 cup shredded sharp cheddar
   cheese ($.75)

Spinach ("Green") Smoothies (page 277) ($1.20)

Heat a 7-inch skillet or omelet pan over high heat. Add a slice of bacon and cook until crisp. Transfer to a paper towel to drain and cool. Crumble when cooled. Pour out fat from pan.

In a mixing bowl, whisk together 3 of the eggs plus 1 tablespoon of milk, and season with of salt and pepper. Pour the eggs into the same skillet where you cooked the bacon. Let the eggs cook for 3 to 4 minutes.

As the eggs begin to firm up in the skillet, take a plastic spatula and run it around the edge of the omelet, tilting the pan if necessary to move the uncooked eggs around, allowing them to finish cooking. When the eggs are almost completely cooked through, add about ⅓ cup of the diced tomatoes, one-fourth of the crumbled bacon, and about ¼ cup of the shredded, sharp cheddar cheese. Using the plastic spatula, fold the omelet in half and cook for another 1 to 2 minutes.

Repeat this process until all 4 omelets are made.

Serve Bacon and Tomato Omelets with Spinach ("Green") Smoothies.

Makes 4 omelets

Cost $4.68

FRUGAL FACT: *Pick two smaller variety tomatoes from your garden and make this for breakfast one cool late-summer morning.*

Ham and Cheese Omelet

¼ cup canola or vegetable oil ($.10)
2 cups diced ham ($1)
12 large eggs ($1.20)
4 tablespoons milk ($.03)

1 cup shredded sharp cheddar cheese
($.75)
salt and pepper

Pumpkin Smoothies (page 276) ($1.25)

Heat a 7-inch skillet or omelet pan over high heat. Add about 1 tablespoon canola or vegetable oil and ½ cup of the diced ham. Sauté over high heat for 3 to 4 minutes.

In a mixing bowl, whisk together 3 of the eggs plus 1 tablespoon of the milk, and season with salt and pepper. Pour the eggs over the sautéed ham, lifting it just after you pour in the eggs, so the eggs can get under the ham. Let the eggs cook for 3 to 4 minutes.

As the eggs begin to firm up in the skillet, take a plastic spatula and run it around the edge of the omelet, tilting the pan if necessary to move the uncooked eggs around, allowing them to finish cooking. When the eggs are almost completely cooked through, add about ¼ cup of shredded, sharp cheddar cheese. Using the plastic spatula, fold the omelet in half and let cook for another 1 to 2 minutes.

Repeat this process until all 4 omelets are made.

Serve Ham and Cheese Omelets with Pumpkin Smoothies.

Makes 4 omelets

Cost $4.33

FRUGAL FACT: *A perfect weekend breakfast any time of year.*

Spinach and Swiss Omelet

....

¼ cup canola or vegetable oil ($.10)
1 cup yellow onion, chopped ($.50)
1 bag (10 ounces) baby spinach ($1.50)
12 eggs ($1.20)

4 tablespoons milk ($.03)
salt and pepper
1 cup shredded Swiss cheese ($.75)

Fresh fruit ($.50)

Heat a 7-inch skillet or omelet pan over high heat. Add about 1 tablespoon of the canola or vegetable oil and ¼ cup chopped onions and 2 large handfuls of spinach. Sauté over high heat for 3 to 4 minutes, or until the spinach has wilted and the onion has turned translucent.

In a mixing bowl, whisk together 3 of the eggs plus 1 tablespoon of the milk, and season with salt and pepper. Pour the eggs over the sautéed spinach and onions, lifting the vegetables just after you pour in the eggs, so the eggs can get under the vegetables. Let the eggs cook for 3 to 4 minutes.

As the eggs begin to firm up around the edge of the skillet, take a plastic spatula and run it around the edge of the omelet, tilting the pan if necessary to move the eggs around, allowing them to finish cooking. When the eggs are almost completely cooked through, add about ¼ cup of shredded Swiss cheese. Using the plastic spatula, fold the omelet in half and let cook for another 1 to 2 minutes.

Repeat this process until all 4 omelets are made.

Serve Spinach and Swiss Omelets with Fresh Fruit.

Makes 4 omelets

Cost $4.58

FRUGAL FACT: *Make this meal for less by using spinach leaves from your garden.*

Bacon and Egg Breakfast Pizza

DOUGH

1 cup lukewarm water
1 cup all-purpose flour ($.20)
1 packet active dry yeast ($.25)
2 tablespoons sugar ($.02)

1 teaspoon salt
2 tablespoons olive oil ($.20)
2 cups whole wheat flour ($.28)
1 teaspoon garlic powder ($.05)

TOPPING

8 large eggs ($.80)
6 bacon slices ($.75)
1 cup homemade (page 255)
  or store-bought salsa
  ($.50)

2 cups shredded Monterey
  Jack cheese ($1.50)

BREAD MACHINE DIRECTIONS FOR THE DOUGH

Place the ingredients for the dough into the bread machine according to manufacturer's directions. Set on the dough cycle.

BY HAND DIRECTIONS FOR THE DOUGH

In a mixing bowl, combine the lukewarm water and 1 cup of the all-purpose flour. Add the yeast, sugar, salt, and oil. Whisk together to make a "spongy" dough. Let sit for 10 to 15 minutes.

Add the 2 cups of whole wheat flour to the sponge and stir with a wooden spoon. When the dough becomes thick enough, knead it by hand for 6 to 8 minutes on a floured surface or in a floured bowl, until it reaches the consistency of soft baby skin. Knead the garlic powder into the dough. Place in a floured or greased bowl and let rise for 45 minutes to 1 hour.

As the dough from the bread machine or the mixing bowl nears its final rising stages, scramble the eggs and cook the bacon slices. Transfer the bacon to paper towels to drain and cool before crumbling.

Once the dough cycle is complete or the dough has doubled in size, punch it down and remove it from the bread machine bowl or mixing bowl. Knead the dough for 2 to 3 minutes, and then roll out on a clean and floured surface into the shape of the baking sheet. Place the rolled out dough onto the prepared baking sheet.

Spread the salsa over the top of the dough, then top with the scrambled eggs and crumbled bacon. Sprinkle the shredded cheese over the entire pizza. Bake the pizza in the preheated oven for 10 to 15 minutes, or until the cheese has melted. Let cool slightly before slicing and serving.

Serve Bacon and Egg Breakfast Pizza.

Makes one 16-inch pizza, or 8 large slices

Cost $4.55

FRUGAL FACT: *If in a time crunch, use a store-bought premade crust in place of the homemade pizza crust.*

Egg in a Nest with Avocado Circle Sandwiches

8 slices whole wheat bread ($.60)

8 large eggs ($.80)

salt and pepper

½ cup homemade (page 255) or store-bought salsa ($.25)

1 avocado, pitted, peeled, and mashed ($.68)

1 teaspoon lime juice ($.02)

1 teaspoon garlic powder ($.05)

½ teaspoon ground cumin ($.03)

4 slices cheddar cheese ($.75)

Preheat a stovetop skillet or griddle, or an electric griddle to 350 degrees. Lightly coat with nonstick cooking spray.

Using a 1½- to 2-circular cookie or biscuit cutter, cut holes in each of the 8 slices of bread. Set the cut bread aside.

Place a slice of bread onto the preheated hot skillet or griddle, then crack the egg into the hole in the middle of the bread. Let fry for 2 to 3 minutes, then flip and let the other side fry for 1 to 2 minutes, or until egg has cooked through. Season to taste with salt and pepper.

In a small bowl, mash the avocado flesh and mix in the lime juice, garlic powder, and ground cumin.

Spread the guacamole on the cut bread circles, then top with salsa and a slice of cheese. Place the other bread circle on top of the cheese, making 4 circles sandwiches. When the eggs in a nest have finished cooking, place the circle sandwiches on the griddle and heat for 2 to 3 minutes on each side, to melt the cheese.

Serve Eggs in a Nest with Avocado Circle Sandwiches.

Makes 8 Eggs in a Nest and 4 Avocado Circle Sandwiches

Cost $3.18

FRUGAL FACT: *A few other ideas to use up the bread circles would be to make them into croutons, freeze them, and use for egg casseroles. Or freeze to use in the Balsamic French Onion Soup (page 199).*

THREE

Breakfast Breads — Waffles, Pancakes, Muffins, and More

Buttermilk Waffles

1¾ cups all-purpose flour ($.35)
2 teaspoons baking powder ($.10)
2 tablespoons brown sugar ($.02)
2 teaspoons ground cinnamon ($.07)
½ teaspoon salt

2 large eggs ($.20)
½ cup canola or vegetable oil ($.20)
1¾ cups buttermilk ($.25)
Butter and syrup for serving ($.25)

Peach-Strawberry Smoothies (page 278) ($2.24)

Preheat a waffle iron according to the manufacturer's instructions.

In a large mixing bowl, combine the flour, baking powder, brown sugar, cinnamon, and salt. Add the eggs, oil, and buttermilk; whisk until a smooth batter forms.

Pour about 1 cup of the batter onto a greased hot waffle iron and cook until the steam no longer escapes from the waffle iron. Check the instruction manual of your waffle iron for proper batter amounts and recommended cooking times. Remove the waffles carefully from the waffle iron. Repeat until all the batter is used.

Serve Buttermilk Waffles with Butter and Syrup and Peach-Strawberry Smoothie.

Makes twelve 4-inch waffles

Cost $3.68

FRUGAL FACT: *Purchase a marked-down quart or half-gallon of buttermilk and make several batches of these buttermilk waffles. For best freezing results, cool waffles completely before freezing in plastic freezer bags.*

FREEZER FRIENDLY

Spiced Pumpkin Waffles

1 cup all-purpose flour ($.20)
½ cup whole wheat flour ($.14)
¼ cup sugar ($.02)
1 tablespoon baking powder ($.15)
½ teaspoon baking soda ($.02)
1 tablespoon pumpkin pie spice ($.15)
½ teaspoon salt

2 large eggs ($.20)
2 cups milk ($.20)
4 tablespoons butter, melted ($.40)
1 cup canned 100 percent pure pumpkin ($.50)
Butter and syrup for serving ($.25)

Fresh fruit ($.50)

Preheat a waffle iron according to the manufacturer's instructions.

In a large mixing bowl, combine the all-purpose flour, whole wheat flour, sugar, baking powder, baking soda, pumpkin pie spice, and salt. Add the eggs, milk, melted butter, and canned pumpkin; whisk until a smooth batter forms.

Pour about 1 cup of the batter onto a greased hot waffle iron and cook until the steam no longer escapes from the waffle iron. Check the instruction manual of your waffle iron for proper batter amounts and recommended cooking times. Remove the waffles carefully from the waffle iron. Repeat until all the batter is used.

Serve Spiced Pumpkin Waffles with Butter and Syrup and Fresh Fruit.

Makes twelve 4-inch waffles

Cost $2.73

FRUGAL FACT: *Coupons for canned pumpkin puree are often released both in the newspaper and online during the holiday season.*

FREEZER FRIENDLY

Banana Nut Waffles

2 medium, ripe bananas ($.40)
1½ cups all-purpose flour ($.30)
2 tablespoons sugar ($.01)
2 teaspoons baking powder ($.10)
1 tablespoon ground cinnamon ($.10)
1 tablespoon ground flaxseed ($.05)
  (optional)

½ teaspoon salt
2 large eggs ($.20)
¼ cup canola or vegetable oil ($.10)
1½ cups milk ($.15)
½ cup walnuts, finely chopped ($.37)
Butter and syrup for serving ($.25)

Mango-Raspberry Smoothies (page 274) ($2.04)

Preheat a waffle iron according to the manufacturer's instructions.

On a small plate, mash the bananas with a fork into a puree.

In a large mixing bowl, combine the flour, sugar, baking powder, cinnamon, ground flaxseed, if using, and the salt. Add the eggs, oil, milk, and mashed bananas; whisk until smooth batter forms. Fold in the finely chopped walnuts.

Pour about 1 cup of the batter into a greased hot waffle iron and cook until the steam no longer escapes from the waffle iron. Check the instruction manual of your waffle iron for proper batter amounts and recommended cooking times. Remove the waffles carefully from the waffle iron. Repeat until all the batter is used.

Serve Banana Nut Waffles with Butter and Syrup and Mango-Raspberry Smoothies.

Makes twelve 4-inch waffles

Cost $4.07

FRUGAL FACT: *Store baking nuts purchased on sale during the holidays in the pantry for up to 6 months, or in the freezer for up to 12 months.*

FREEZER FRIENDLY

Whole Wheat Apple Waffles

2 small apples, peeled, cored, and finely
   chopped into ⅛-inch pieces ($.50)
1 teaspoon lemon juice ($.02)
2 teaspoons brown sugar ($.02)
1 cup whole wheat flour ($.28)
½ cup all-purpose flour ($.10)
2 teaspoons baking powder ($.10)

1 teaspoon ground cinnamon ($.05)
½ teaspoon salt
2 large eggs ($.20)
¼ cup canola or vegetable oil ($.10)
1 tablespoon maple syrup ($.03)
1½ cups milk ($.15)
Butter and maple syrup for serving ($.25)

Fresh fruit ($.50)

Preheat a waffle iron according to the manufacturer's instructions.

In a small mixing bowl, toss the diced apples with the lemon juice and the brown sugar.

In a large mixing bowl, combine the whole wheat flour, all-purpose flour, baking powder, cinnamon, and salt. Add the eggs, oil, syrup, and milk; whisk until a smooth batter forms. Fold in the chopped apples.

Pour about 1 cup of the batter onto a greased hot waffle iron and cook until the steam no longer escapes from the waffle iron. Check the instruction manual of your waffle iron for proper batter amounts and recommended cooking times. Remove the waffles carefully from the waffle iron. Repeat until all the batter is used.

Serve Whole Wheat Apple Waffles with Butter and Maple Syrup and Fresh Fruit.

Makes twelve 4-inch waffles

Cost $2.30

FRUGAL FACT: *Watch for coupons for margarine and match with a sale price to get free or nearly free containers of margarine.*

FREEZER FRIENDLY

Pumpkin Chocolate Chip Waffles

1½ cups whole wheat flour ($.42)
¼ cup firmly packed brown sugar ($.10)
2 teaspoons baking powder ($.10)
1 teaspoon baking soda ($.02)
2 teaspoons pumpkin pie spice ($.10)
½ teaspoon salt
2 large eggs ($.20)

1¾ cups milk ($.17)
4 tablespoons butter, melted ($.40)
1 cup canned 100 percent pure pumpkin puree ($.50)
1½ cups mini chocolate chips ($1)
Butter and maple syrup for serving ($.25)

Fresh fruit ($.50)

Preheat a waffle iron according to the manufacturer's instructions.

In a large mixing bowl, combine the flour, sugar, baking powder, baking soda, pumpkin pie spice, and salt. Add the eggs, milk, melted butter, and canned pumpkin; whisk until a smooth batter forms. Fold in the mini chocolate chips.

Pour about 1 cup of the batter into a greased hot waffle iron and cook until the steam no longer escapes from the waffle iron. Check the instruction manual of your waffle iron for proper batter amounts and recommended cooking times. Remove the waffles carefully from the waffle iron. Repeat until all the batter is used.

Serve Pumpkin Chocolate Chip Waffles with Butter and Syrup and Fresh Fruit.

Makes twelve 4-inch waffles

Cost $3.76

FRUGAL FACT: *My "never-pay-more-than" price for a bag of baking chips is $1.49.*

FREEZER FRIENDLY

Half Whole Wheat Pancakes

1 cup whole wheat flour ($.28)
1 cup all-purpose flour ($.20)
3 tablespoons sugar ($.02)
2 teaspoons baking powder ($.10)
½ teaspoon salt

1 large egg ($.10)
3 tablespoons canola or vegetable oil ($.08)
1⅔ cups milk ($.17)
Butter and syrup for serving ($.25)

Strawberry-Banana Smoothies (page 273) ($1.74)

Preheat an electric griddle to 300 degrees, or warm a skillet over medium-high heat; lightly coat with nonstick cooking spray.

In a large mixing bowl, combine the whole wheat flour, all-purpose flour, sugar, baking powder, and salt. Add the egg, oil, and milk and whisk until a smooth batter forms.

Using a ¼ cup measuring cup, pour the batter in 4-inch circles onto the hot griddle or skillet. Flip the pancakes with a spatula once bubbles form on the surface of the batter. When cooked through, remove the pancakes from griddle or skillet. Keep them warm on a plate, covered with a clean dish towel. Continue making pancakes until the batter is used.

Serve Half Wheat Waffles with Butter and Syrup and Fresh Fruit.

Makes sixteen 4-inch pancakes

Cost $2.94

FRUGAL FACT: *Cool pancakes completely before freezing, and they will not stick together in the plastic freezer bags.*

FREEZER FRIENDLY

Oatmeal Pancakes

½ cup quick-cooking oats ($.10)
½ cup whole wheat flour ($.14)
½ cup all-purpose flour ($.10)
¼ cup sugar ($.03)
2 teaspoons baking powder ($.10)
½ teaspoon salt

1 large egg ($.10)
3 tablespoons canola or vegetable oil ($.08)
1¼ cups milk ($.12)
Butter and syrup for serving ($.25)

Spinach ("Green") Smoothies (page 277) ($1.20)

Preheat an electric griddle to 300 degrees, or warm a skillet over medium-high heat; lightly coat with nonstick cooking spray.

In a coffee bean grinder or a mini food processor, grind the oats into a loose powder.

In a large mixing bowl, combine the ground oats, whole wheat flour, all-purpose flour, sugar, baking powder, and salt. Add the egg, oil, and milk and whisk until a smooth batter forms.

Using a ¼ cup measuring cup, pour the batter in 4-inch circles onto the hot griddle or skillet. Flip the pancakes with a spatula once bubbles form on the surface of the batter. When cooked through, remove the pancakes from griddle or skillet. Keep them warm on a plate, covered with a clean dish towel. Continue making pancakes until the batter is used.

Serve Oatmeal Pancakes with Butter and Syrup and Spinach ("Green") Smoothies.

Makes sixteen 4-inch pancakes

Cost $2.22

FRUGAL FACT: *Use the plastic bags from store-bought bread loaves to freeze your pancakes.*

FREEZER FRIENDLY

Apple Cinnamon Pancakes

1 apple, peeled, cored, and finely chopped into ⅛-inch pieces ($.25)

2 tablespoons brown sugar ($.02)

½ teaspoon ground cinnamon ($.03)

1 cup whole wheat flour ($.28)

1 cup all-purpose flour ($.20)

2 tablespoons granulated sugar ($.01)

2 teaspoons baking powder ($.10)

½ teaspoon salt

1 large egg ($.10)

3 tablespoons canola or vegetable oil ($.08)

1¼ cups milk ($.12)

Butter and syrup for serving ($.25)

Blueberry Smoothies (page 275) ($1.89)

Preheat an electric griddle to 300 degrees, or warm a skillet over medium-high heat; lightly coat with nonstick cooking spray.

In a small bowl, toss the apples with the brown sugar and cinnamon.

In a large mixing bowl, combine the whole wheat flour, all-purpose flour, granulated sugar, baking powder, and salt. Add the egg, oil, and milk and whisk until a smooth batter forms. Fold in the apple mixture.

Using a ¼ cup measuring cup, pour the batter in 4-inch circles onto the hot griddle or skillet. Flip the pancakes with a spatula once the bubbles form on the surface of the batter. When cooked through, remove the pancakes from the griddle or skillet. Keep them warm on a plate, covered with a clean dish towel. Continue making pancakes until the batter is used.

Serve Apple Cinnamon Pancakes with Butter and Syrup and Blueberry Smoothies.

Makes sixteen 4-inch pancakes

Cost $3.33

FRUGAL FACT: *If you find a fantastic price on apples and don't want to let them go to waste, peel and chop the apples into itty-bitty pieces and freeze in 1 cup portions to use for baking muffins and making waffles or pancakes.*

FREEZER FRIENDLY

Maple Pecan Pancakes

1 cup whole wheat flour ($.28)
½ cup all-purpose flour ($.10)
¼ cup sugar ($.03)
2 teaspoons baking powder ($.10)
½ teaspoon ground cinnamon ($.03)
½ teaspoon salt
3 tablespoons maple syrup ($.50)

1 large egg ($.10)
2 tablespoons canola or vegetable oil ($.05)
1¼ cups milk ($.12)
½ cup chopped pecans ($.75)
Butter and maple syrup for serving ($1)

Fresh fruit ($.50)

Preheat an electric griddle to 300 degrees, or warm a skillet over medium-high heat; lightly coat with nonstick cooking spray.

In a large mixing bowl, combine the whole wheat flour, all-purpose flour, sugar, baking powder, cinnamon and salt. Add the maple syrup, egg, oil, and milk and whisk until a smooth batter forms. Fold in the chopped pecans.

Using a ¼ cup measuring cup, pour the batter in 4-inch circles onto the hot griddle or skillet. Flip the pancakes with a spatula once bubbles form on the surface of the batter. When cooked through, remove the pancakes from griddle or skillet. Keep them warm on a plate, covered with a clean dish towel. Continue making pancakes until the batter is used.

Serve Maple Pecan Pancakes with Butter and Maple Syrup and Fresh Fruit.

Makes sixteen 4-inch pancakes

Cost $3.56

FRUGAL FACT: *Maple syrup prices are generally lower at a local farmers' market than what you'll see in a grocery store.*

FREEZER FRIENDLY

Pumpkin Pancakes

1 cup whole wheat flour ($.28)
1 cup all-purpose flour ($.20)
2 teaspoons baking powder ($.10)
3 tablespoons brown sugar ($.03)
1 teaspoon baking soda ($.02)
1 teaspoon ground cinnamon ($.05)
½ teaspoon ground ginger ($.05)
½ teaspoon ground allspice ($.05)

½ teaspoon salt
1 large egg ($.10)
2 tablespoons canola or vegetable oil ($.05)
1¾ cups milk ($.17)
1 cup canned 100 percent pure pumpkin puree ($.50)
Butter and maple syrup for serving ($1)

Fresh fruit ($.50)

Preheat an electric griddle to 300 degrees, or warm a skillet over medium high-heat; lightly coat with nonstick cooking spray.

In a large mixing bowl, combine the whole wheat flour, all-purpose flour, baking powder, sugar, baking soda, cinnamon, ginger, allspice, and salt. Add the egg, oil, milk, and canned pumpkin puree; whisk until a smooth batter forms.

Using a ¼ cup measuring cup, pour the batter in 4-inch circles onto the hot griddle or skillet. Flip the pancakes with a spatula once bubbles form on the surface of the batter. When cooked through, remove the pancakes from the griddle or skillet. Keep them warm on a plate, covered with a clean dish towel. Continue making pancakes until the batter is used.

Serve Pumpkin Pancakes with Butter and Maple Syrup and Fresh Fruit.

Makes sixteen 4-inch pancakes

Cost $3.10

FRUGAL FACT: *Thaw frozen pancakes by placing them in the fridge the night before, or reheating them in the toaster if you forget to thaw them overnight.*

FREEZER FRIENDLY

Ginger Maple Pancakes

....

1 cup whole wheat flour ($.28)
1 cup all-purpose flour ($.20)
2 teaspoons baking powder ($.10)
1 teaspoon ground cinnamon ($.05)
1 teaspoon ground ginger ($.10)
½ teaspoon salt

4 tablespoons maple syrup ($.65)
2 large eggs ($.20)
4 tablespoons butter, melted ($.40)
2 cups milk ($.20)
Butter and maple syrup for serving ($1)

Fresh fruit ($.50)

Preheat an electric griddle to 300 degrees, or warm a skillet over medium-high heat; lightly coat with nonstick cooking spray.

In a large mixing bowl, combine the whole wheat flour, all-purpose flour, baking powder, cinnamon, ginger, and salt. Add the maple syrup, eggs, melted butter, and milk and whisk until a smooth batter forms.

Using a ¼ cup measuring cup, pour the batter in 4-inch circles onto the hot griddle or skillet. Flip the pancakes with a spatula once bubbles form on the surface of the batter. When cooked through, remove the pancakes from the griddle or skillet. Keep them warm on a plate, covered with a clean dish towel. Continue making pancakes until the batter is used.

Serve Ginger Maple Pancakes with Butter and Maple Syrup and Fresh Fruit.

Makes sixteen 4-inch pancakes

Cost $3.68

FRUGAL FACT: *Eat these pancakes with scrambled eggs and fresh fruit for an easy dinner meal on a busy evening.*

FREEZER FRIENDLY

Chocolate Chip Raspberry Pancakes

1 cup raspberries, crushed ($.50)
1 cup whole wheat flour ($.28)
1 cup all-purpose flour ($.20)
2 teaspoons baking powder ($.10)
3 tablespoons ground flaxseed ($.15) (optional)
¼ cup ground almonds ($.37)
½ teaspoon salt

1 large egg ($.10)
3 tablespoons canola or vegetable oil ($.08)
1¾ cups milk ($.17)
¾ cup chocolate chips (mini chips work best) ($.50)
Butter and syrup for serving ($.25)

Fresh fruit ($.50)

Preheat an electric griddle to 300 degrees, or warm a skillet over medium-high heat; lightly coat with nonstick cooking spray.

Rinse the raspberries and pat dry. In a small bowl, use a fork to gently crush the raspberries, but not into a puree.

In a large mixing bowl, combine the whole wheat flour, all-purpose flour, baking powder, ground flaxseed, if using, and the ground almonds and salt. Add the egg, oil, and milk; whisk until a smooth batter forms. Fold in the crushed raspberries and chocolate chips.

Using a ¼ cup measuring cup, pour the batter in 4-inch circles onto the hot griddle or skillet. Flip the pancakes with a spatula once bubbles form on the surface of the batter. When cooked through, remove the pancakes from griddle or skillet. Keep them warm on a plate, covered with a clean dish towel. Continue making pancakes until the batter is used.

Serve Chocolate Chip Raspberry Pancakes with Butter and Syrup and Fresh Fruit.

Makes twelve 4-inch pancakes

Cost $3.20

FRUGAL FACT: *Look out for chocolate chip and other baking goods coupons in the newspaper and online before, during, and after the holiday baking season. Stock up so the items will last into the next year.*

FREEZER FRIENDLY

Drop Biscuits with Cinnamon Butter

BISCUITS

1 cup whole wheat flour ($.28)
1 cup all-purpose flour ($.20)
1 tablespoon sugar ($.10)
1 tablespoon baking powder ($.15)

½ teaspoon salt
4 tablespoons butter or margarine,
   melted ($.40)
1 cup milk ($.10)

CINNAMON BUTTER

1 tablespoon honey ($.10)
2 tablespoons butter ($.20)

½ teaspoon ground cinnamon ($.02)

Fresh fruit ($.50)

Preheat the oven to 400 degrees. Lightly coat a baking sheet with nonstick cooking spray.

In a large mixing bowl, combine the whole wheat flour, all-purpose flour, sugar, baking powder, and salt. Stir in the melted butter and milk; combine until a biscuit batter forms.

Drop spoonfuls of the biscuit batter onto the prepared baking sheet.

Bake the biscuits in the preheated oven for 10 to 12 minutes, or until golden on top. Let cool on a wire rack before serving.

In a small bowl, stir together the honey, butter, and cinnamon. Slather on the hot biscuits.

Serve Drop Biscuits with Cinnamon Butter and Fresh Fruit.

Makes 12 biscuits

Cost $2.05

FRUGAL FACT: *Triple or quadruple this batch and stash the extra biscuits in the freezer and the extra Cinnamon Butter in the refrigerator for a quick "on-the-go" breakfast. If you prefer your biscuits warm from the oven, make an extra batch and freeze the dough (directions on page 21).*

Cheesy Drop Biscuits

3 cups all-purpose flour ($.60)
1 tablespoon baking powder ($.15)
1 tablespoon sugar ($.01)
1 teaspoon salt

⅔ cup cold butter, diced ($1.10)
1½ cups milk ($.15)
1 cup shredded cheddar cheese ($.75)

Fresh fruit ($.50)

Preheat the oven to 400 degrees. Lightly coat a baking sheet with nonstick cooking spray.

In a large mixing bowl, sift together the flour, baking powder, sugar, and salt. Using a pastry blender or two knives, cut the butter into the flour mixture until little crumbles form. Slowly stir the milk into the flour and butter. Once a loose batter forms, fold in the shredded cheese.

Drop spoonfuls of biscuit batter onto the prepared baking sheet.

Bake the biscuits in the preheated oven for 8 to 10 minutes, or until golden on top. Let cool on a wire rack before serving.

Serve Cheesy Drop Biscuits with Fresh Fruit.

Makes 12 biscuits

Cost $3.26

FRUGAL FACT: *In case you forget to thaw your cheese before making this recipe, use shredded cheese straight from the freezer. Thawing the cheese is not necessary when adding to the recipe.*

FREEZER FRIENDLY ■ *"ON-THE-GO" BREAKFAST*

Buttermilk Biscuits

2 cups all-purpose flour ($.40)
2 teaspoons baking powder ($.10)
½ teaspoon baking soda ($.01)
1 teaspoon salt

½ cup cold butter, diced ($.80)
¾ cup buttermilk ($.20)
Jam and butter for serving ($.25)

Peach-Strawberry Smoothies (page 278) ($2.24)

Preheat the oven to 400 degrees. Lightly coat a baking sheet with nonstick cooking spray.

In a large mixing bowl, sift together the flour, baking powder, baking soda, and salt. Using a pastry blender or two knives, cut the butter into the flour mixture until little crumbles form. Slowly stir the milk into the flour and butter. Using your hand, lightly knead the biscuit dough together, forming a ball. Separate the dough ball into three balls. Using your hand or a rolling pin, flatten the dough to about ½ inch thick. Cut out circles with a cookie cutter or biscuit cutter. Place the biscuit circles on the prepared baking sheet.

Bake the biscuits in the preheated oven for 8 to 10 minutes, or until golden brown on top. Let cool on a wire rack before serving.

Serve Buttermilk Biscuits with Jam and Butter and favorite Fresh Fruit.

Makes 12 biscuits

Cost $4.00

FRUGAL FACT: *Increase the milk to 1 cup and make "drop biscuits." Follow the directions on the Cheesy Drop Biscuits recipe (page 101) for baking.*

FREEZER FRIENDLY ■ *"ON-THE-GO" BREAKFAST*

Sour Cream and Chive Drop Biscuits

2½ cups all-purpose flour ($.50)
2 tablespoons baking powder ($.15)
1 teaspoon salt
½ cup sour cream ($.25)
1 cup milk ($.10)

3 tablespoons dried chives or fresh
  chopped chives ($.25)
1 cup shredded cheddar cheese ($.75)

Fresh fruit ($.50)

Preheat the oven to 400 degrees. Lightly coat a baking sheet with nonstick cooking spray.

In a large mixing bowl, sift together the flour, baking powder, and salt. Stir the sour cream and the milk into the flour mixture. Once a loose batter forms, fold in the chives and shredded cheese.

Drop spoonfuls of the biscuit batter onto the prepared baking sheet.

Bake the biscuits in the preheated oven for 8 to 10 minutes, or until golden on top. Let cool on a wire rack before serving.

Serve Sour Cream and Chive Drop Biscuits with favorite Fresh Fruit.

Makes 12 biscuits

Cost $2.50

FRUGAL FACT: *Sour cream can often be purchased for free or nearly free by combining coupons with $1 sale prices.*

FREEZER FRIENDLY ■ *"ON-THE-GO" BREAKFAST*

Apple Bars

1 cup all-purpose flour ($.20)
1 cup whole wheat flour ($.28)
1 teaspoon baking soda ($.03)
1 teaspoon ground cinnamon ($.05)
½ teaspoon ground allspice ($.02)
½ teaspoon salt
¼ cup canola or vegetable oil ($.10)
¼ cup applesauce ($.07)

½ cup milk ($.05)
¾ cup firmly packed brown sugar ($.20)
4 large eggs ($.40)
2 teaspoons vanilla extract ($.10)
2 lunch box–size apples, peeled, cored, and chopped ($.50)
½ cup walnuts, chopped ($.37) (optional)

Fresh fruit ($.50)

Preheat the oven to 350 degrees. Lightly coat a 15 × 10 × 1-inch baking sheet with nonstick cooking spray.

In a mixing bowl, whisk together the all-purpose flour, whole wheat flour, baking soda, cinnamon, allspice, and salt. Set aside. In the bowl of a stand mixer or in a large mixing bowl, add the oil, applesauce, milk, brown sugar, eggs, and vanilla extract. Mix until smooth. Add the dry ingredients to the wet ingredients and mix until a batter forms. Fold in the chopped apples and walnuts (if using). Pour the batter into the prepared baking sheet.

Bake the apple bars in the preheated oven for 25 to 30 minutes, or until toothpick inserted into the center comes out clean. Let cool on a wire rack before cutting and serving.

Serve Apple Bars with favorite Fresh Fruit.

Makes 24 breakfast bars

Cost $2.87

FRUGAL FACT: *This is a great recipe for a batch cooking prep hour, or to bake while eating dinner. The bars bake, freeze, and thaw well.*

FREEZER FRIENDLY ■ *"ON-THE-GO" BREAKFAST*

Cranberry-Raisin Loaf Bread

2 large eggs ($.20)
⅓ cup canola or vegetable oil ($.15)
¾ cup milk ($.08)
½ cup firmly packed brown sugar ($.12)
1 teaspoon vanilla extract ($.05)
1 cup all-purpose flour ($.20)

1 cup whole wheat flour ($.28)
2 teaspoons baking powder ($.10)
1 teaspoon baking soda ($.03)
1 teaspoon ground cinnamon ($.05)
½ teaspoon salt
1 cup raisins ($.75)
1 cup dried cranberries ($.75)

4 hard-boiled eggs ($.40)

Preheat the oven to 350 degrees. Lightly coat a 9 × 5-inch loaf pan with nonstick cooking spray.

In the bowl of a stand mixer or in a large mixing bowl, beat together the eggs, oil, milk, brown sugar, and vanilla.

In another mixing bowl, whisk together the all-purpose flour, whole wheat flour, baking powder, baking soda, cinnamon, and salt. Pour the dry ingredients into the bowl of the stand mixer or large mixing bowl and mix with the wet ingredients until the batter is smooth. Fold in the raisins and the cranberries. Pour the batter into the prepared loaf pan.

Bake the loaf in the preheated oven for 45 to 55 minutes, reducing the oven temperature to 300 for the last 10 to 15 minutes of baking. The loaf is done when a knife inserted in the center of the loaf comes out clean. Let cool on a wire rack before slicing and serving.

Serve Cranberry-Raisin Loaf Bread with Hard-boiled Eggs.

Makes 1 loaf

Cost $3.16

FRUGAL FACT: *The best sale price I have found for dried cranberries is $1 per cup, and the best price for raisins around $.75 per cup.*

FREEZER FRIENDLY ■ *"ON-THE-GO" BREAKFAST*

Banana Blueberry Loaf Bread

3 cups all-purpose white flour ($.60)
1 cup whole wheat flour ($.28)
1 tablespoon baking powder ($.15)
1 teaspoon salt
4 eggs ($.40)
½ cup granulated sugar ($.10)

½ cup firmly packed brown sugar ($.12)
4 tablespoons canola or vegetable oil ($.10)
1 teaspoon vanilla extract ($.05)
¾ cup milk ($.07)
3 bananas, mashed ($.60)
2 cups blueberries ($1)

4 hard-boiled eggs ($.40)

Preheat the oven to 350 degrees. Lightly coat two 9 × 5-inch loaf pans with nonstick cooking spray. Set aside.

In a large mixing bowl, whisk together the all-purpose flour, whole wheat flour, baking powder, and salt. Set aside.

In the bowl of a stand mixer or in a large mixing bowl using a hand mixer, beat together the eggs, granulated sugar, brown sugar, oil, vanilla, milk, and the mashed bananas until well combined. Mix in the flour mixture until a smooth batter forms. Gently fold in the blueberries by hand.

Pour the batter into the prepared pans. Bake the loaves in the preheated oven for 55 to 60 minutes, or until a knife inserted in the centers of the loaves comes out clean. Let cool on a wire rack before serving.

Serve Banana Blueberry Loaf Bread with Hard-boiled Eggs.

Makes 2 loaves

Cost $3.87

FRUGAL FACT: *If you can't use your overly ripe bananas right away, peel them and freeze them to use later in banana bread or muffin recipes.*

FREEZER FRIENDLY ■ *"ON-THE-GO" BREAKFAST*

Whole Wheat Toasting Bread

1 cup warm milk ($.10)
1 cup all-purpose flour ($.20)
1 packet active dry yeast ($.25)
2 tablespoons sugar ($.01)
1 teaspoon salt

¼ cup canola or vegetable oil ($.10)
2 cups whole wheat flour ($.56)
1 large egg, lightly beaten ($.10)
½ cup quick-cooking oats ($.10)
Butter and jam or jelly for serving ($.25)

4 hard-boiled eggs ($.40)

BREAD MACHINE DIRECTIONS

Place the ingredients in the order listed into the bread machine. Set on the whole wheat bread cycle and bake. Let cool completely before removing from the bread pan. When cooled, slice with bread knife.

Toast the bread in a toaster or toaster oven and serve with butter and your favorite jam or jelly.

BY HAND DIRECTIONS

Lightly coat a 9 × 5-inch loaf pan with nonstick cooking spray.

In a large mixing bowl, combine warm milk plus the 1 cup all-purpose of flour. Add the yeast, sugar, salt, and oil. Whisk together. This will make a "spongy" dough. Let sit for 10 to 15 minutes.

Add 1½ cups of the whole wheat flour and the beaten egg to the spongy dough and stir with wooden spoon. Then, knead in the remaining flour 2 tablespoons of flour at a time, until the dough can be handled easily and kneaded into a large ball. Knead the quick-cooking oats into the dough ball. Place the dough into the prepared loaf pan. Set aside and let rise for 30 minutes to 1 hour in a warm place.

Preheat the oven to 350 degrees.

Bake the bread in the preheated oven for 20 to 25 minutes, or until golden brown on top and sounds hollow when the bottom is rapped. Remove from oven and let cool on wire rack. Slice with a bread knife when cooled.

Serve Whole Wheat Toasting Bread with Butter and Jam or Jelly and Hard-boiled Eggs.

Makes one 1½-pound loaf; 12 slices

Cost $2.07

FRUGAL FACT: *Store yeast in the freezer to keep it fresh for a year.*

Whole Wheat Cinnamon Rolls with Flaxseed

ROLLS

1 packet active dry yeast ($.25)
1 teaspoon sugar ($.01)
⅓ cup warm water
1 cup milk ($.10)
1 teaspoon vanilla extract ($.05)
2 tablespoons butter or margarine, melted ($.20)
1 large egg ($.10)

¼ cup sugar ($.03)
1 teaspoon salt
½ cup all-purpose flour, plus ¼ cup for kneading and rolling ($.15)
3 cups whole wheat flour ($.84)
½ cup butter or margarine, softened ($.80)

CINNAMON FILLING

¼ cup firmly packed brown sugar ($.06)
¼ cup ground flaxseed ($.50)

1 tablespoon ground cinnamon ($.15)

Spinach ("Green") Smoothies (page 277) ($1.20)

In the bowl of a stand mixer or in a large mixing bowl, add the yeast, sugar, and warm water. Let proof.

In a small mixing bowl or a 2-cup spouted measuring cup, add the milk, vanilla, melted butter, and egg. Stir lightly with a fork.

In a medium mixing bowl, whisk together the sugar, salt, ½ cup all-purpose flour, and the wheat flour.

Add the milk mixture to the proofed yeast and mix for 1 to 2 minutes. Then add the flour mixture 1 cup at a time, mixing for 30 seconds to 1 minute each time flour is added to the mixing bowl.

Once all the flour is added to the mixing bowl, knead the dough with your hands on a clean, floured work surface for approximately 5 to 8 minutes, or until the dough ball is smooth. If using a stand mixer, knead with the kneading hook for 5 to 8 minutes. Remove the dough ball from the bowl it is in and then grease that same bowl with butter. Place the dough ball back into the greased bowl and place in a warm location in your kitchen. Cover the bowl with a towel and let rise for 1 hour.

While rising, set out the butter or margarine to soften and prepare the cinnamon filling: In a small bowl, toss together the brown sugar, ground flaxseed, and cinnamon and set aside.

Preheat the oven to 350 degrees. Coat a large baking sheet with nonstick cooking spray.

Once the dough has doubled in size, punch it down and let sit for 10 minutes. After 10 minutes, gently knead the dough for 1 minute and then set it on a floured surface. Roll it out into an 8 × 15-inch rectangle. Spread the softened butter or margarine over the dough and then evenly sprinkle the cinnamon mixture over the butter. Roll the dough up lengthwise and pinch together the ends. Cut the dough into 12 rolls, using dental floss or a sharp knife.

Place the cut cinnamon rolls onto the prepared baking sheet and let rise in a warm place for 20 to 30 minutes.

Bake the cinnamon rolls in the preheated oven for 14 to 18 minutes, or until they begin to golden brown on top. Let cool on a wire rack before serving.

Serve Whole Wheat Cinnamon Rolls with Flaxseed with Spinach ("Green") Smoothies.

Makes 12 cinnamon rolls

Cost $4.44

FRUGAL FACT: *This is another great recipe to double and then freeze the extra cinnamon rolls for an "on-the-go" breakfast.*

FREEZER FRIENDLY ■ *"ON-THE-GO BREAKFAST"*

Southwest Sausage Muffins

....

½ pound all-natural pork sausage ($1)
2¼ cup all-purpose flour ($.43)
1 tablespoon baking powder ($.15)
1 teaspoon salt
2 large eggs ($.20)
1 tablespoon canola or vegetable oil
  ($.03)

1¼ cups milk ($.12)
1 can (4 ounces) green chilies, drained
  ($.59)
1 cup corn kernels ($.50)
½ cup shredded cheddar or pepper
  jack cheese ($.37)

Fresh fruit ($.50)

Preheat the oven to 350 degrees. Lightly coat 12 wells of a regular-size muffin pan with nonstick cooking spray, or line with paper liners.

In a large skillet, brown the pork sausage, crumbling it as you cook it. Drain and set aside on a paper towel to absorb excess grease.

In a large mixing bowl, whisk together the flour, baking powder, and salt. Whisk in the eggs, oil, and milk until a batter forms. Fold in the cooked sausage crumbles and the drained green chilies, corn kernels, and shredded cheese.

Fill the prepared muffin wells up to the top with the batter. Bake the muffins in the preheated oven for 18 to 22 minutes, or until they begin to turn golden on top. Let cool on a wire rack before serving.

Serve Southwest Sausage Muffins with Fresh Fruit.

Makes 12 muffins

Cost $3.89

FRUGAL FACT: *Be sure to stock up on cans of green chilies when you see them on sale. My "never-pay-more-than" price for green chilies is $.59 per can.*

FREEZER FRIENDLY ■ *"ON-THE-GO" BREAKFAST*

Cheesy Sausage Muffins

½ pound all-natural pork sausage ($1)
2 cups all-purpose flour ($.40)
2 teaspoons baking powder ($.10)
1 teaspoon salt
2 large eggs ($.20)

¼ cup canola or vegetable oil ($.10)
1 cup milk ($.10)
1 cup shredded cheddar or Monterey
   Jack cheese ($.75)

Fresh fruit ($.50)

Preheat the oven to 350 degrees. Lightly coat 12 wells of a regular-size muffin pan with nonstick cooking spray, or line with paper liners.

In a large skillet, brown the pork sausage, crumbling it as you cook it. Drain and set aside on a paper towel to absorb excess fat.

In a large mixing bowl, whisk together the flour, baking powder, and salt. Whisk in the eggs, oil, and milk until a batter forms. Fold in the cooked sausage crumbles and shredded cheese.

Fill the prepared muffin wells up to the top with the batter. Bake the muffins in the preheated oven for 18 to 22 minutes, or until they begin to turn golden on top. Let cool on a wire rack before serving.

Serve Cheesy Sausage Muffins with Fresh Fruit.

Makes 12 muffins

Cost $3.15

FRUGAL FACT: *If using a 1-pound roll of all-natural pork sausage, brown the entire pound and double this recipe and stash the extra sausage muffins in the freezer. Another option would be to freeze the other half-pound of cooked sausage for future use.*

FREEZER FRIENDLY ■ *"ON-THE-GO" BREAKFAST*

Lemon Blueberry Muffins

2¼ cups all-purpose flour ($.45)
1 teaspoon baking powder ($.05)
1 teaspoon baking soda ($.03)
½ teaspoon salt
2 large eggs ($.20)

½ cup sugar ($.05)
¾ cup milk ($.08)
1 teaspoon vanilla extract ($.05)
3 tablespoons lemon juice ($.15)
1 cup blueberries ($.50)

Fresh fruit ($.50)

Preheat the oven to 350 degrees. Lightly coat 12 wells of a regular-size muffin pan with nonstick cooking spray, or line with paper liners.

In a small mixing bowl, whisk together the flour, baking powder, baking soda, and salt.

In a large mixing bowl or the bowl of a stand mixer, beat the eggs, sugar, milk, vanilla, and lemon juice until well blended. Add the flour mixture and beat until a batter forms. Gently fold in the blueberries by hand.

Fill the prepared muffin wells three-quarters full with the batter. Bake the muffins in the preheated oven for 18 to 22 minutes, or until a toothpick inserted in the centers of the muffins comes out clean. Let cool on a wire rack before serving.

Serve Lemon Blueberry Muffins with Fresh Fruit.

Makes 12 muffins

Cost $1.96

FRUGAL FACT: *When blueberry prices drop to around the $1 mark, be sure to stock up and quick freeze what you can't use right away. Frozen blueberries are perfect for baking and for smoothies.*

FREEZER FRIENDLY ■ *"ON-THE-GO" BREAKFAST*

Zucchini-Carrot Muffins

1 cup all-purpose flour ($.20)
1 cup whole wheat flour ($.28)
2 teaspoons ground cinnamon ($.10)
2 teaspoons baking powder ($.10)
1 teaspoon baking soda ($.03)
½ teaspoon salt

4 large eggs ($.40)
½ cup firmly packed brown sugar ($.12)
¼ cup canola or vegetable oil ($.10)
¼ cup applesauce ($.07)
1 medium zucchini, shredded ($.79)
2 carrots, peeled and shredded ($.20)

Pumpkin Smoothies (page 276) ($1.25)

Preheat the oven to 350 degrees. Lightly coat 24 wells of a regular-size muffin pan with nonstick cooking spray, or line with paper liners.

In a small mixing bowl, whisk together the flours, cinnamon, baking powder, baking soda, and salt.

In a large mixing bowl or the bowl of a stand mixer, beat the eggs, brown sugar, oil, and applesauce until well blended. Add the flour mixture and beat until a batter forms. Gently fold in the shredded zucchini and carrots.

Fill the prepared muffin wells three-quarters full with the batter. Bake the muffins in the preheated oven for 18 to 22 minutes, or until toothpick inserted in the centers of the muffins comes out clean. Let cool on a wire rack before serving.

Serve Zucchini-Carrot Muffins with Pumpkin Smoothies.

Makes 24 muffins

Cost $3.64

FRUGAL FACT: *During the mid to late summer, purchase extra zucchini when they are at their lowest price. Shred them and then freeze the shredded zucchini in 1- and 2-cup portions. Then you can make these muffins in the winter and not have to pay the high off-season prices for zucchini.*

FREEZER FRIENDLY ■ *"ON-THE-GO" BREAKFAST*

Pumpkin Nut Muffins

1 cup all-purpose flour ($.20)
½ cup whole wheat flour ($.14)
1 teaspoon baking powder ($.05)
2 teaspoon pumpkin pie spice ($.10)
½ teaspoon salt
2 large eggs ($.20)
½ cup granulated sugar ($.05)

½ cup applesauce ($.12)
⅓ cup canola or vegetable oil ($.15)
1 cup canned 100 percent pure pumpkin puree ($1)
1 cup chopped walnuts ($.75)
1 teaspoon brown sugar ($.01)
1 teaspoon ground ginger ($.05)

Fresh fruit ($.50)

Preheat the oven to 350 degrees. Lightly coat 12 wells of a regular-size muffin pan with nonstick cooking spray, or line with paper liners.

In a small mixing bowl, whisk together the all-purpose flour, whole wheat flour, baking powder, pumpkin pie spice, and salt.

In the bowl of a stand mixer or a large mixing bowl, beat the eggs, granulated sugar, applesauce, oil, and pumpkin puree until smooth. Add the flour mixture and beat until a batter forms. (Set the flour bowl aside.)

In the same small mixing bowl used for the flour, toss the walnuts with the brown sugar and ginger. Gently fold the coated walnuts into the batter.

Fill the prepared muffin wells three-quarters full with the batter. Bake the muffins in the preheated oven for 20 to 24 minutes, or until a toothpick in the centers of the muffins comes out clean. Let cool on a wire rack before serving.

Serve Pumpkin Nut Muffins with Fresh Fruit.

Makes 12 muffins

Cost $3.32

FRUGAL FACT: *Adding coated walnuts into the muffins give them both a flavor boost and a protein boost.*

FREEZER FRIENDLY ■ *"ON-THE-GO" BREAKFAST*

Blueberry Oat Muffins

1 cup-quick cooking oats ($.12)
1 cup plus 1 teaspoon all-purpose flour
    ($.21)
½ cup whole wheat flour ($.14)
2 teaspoons baking powder ($.10)
1 teaspoon baking soda ($.03)
½ teaspoon ground cinnamon ($.02)
½ teaspoon salt

1 large egg ($.10)
½ cup firmly packed brown sugar ($.12)
3 tablespoons canola or vegetable oil
    ($.08)
1 teaspoon vanilla extract ($.05)
1 cup milk ($.10)
2 cups blueberries ($1)

Fresh fruit ($.50)

Preheat the oven to 350 degrees. Lightly coat 12 wells of a regular-size muffin pan with nonstick cooking spray, or line with paper liners.

In a small mixing bowl, whisk together the oats, 1 cup of all-purpose flour, whole wheat flour, baking powder, baking soda, cinnamon, and salt.

In a large mixing bowl or the bowl of a stand mixer, beat the egg, brown sugar, oil, vanilla, and milk until well blended. Add the flour mixture and beat until a batter forms. Set aside the flour bowl.

In the same small mixing bowl used for the flour, toss the blueberries with the remaining 1 teaspoon all-purpose flour. Gently fold the coated blueberries into the batter.

Fill the prepared muffin wells three-quarters full with the batter. Bake the muffins in the preheated oven for 18 to 22 minutes, or until toothpick inserted in the centers of the muffins comes out clean. Let cool on a wire rack before serving.

Serve Blueberry Oat Muffins with Fresh Fruit.

Makes 12 muffins

Cost $2.57

FRUGAL FACT: *Coating the blueberries in flour helps them "float" in the batter and not fall to the bottom of the muffin cup while baking.*

FREEZER FRIENDLY ■ *"ON-THE-GO" BREAKFAST*

Cinnamon Butternut Squash Muffins

1 cup all-purpose flour ($.20)
1 cup whole wheat flour ($.28)
2 teaspoons ground cinnamon ($.10)
2 teaspoons baking powder ($.10)
1 teaspoon baking soda ($.03)
1 teaspoon salt
4 large eggs ($.40)

⅓ cup granulated sugar ($.04)
⅓ cup applesauce ($.10)
⅓ cup canola or vegetable oil ($.20)
1 ripe banana, mashed ($.20)
1 cup cooked butternut squash, mashed ($.50)

OPTIONAL TOPPING

¼ cup firmly packed brown sugar ($.06) (optional)

1 teaspoon ground cinnamon ($.05) (optional)

Fresh fruit ($.50)

Preheat the oven to 350 degrees. Lightly coat 24 wells of a regular-size muffin pan with nonstick cooking spray, or line with paper liners.

In a small mixing bowl, whisk together the all-purpose flour, whole wheat flour, cinnamon, baking powder, baking soda, and salt.

In the bowl of a stand mixer or a large mixing bowl, beat the eggs, granulated sugar, applesauce, and oil until well blended. Add the flour mixture and beat until a batter forms. Stir the mashed banana and butternut squash into the batter. In a small bowl, toss together the brown sugar and cinnamon, if using.

Fill the prepared muffin wells three-quarters full with the batter. Sprinkle the brown sugar–cinnamon mixture over the batter in each muffin cup, if using. Bake the muffins in the preheated oven for 18 to 22 minutes, or until a toothpick inserted in the centers of the muffins comes out clean. Let cool on a wire rack before serving.

Serve Cinnamon Butternut Squash Muffins with Fresh Fruit.

Makes 24 muffins

Cost $2.76

FRUGAL FACT: *These muffins are a perfect way to use up baked butternut squash left-over from dinner.*

FREEZER FRIENDLY ■ *"ON-THE-GO" BREAKFAST*

Sweet Bran Muffins

2 cups All-Bran cereal ($.50)
½ cup all-purpose flour ($.10)
¾ cup whole wheat flour ($.21)
1 tablespoon ground cinnamon
  ($.15)
1 teaspoon baking soda ($.03)
½ teaspoon salt
2 large eggs ($.20)

½ cup firmly packed brown sugar ($.12)
¼ cup butter or margarine, melted
  ($.40)
1 cup milk ($.10)
2 teaspoons vanilla extract ($.10)
1 cup raisins, or other dried fruit ($1)
Sugar for sprinkling ($.01)

4 hard-boiled eggs ($.40)

Preheat the oven to 375 degrees. Lightly coat 12 wells of a regular-size muffin pan with nonstick cooking spray, or line with paper liners.

In a grinder or food processor, grind the All-Bran cereal.

In a small mixing bowl, whisk together the ground All-Bran cereal, all-purpose flour, whole wheat flour, cinnamon, baking soda, and salt.

In the bowl of a stand mixer or a large mixing bowl, beat the eggs, brown sugar, melted butter or margarine, milk, and vanilla until well blended. Add the flour mixture and beat until batter forms. Gently fold in the raisins.

Fill the prepared muffin wells three-quarters full with the batter. Sprinkle sugar over the top of each muffin. Bake the muffins in the preheated oven for 18 to 22 minutes, or until a toothpick inserted in the centers of the muffins comes out clean. Let cool on a wire rack before serving.

Serve Sweet Bran Muffins with Hard-boiled Eggs.

Makes 12 muffins

Cost $3.32

FRUGAL FACT: *My "never pay more than" price for a box of cereal is $1 per box. Match up high-value coupons with sale prices to get the best deals. And watch those drugstore ads, as sometimes cereal prices are less there than at the grocery store.*

FREEZER FRIENDLY ■ *"ON-THE-GO" BREAKFAST*

English Muffins Toppings

6 English muffins ($1)

TOPPING IDEAS PER ENGLISH MUFFIN ($.50 TO $1)

1 tablespoon peanut butter and 2 thin apple slices with a sprinkle of cinnamon ($.75)

1 tablespoon peanut butter drizzled with 1 teaspoon honey ($.50)

1 tablespoon cream cheese and a dollop of salsa ($.75)

1 tablespoon Roasted Garlic Hummus (page 271) and a slice of tomato ($1)

Dollop of cottage cheese and a slice of tomato ($1)

1 teaspoon butter and a dollop of cranberry sauce ($.50)

Fresh fruit ($.50)

Open English muffins and toast the halves. Spread with the desired toppings.

Grab a piece of fresh fruit for an "on-the-go" breakfast.

Serve English Muffins with Fresh Fruit.

Makes 4 to 6 breakfast servings

Cost $2 to $2.50

FRUGAL FACT: *Stash "reduced-for-quick-sale" English muffins in the freezer. Thaw in the microwave or toaster oven.*

"ON-THE-GO" BREAKFAST

Bagel Toppings

6 bagels ($1.19)

TOPPING IDEAS PER BAGEL ($.50 TO $1.50)

1 tablespoon peanut butter and 6 to 8 banana slices ($.75)

1 tablespoon salsa and 1 slice cheddar cheese ($1)

1 tablespoon cream cheese, 1 slice of tomato, and 1 slice provolone cheese ($1.50)

About one-fourth of an avocado, smashed with salt and pepper ($1)

1 tablespoon cream cheese drizzled with 1 teaspoon honey ($.50)

Fresh fruit ($.50)

Open the bagels and toast the halves. Spread with the desired toppings. Place in a toaster oven or under the broiler to melt cheese, if necessary.

Serve Bagels with your favorite Toppings and Fresh Fruit for an "on-the-go" breakfast.

Makes 4 to 6 breakfast servings

Cost $2.19 to $3.19

FRUGAL FACT: *Watch the prices on bagels and stock up the freezer for quick and easy breakfasts.*

"ON-THE-GO" BREAKFAST

FOUR

Breakfast Tacos and Breakfast Sandwiches

Potato, Egg, and Cheese Breakfast Tacos

1 tablespoon canola oil ($.03)
6 small white potatoes, peeled and diced
   into ¼-inch pieces ($.80)
8 large eggs ($.80)

¼ cup milk ($.03)
salt and pepper
8 burrito-size, flour tortillas ($1)
1 cup shredded cheddar cheese ($.67)

1 orange and 1 apple, cut into quarters ($.50)

Heat the oil in a large skillet. Add the diced potatoes and sauté for 6 to 7 minutes, or until softened.

While the potatoes are sautéing, whisk together the eggs, milk, and salt and pepper to taste in a medium mixing bowl. Transfer the cooked potatoes to a plate, and set aside.

In the same skillet that you used to sauté the potatoes, scramble the eggs. When they are almost cooked, add the cooked potatoes to the skillet and combine with the scrambled eggs.

Heat the tortillas for a minute in the microwave, or wrap in aluminum foil and place in a 300-degree oven for 10 minutes.

Scoop the potato-egg mixture onto the 8 warmed tortillas dividing it equally. Sprinkle a pinch of shredded cheese over the potato-egg mixture. Roll up the tortillas and serve immediately, or freeze. If freezing, it is not necessary to warm the tortillas before assembling.

Serve Potato, Egg, and Cheese Breakfast Tacos with Orange and Apple Slices.

Makes 8 breakfast tacos

Cost $3.83

FRUGAL FACT: *Serve seasonal fruits with breakfast to keep overall meal costs down.*

FREEZER FRIENDLY

Sausage, Egg, and Cheese Breakfast Tacos

1 pound all-natural mild pork sausage ($1.99)

8 large eggs ($.80)

¼ cup milk ($.03)

salt and pepper

8 burrito-size, flour tortillas ($1)

1 cup shredded cheddar or Mexican blend cheese ($.67)

2 apples, sliced ($.50)

In a large skillet, brown the sausage, crumbling it as you cook it. Transfer the browned sausage to a nearby plate with a paper towel, to absorb excess fat.

While the sausage is browning, whisk together the eggs, milk, and salt and pepper to taste in a medium mixing bowl.

In the same skillet that you used to brown the sausage, scramble the eggs. When they are almost cooked, return the browned sausage to the skillet and combine with the scrambled eggs.

Heat the tortillas for a minute in the microwave, or wrap in aluminum foil and place in a 300-degree oven for 10 minutes.

Scoop the sausage-egg mixture onto 8 the warm tortillas dividing it equally. Sprinkle a pinch of shredded cheese over the sausage-egg mixture. Roll up the tortillas and serve immediately, or freeze. If freezing, it is not necessary to warm the tortillas before assembling.

Serve Sausage, Egg, and Cheese Tacos with Apple Slices.

Makes 8 breakfast tacos

Cost $4.99

FRUGAL FACT: *Look for BOGO (buy-one-get-one-free) sales on sausage. Sausage can be frozen in its package if you don't plan to use it right away. Thaw frozen sausage quickly by placing it in a bowl of warm water.*

FREEZER FRIENDLY

Salsa Breakfast Tacos

8 large eggs ($.80)
¼ cup milk ($.03)
1 teaspoon ground cumin ($.05)
salt and pepper
1 tablespoon canola or vegetable oil ($.03)

1 cup homemade (page 255) or store-bought salsa ($.50)
1 cup shredded cheddar or Mexican blend cheese ($.67)
8 burrito-size, flour tortillas ($1)

4 bananas ($.80)

In a mixing bowl, whisk together the eggs, milk, ground cumin, and season with salt and pepper.

Heat the oil in a large skillet, and place over medium-high heat. Pour in the egg mixture and scramble. Once the eggs are nearly cooked, add the salsa. Turn down heat and let simmer for 5 to 7 minutes, allowing some of the liquid from the salsa to evaporate.

Add the shredded cheese to the salsa-egg mixture and let cook until the cheese melts.

Heat the tortillas for a minute in the microwave, or wrap in aluminum foil and place in a 300-degree oven for 10 minutes.

Scoop the salsa-egg mixture onto the 8 warm tortillas dividing it equally. Roll up the tortillas and serve immediately, or freeze. If freezing, it is not necessary to warm the tortillas before assembling.

Serve Salsa Breakfast Burritos with Bananas.

Makes 8 breakfast burritos

Cost $3.88

FRUGAL FACT: *Clip and file those name-brand salsa coupons and match them up with a sale price to get large jars of salsa for less than $1.*

FREEZER FRIENDLY

Chorizo Breakfast Tacos

....

½ pound chorizo sausage ($1.49)
8 large eggs ($.80)
¼ cup milk ($.03)
salt and pepper

1 cup shredded Monterey Jack cheese
 ($.67)
Dashes of hot sauce ($.10)
8 burrito-size, flour tortillas ($1)

½ cantaloupe, cut into wedges ($.75)

In a large skillet, brown and crumble the chorizo sausage. Transfer the browned sausage to a plate lined with a paper towels, to absorb excess fat.

While the sausage is browning, whisk together the eggs, milk, and salt and pepper in a medium mixing bowl.

In the same skillet that you used to brown the sausage, scramble the eggs. When they are almost cooked, add the browned sausage and the shredded cheese to the skillet and combine with the scrambled eggs. Cook until the cheese melts.

Heat the tortillas for a minute in the microwave, or wrap in aluminum foil and place in a 300-degree oven for 10 minutes.

Scoop the chorizo-egg mixture onto the 8 warm tortillas dividing it equally. Add a dash or two of hot sauce to the chorizo-egg mixture on each tortilla. Roll up the tortillas and serve immediately, or freeze. If freezing, it is not necessary to warm the tortillas before assembling.

Serve Chorizo Breakfast Tacos with Cantaloupe Wedges.

Makes 8 breakfast tacos

Cost $4.84

FRUGAL FACT: *Look for chorizo sausage at an international or ethnic market if you can't find it at your regular supermarket.*

FREEZER FRIENDLY

Bacon, Avocado, and Cheese Breakfast Tacos

6 large eggs ($.60)
¼ cup milk ($.03)
salt and pepper
1 tablespoon canola or vegetable oil ($.03)

1 large avocado, sliced ($.75)
8 burrito-size, flour tortillas ($1)
8 cooked bacon slices ($.99)
4 slices provolone cheese ($.67)

¼ honeydew melon, cut into wedges ($.75)

In a mixing bowl, whisk together the eggs, milk, and salt and pepper.

Heat the oil in a large skillet, and place over medium-high heat. Pour in the egg mixture and scramble.

Cut around the avocado lengthwise. Open it up and remove the pit. Make several lengthwise slices in the flesh of the avocado. Using a spoon, carefully scoop out the slices.

Heat the tortillas for a minute in the microwave, or wrap in aluminum foil and place in a 300-degree oven for 10 minutes.

Lay out warm tortillas on a clean countertop. Scoop the scrambled eggs onto the tortillas dividing it equally. Add 1 slice of cooked bacon, ½ slice cheese, and 1 to 2 slices of avocado to each tortilla. Roll up the tortillas and serve immediately, or freeze. If freezing, it is not necessary to warm the tortillas before assembling.

Serve Bacon, Avocado, and Cheese Breakfast Taco with Honeydew Melon Wedges.

Makes 8 breakfast tacos

Cost $4.82

FRUGAL FACT: *Be sure to buy a few extra avocados when they go on sale for less than $1.*

FREEZER FRIENDLY

Ham and Swiss Breakfast Wraps

8 large eggs ($.80)
¼ cup milk ($.03)
2 teaspoons dried chives ($.20)
salt and pepper
1 tablespoon canola or vegetable oil
   ($.03)

2 cups cooked and diced ham ($1.50)
8 burrito-size, flour tortillas ($1)
4 slices Swiss cheese, cut in half ($.67)

4 cups pineapple chunks ($.75)

In a mixing bowl, whisk together the eggs, milk, dried chives, and salt and pepper to taste.

In a large skillet, heat the oil over medium-high heat. Pour in the egg mixture and scramble. When the eggs are nearly cooked, stir in the diced ham.

Heat the tortillas for a minute in the microwave, or wrap in aluminum foil and place in a 300-degree oven for 10 minutes.

Lay out the 8 warm tortillas on a clean countertop and add a half slice of Swiss cheese onto each tortilla. Scoop the ham-egg mixture onto the tortillas, dividing it equally. Roll up the tortillas. Serve immediately, or freeze. If freezing, it is not necessary to warm the tortillas before assembling.

Serve Ham and Swiss Breakfast Wraps with Pineapple Chunks.

Makes 8 breakfast wraps

Cost $4.98

FRUGAL FACT: *Dice up the leftover ham from your holiday feast and make these delicious breakfast wraps the next morning.*

FREEZER FRIENDLY

Bean and Cheese Breakfast Tacos

2 cans (15 ounces each) refried beans ($1.50)

8 burrito-size whole wheat tortillas ($1)

1 cup shredded sharp cheddar cheese ($.67)

½ cantaloupe, cut in wedges ($.75)

Place the refried beans into a large microwave-safe bowl. Microwave them on high power for 1 to 2 minutes, or until heated through.

Heat the tortillas for a minute in the microwave, or wrap in aluminum foil and place in a 300-degree oven for 10 minutes.

Lay out the 8 tortillas on a clean countertop. Spoon the warmed refried beans on each tortilla, dividing it equally. Sprinkle with a pinch of the shredded cheese. Roll up the tortillas and serve immediately, or freeze. If freezing, it is not necessary to warm the tortillas before assembling.

Serve Bean and Cheese Breakfast Tacos with Cantaloupe Wedges.

Makes 8 breakfast tacos

Cost $3.92

FRUGAL FACT: *Making homemade refried beans is the most frugal option for these breakfast tacos. But if you don't want to make your own, then watch for prices of $.75 or less for canned refried beans.*

FREEZER FRIENDLY

Sausage Eggwiches

2 tablespoons canola or vegetable oil ($.06)
6 large eggs ($.60)
½ pound all-natural pork sausage in a roll ($.99)

6 slices cheddar cheese ($1)
6 English muffins ($.99)

2 clementines ($.50)

In a large skillet, heat the oil. Fry each of the 6 eggs and set aside on a plate.

Slice the sausage roll into six ⅓-inch-thick circles. Fry the sausage patties in the same skillet that you used to cook the eggs until cooked through.

Assemble the sandwiches. Place a fried egg, a cooked sausage patty, and a slice of cheese onto bottom half of each English muffin. Place in a toaster oven or under the broiler for 3 to 4 minutes, or until the cheese melts. Add the top half of the English muffin.

Serve Sausage Eggwiches with clementines.

Makes 6 eggwiches

Cost $4.14

FRUGAL FACT: *Store-brand English muffins are often on sale around $1.*

FREEZER FRIENDLY

Hawaiian Ham-wiches

2 tablespoons canola or vegetable oil ($.06)

6 large eggs ($.60)

6 slices leftover ham ($.99)

6 pineapple slices ($.25)

6 slices sharp cheddar or Swiss cheese ($1)

6 English muffins ($.99)

2 pears, sliced ($.99)

In a large skillet, heat the oil. Fry each of the 6 eggs and set aside on a plate.

In the same skillet that you used to cook the eggs, heat the ham slices.

Assemble the sandwiches. Place a fried egg, a warm slice of ham, and a slice of cheese onto the bottom half of each English muffin. Place in a toaster oven or under the broiler for 3 to 4 minutes, or until the cheese melts. Toast the top half of the English muffin and add.

Serve Hawaiian Ham-wiches with Pear Slices.

Makes 6 ham-wiches

Cost $4.88

FRUGAL FACT: *Freeze leftover holiday ham in slices and in diced pieces, for use in a variety of recipes once the holidays have passed.*

FREEZER FRIENDLY

Bacon, Egg, and Cheese Bagel Melts

2 tablespoons canola or vegetable oil ($.06)

6 eggs ($.60)

12 slices bacon ($1.50)

6 slices sharp cheddar cheese ($1)

6 bagels ($1.19)

2 small peaches, sliced ($.60)

In a large skillet, heat the oil. Fry each of the 6 eggs and set aside on a plate.

Cook the bacon in the same skillet that you used to cook the eggs or in the microwave. To cook in the microwave, place the bacon on a microwave-safe plate, lined with 2 paper towels. Cover the bacon with another paper towel. Microwave the bacon on high for 4 to 5 minutes, or until crisp. Transfer the bacon to clean paper towels to drain.

Assemble the sandwiches. Place a fried egg, the cooked bacon, and a slice of cheese onto bottom half of each bagel. Place in toaster oven or under the broiler for 3 to 4 minutes or until the cheese melts. Toast the top half of the bagel and add to the sandwich, or eat open faced.

Serve Bacon, Egg, and Cheese Bagel Melts with Peach Slices.

Makes 6 bagel melts

Cost $4.95

FRUGAL FACT: *Store-brand bagels are often on sale around $1. And keep an eye out for REDUCED FOR QUICK SALE stickers, and stash bagels in the freezer.*

FREEZER FRIENDLY

PART II

Lunches: At Home and On-the-Go

Ah, lunches. lunches, lunches, lunches.

Lunchtime has always been the most frustrating meal for me to manage each day. It's the forgotten meal. At least around here it's the forgotten meal. It seems that lunch gets thrown together at the last minute. *Oh, I'll just have leftovers or a PBJ.* More often that for the other meals, I find myself opening the refrigerator door to survey its contents, only to close it and wish I could reach for a magic wand.

If I had one, I would keep my magic wand in the drawer right next to the fridge. Wave. Wave. Wave and *POOF!* Open the refrigerator door and find that the wraps have made themselves, the carrots peeled themselves, the grapes jumped onto the plate, and lunch is ready for me. Wouldn't that be amazing!

Seriously though, lunch really is a versatile meal because anything goes. You can make a simple sandwich or salad, but you can also make breakfast for lunch, or a more dinnerlike hot lunch, too. And of course, you can reheat leftovers for lunch.

Let's get creative and move away from Peanut Butter and Jelly and boxed Macaroni and Cheese, shall we?! If you are going to spend 10 minutes making a box of "mac and cheese" or 5 minutes on the PBJ assembly line, you might as well make something new and different in those 10 minutes, right? I've got loads of meal ideas that you could prepare in the same amount of time it takes to boil noodles and mix together some cheese sauce. (Please note: I have nothing against "mac and cheese" or PBJs . . . it just gets old after a while!)

It's time to stir it up (pun intended). In this chapter I'll share time and money-saving tips, as well as outline some options for batch cooking and batch chopping ingredients for lunches. I'll also often advise on the ins and outs of eating lunch at work, at school or day care, as well as at home. And finally, I'll address some of the most common frustrations that people have surrounding the lunch hour.

The theme that you will notice throughout this chapter is one I introduced in the breakfasts chapter. The key to saving your time, money, and sanity when noon rolls around is **being one step ahead of yourself**. I'm saying it again now, and I'll probably say it again before the book has ended . . . when working on one meal or snack, be thinking about the next meal and how you can start preparing for it when you have a spare moment in the kitchen.

Time-Saving Tips for the Lunch Hour

Whether you are eating lunch at home, at the office, or at school, the time for actually eating your lunch is generally limited. Due to rigid academic schedules, the lunch hour at school is cut to as little as 20 minutes. Layoffs at the office have doubled the workload for many workers, leaving them eating lunch at the computer while they respond to e-mails, before running off to a 1 P.M. client meeting. Even at home, lunch can be rushed depending on the kids' daily activities and schedules.

We need both fast-to-pack and fast-to-eat foods in our lunch boxes. Below are a few ideas for making the lunch-packing process a bit faster.

BATCH COOKING, CHOPPING AND MAKE-AHEAD FOODS

Being able to pack a lunch box in 30 seconds or less would be wonderful, wouldn't it!?

The basic principles of batch cooking and batch chopping described in Breakfast: At-Home and On-the-Go chapter apply to lunch foods as well. Grab a premade wrap, an apple, a handful of carrots or celery sticks, and a cookie from the freezer—30 seconds and done—with no major blip in the morning routine.

The only way to make this happen, both on a budget and with healthy foods, is to plan ahead and do some batch cooking and chopping. If you are willing to do a few minutes of prep work at the start of each school or work week, you'll be on your way to packing your lunch on the weekdays in less than a minute!

Packing a fresh fruit or vegetables into your lunch box is essential, but the thought of getting out the knives and cutting board every single day is daunting. Chances are you'll just skip the fresh fruit if you don't have the time, or know how, to cut the fruit. Let's just take out that cutting board once, maybe twice, during the week and you won't have to skip out on those vital nutrients.

To store your batch chopped veggies to keep them fresh, place the chopped veggies in a small plastic container and sprinkle with some water. This will keep them fresh and moist. If you notice that your carrots or celery are drying out a bit, then fill a plastic container with enough water to submerge the carrots or celery. They can then soak up the water they need to stay fresh. Store cut vegetables in water no longer than 4 to 5 days in the refrigerator.

I like to cut up a few pieces of fruit and make up a fruit salad at the start of each week, and then another in the middle of the week. When adding diced apples or sliced bananas to the fruit salad, toss them with some lemon juice to keep the fruit from browning. You can then use your fruit salad for Fruit Kebabs with Yogurt Dip (page 269) or mix with a yogurt dressing (page 243).

In addition to chopping veggies and cutting fruit for lunch boxes or lunch plates, I have found that batch cooking several other ingredients can be helpful for throwing together a quick lunch.

- Batch-Cooking Dried Beans. Cooking with dried beans costs at least half as much using canned beans. Instead of cooking 1 cup at a time to get the beans I need for a recipe, I cook the entire bag, then cool the cooked beans and freeze in 1- or-2 cup portions. I usually will cook 2 or 3 bags worth of beans while I'm at it—saves both time and energy, especially when it comes to cleanup. To cook the dried beans, soak them overnight or for at least 2 hours in hot water. Then rinse the beans and place them in a large saucepan. Add water to the beans, covering them with about 2 inches of water. Bring to a boil, and then reduce heat to low and cook for 1 hour to 1 hour and 15 minutes. Drain the beans in a colander and rinse with cool water. Let cool completely in the colander before placing into plastic bags to freeze.

- Batch-Grilling Chicken Breasts. If you are grilling chicken breasts for dinner one night, why not grill a few extras to slice or dice and throw in the freezer. Then you'll have diced chicken ready for a quick pasta salad, or some sliced chicken to put on a salad or in a wrap. To thaw, set in the refrigerator the night before, or defrost in the microwave.

- Batch-Grilling Burgers. The same goes for burgers. If you are grilling hamburgers, grill a dozen extra to keep in the freezer for a fun summertime picnic with the kids. You'll get the great taste of a burger without having to turn on the grill. To thaw, set in the refrigerator the night before and reheat in the microwave, or defrost and reheat in the microwave.

There are other lunch foods that freeze well and would work well for batch cooking. Here are some other ideas of foods that could be kept in the freezer for a quick lunch: freeze Pepperoni Calzones (page 194) after they have been baked, chicken salad wrapped in tortillas (chicken salad recipes on pages 158 to 161), make the Spicy Sloppy Joes (page 213) and freeze just the meat and sauce. Reheat and then add to the bread or bun just before serving. Plan to make these during an hour prep session, or during the time you spend in the kitchen getting dinner ready.

Also, if you see a loaf of bread marked down for quick sale, buy it and set up a PBJ assembly line. Make up the 10 to 12 sandwiches, and then freeze them in sandwich baggies. And of course, making an extra batch of cookies or muffins and freezing them will help cut down on the time it takes to throw together a lunch for the road.

SLOW-COOKER ADAPTABLE

Many recipes in the Hot Lunches chapter in this cookbook are slow-cooker adaptable. If you need food to be ready when you wake up, to take to work or school, consider slow cooking your food overnight. It will be ready for you on the counter in the morning when you wake up. While you may not enjoy waking up to the smell of chili in your house, you probably won't remember at noon when you take that first bite of delicious chili from the thermos. Using the slow cooker can be a huge time saver.

The following recipes from Chapter Six are slow-cooker adaptable.

- Twice-Baked, Fully Loaded Baked Potato Soup (page 202) – Place all ingredients in the slow cooker with an extra cup of liquid and cook on low for 8 to 10 hours.

- Thyme Chicken Noodle Soup (page 201) – Add all ingredients except the pasta noodles to the slow cooker and set on low for 10 hours. If desired, add diced chicken breast that has not been cooked yet. Add the pasta right when you wake up and it will be ready about 30 minutes later.

- Baked Parmesan Chicken Fingers (page 204)– Prepare the chicken tenderloins as directed. Spray the base of the slow cooker with nonstick cooking spray and add the chicken fingers in a single layer. If you need to add another layer of chicken fingers, place a piece of aluminum foil with lots of little holes punched in it to allow the steam to escape and keep the chicken fingers crispy. Cook on high for 2 to 4 hours. Start these after breakfast and they'll be ready in time for an At-Home Lunch.

- Chuckwagon Chili (page 210) – Brown the ground beef, then place all ingredients except the pasta in the slow cooker. Set on low for 8 hours overnight or 4 hours in the morning. Add pasta plus 1 cup of boiling water about 30 minutes before serving.

- Cincinnati-Style Chili (page 211) – Brown the ground beef, and then place all the ingredients except the pasta and cheese in the slow cooker. Set on low for 8 hours overnight or 4 hours in the morning. Serve with leftover spaghetti noodles and shredded cheese.

- White Bean Chili (page 212) – If you wish to make this chili using dried white beans, then add an additional 2 cups of liquid to the recipe. The beans will soak up that liquid as they cook.

- Salsa and Black Bean Chicken (page 214) – Place the chicken in the base of the slow cooker and cover with the beans and salsa mixture. Set on low and cook for 8 hours overnight.

If using your slow cooker overnight, be sure it switches to a default warm setting when the cooking cycle has finished. If you have a fancy slow cooker with a start timer, then set your food to start cooking at the time you wish, so it will be ready at the desired hour. When it's time to head out the door for a busy day at work or school, scoop out some soup, chili, or chicken from the slow cooker, put it into a thermos, and be on your way. No need to spend $8 on lunch from the deli down the street!

Money-Saving Tips for the Lunch Hour

While time is of the essence, so is money. Let's talk about a few strategies that will help save you a little extra "green" each week at the grocery store.

When at the grocery store, buy only the produce that is on sale that week, plus a few of your regular favorites like bananas, a bag of apples, and a head of lettuce. If you see that mangoes or pineapple are on sale, but you are not sure how to choose a good one from the produce stand, then look on www.5dollardinners.com for instructions and details on selecting the best fruit. And if you don't know how to cut a mango, or a pineapple, then I'll show you on the Web site too. Don't be afraid to try new fruits and vegetables that are on sale just because you don't know how to choose them or cut them. Educate yourself and then start enjoying those mangoes, or that fresh pineapple.

Also, practice strategic couponing and match those coupons with a sale price. This will help you save $10 to $20 a week on deli meats, bread, sliced cheese, yogurts, and other lunch ingredients.

I don't think I need to tell you that convenience foods cost more. But just to be clear on the matter, I'd like to show you how much you would save by chopping and dicing your own vegetables versus buying the prepackaged healthy convenience foods, like baby carrots or the individual little raisin boxes.

Here is a cost comparison of just a few popular lunch box items—prepackaged versus make-and-pack your own.

- **Carrots**: 1 pound bag of baby carrots $1.77 versus 1-pound bag of whole carrots $.67—Take 3 minutes to peel and cut into carrot sticks
  - ○ $1 a week = $36 savings on the year (for the 36 weeks of school)

- **Raisins**: Large 15-ounce box of raisins $2.49 v. 6-pack of the 1.25 ounce mini boxes $1.99—Divide out raisins into small containers instead of using the little boxes.
  - ○ $1 a week = $36 savings

- **Jell-O or pudding:** $.72 for Jell-O box v. $1.89 for Jell-O cups—Mix a large bowl and then divide it out into smaller reusable containers before it sets in the refrigerator
  - ○ $1.15 a week = $41.40 savings

- **Cheese Cubes:** 16-ounce cheese block $2.99 v. 7-ounce prepackaged cut cheese $2.50—Take 3 minutes to cut the cheese block and place in a storage bag in the refrigerator.
  - ○ $2 a week per ounce = $72 savings

The overall cost savings for the school year for each lunch box could be as much as $300, depending on the foods and how much preparing you do at home. By doing a little busywork as you assemble lunch boxes and write up your meal plan for the week, or while supervising homework hour, you are saving yourself quite a bit of money. If you are packing several lunch boxes every day, the potential savings could reach into the thousands of dollars. And just think about the savings from packing a lunch over the course of *twelve* school years!

So we have established that by staying ahead of yourself in the kitchen and chopping up your own fruits and veggies you will definitely cut grocery costs and help streamline the time it takes to put together lunches in the middle of the week. But do you know what you'll be having for lunch tomorrow? (I probably don't.)

Meal Planning for the Lunch Hour

Guilty. Guilty as charged. The Crime: Failure to Write Meal Plan for Lunch.

I'll be preaching to myself for the next few paragraphs. I am the worst meal planner for lunch. Dinner, breakfast, snacks . . . I've got those under control. But lunch is the most difficult for me. It probably has something to do with the fact that our family eats different things for lunch each day. My husband typically takes a sandwich, an apple, a yogurt, and a baked goodie in his lunch bag. The kids and I are generally at home and have leftovers, sandwiches, salads, wraps, or whatever the magic wand fixes for us.

When I get my act together, this is what I'll tell myself when it comes to meal planning for lunch. *Ahem.*

Just as with breakfast, set up themes for the weekdays. Have a Tuna Day, a Hot Lunches Day, a Wraps Day, a PBJ Day (see page 197 for some new fun PBJ ideas), and a Salads Day. Also, keep an arsenal of fresh fruit and veggies in the fridge, along with some nuts, granolas, finger foods, and simple snacks on hand to go along with the "main dish." This will speed up the lunch-packing process and reduce the meal planning stress as well.

If no one is complaining about having "the same old thing for lunch," then stick with it as long as you can. But it might be nice to change things up every now and again to keep everyone on their toes. Make one day of the week the "New Lunch Day," where you send a new meal in your family's lunch boxes. I recommend getting input for your family as to what new meals they would like to have in their lunch boxes; otherwise you might end up with an uneaten lunch and a hungry, cranky kid when they get home from school.

Meal planning for lunch can be anything from a strict plan, complete with detailed batch cooking plans to a themed day of the week to just throwing together a lunch based on what you've got. Do what works for you!

Now let's look a little more closely at what lunch looks like at work, at school, and at home.

Brown Bag for Work

While we all know that it's cheaper to bring your lunch to work, let's take a quick peek at how much you could save by brown bagging it to work. It only costs on average $1.25 to $1.50 for lunch for 1 person if you pack your own. A sandwich and some chips or a piece of fruit plus a drink from the deli down the street can run anywhere from $7 to $9. With 22 workdays in every month, you could save yourself as little as $176 a month by toting your own. That's a savings of over $2,000 for the entire year.

EATING AT YOUR DESK

Please step away from your desk to eat lunch. It might just bring you the peace of mind you need to finish up the workday.

Should you eat at your desk or should you step away? I recommend stepping away and moving to a new location to eat lunch. Not only will it provide a change of scenery, it will give your mind some space to breathe and relax. You can't check your e-mail, at least not from your computer. You can't pick up the phone when someone calls. You can't be looking through your files while munching on your apple.

And if you must eat at your desk, at least set the computer to hibernate mode, and pretend you are picnicking on the beach on a tropical isle.

WHAT ABOUT TAKING A SHORTER LUNCH BREAK?

Most companies allow for an hour for lunch, but what about shortening your lunch break and shave off those minutes from the end of the workday to get home to your family. Of course, this is dependent on the boss, the company policy, and your position. I am all for family time, so if workdays could be cut short with a shorter lunch break, then go for it.

FORGETTING YOUR LUNCH

Quite often I'll open the refrigerator to get the milk out for breakfast, only to find my husband's packed lunch bag, forgotten as he ran out the door for work. If you live nearby and can return home to pick it up, or your spouse can bring it by later in the morning, then make those arrangements. If you live too far from the office and it's not cost- or time-effective to bring the lunch by that morning, then unfortunately, you'll be left with one option: eating out.

While packing your lunch the evening before certainly helps with the rush out the door factor, but it won't help with the "Oops-I-forgot-it!" factor.

WHAT TO PACK FOR THE OFFICE

Because every office lunchroom setup is different, deciding what to pack for lunch will very much depend on the individual situation. Some companies are equipped with an entire kitchen, where you could even prepare some food from scratch if you brought all the necessary ingredients. Other office buildings just have a microwave and a drink machine. Some eating spaces are just tables in front of vending machines.

For the most part, all of the different types of foods featured in the lunch recipe chapters that follow are suitable for an office bound lunch box. If you typically work late in the afternoon or have a late dinner, it might be wise to pack a small snack to tide you over until dinner time. This will also keep you from wandering over to the snack machine and spending too much on a high calorie, sugar laden snack that will leave your stomach feeling empty and you feeling guilty about spending $1.25 on 4 cookies.

If you have access to a microwave at the office, then the occasional can of soup or prepackaged frozen meal can be a nice change to the lunch-packing routine, both in not having to think about what to pack and not having to take the time to prepare a lunch box. I do not recommend making this a regular practice, because of the additives and preservatives commonly found in prepared soups and frozen meals.

KEEPING THINGS COOL

It's not uncommon to find cheese cubes, mayonnaise-based salads, or coleslaws inside a lunch box. Those foods need to be kept cool to be safe to eat, come lunchtime. The best way to keep the contents cool is to add a frozen ice pack. These can be found at the discount store for less than $1. It might be prudent to buy at least 2 ice packs per lunch box, as you'll need back up for when they are lost, damaged, or forgotten.

EATING OUT FOR LUNCH

Sometime eating out for lunch is a nice break. In order to keep eating out for lunch from becoming a habit that you might not be able to afford, I recommend setting aside some cash at the start of every month to use just for the deli. Use a cash envelope system, or tuck a $20 bill or two into a secret place in your wallet. The use of cash will keep you accountable to your budget and keep your lunchtime spending under control.

So we've got work covered for the "big people," but what about when the "little people" go to work. They need the proper fuel to get through the rest of their work/school day. And their teachers will thank you if you send a healthy lunch, low in sugar. (Can you imagine a classroom full of children who ate sugary fruit snacks, chocolate pudding, and a bag of chips for lunch? Yikes!)

Lunch Box for School and Day care

These days, the average school lunch box and its contents will experience scrutiny, peer pressure, feelings of inadequacy, and even failure. And chances are your child will experience the same feelings around the lunchroom table if their lunch isn't "as cool as" their friend's lunch. With all the different types of sugar laden convenience snack foods available now, it makes the "healthy" lunchbox look so unappealing to all the little people sitting around the lunch table.

Not only is there the peer pressure among the kids, there's the "teacher-parent" lunch-box pressure too. While it's never spoken, your child's teacher knows right away which parents are *these* parents and which are *those* parents. *These* kinds of parents send whatever foods will appease their child, even if it means they are bouncing off the classroom walls during the afternoon. *Those* kinds of parents swim against the current and send healthy snacks and veggies in their child's lunch box.

(For the record, I am one of *those* moms. And I'm OK with that. And so are the boys. We talk about the importance of eating healthy and how comparing food is not necessary, and that it's best just to enjoy your own food.)

The type of lunch box or bag that you choose to send with your child to school depends in large part on your style in the kitchen. You could send a brown bag–style lunch with a wrap or sandwich, a piece of fruit, and a cookie. An ever-growing trend in the United States is the bento lunch box. A bento box is a rectangular box that contains smaller reusable plastic containers with different types of foods. It is common to have a themed bento box based on a holiday or color theme, or a decorative bento box making creative little surprises (see below).

Another option is the tin lunchbox that comes with a thermos for juice or soup. Send some juice or a hot soup for lunch, along with a variety of other small snacks or a sandwich and a fruit or veggie. You could also use a soft-sided thermal style lunch bag, designed to keep the food inside cool longer than a traditional lunch box.

A few ideas for what to put into your child's lunchbox:

- Sandwich, Wrap, or Quesadilla (Chapter 5)

- Peanut Butter Surprise Sandwiches (page 197)

- Pantry Trail Mix (page 266)

- Dehydrated Fruit (page 267)

- Muffin Tin Snacks (page 268)

- Yogurt cups

- Whole wheat crackers and cheese slices or cheese cubes

- Garlic Toast with Roasted Garlic Hummus (page 271)

- Tortilla Chips with Guacamole

- Veggies Crudités: Carrot Sticks, Celery Sticks, Broccoli, Cherry Tomatoes

- Finger Fruits: Berries, Grapes, Diced Mango, Pineapple, Apples (tossed in lemon juice), Banana Slices (tossed in lemon juice), mandarin orange slices, diced peaches

- Whole Grain Cereals or Granolas (pages 41 to 44)

- Popcorn, muffins, or cookies from the Snacks Chapter (page 264)

And a few creative ideas that are sure to surprise your child when they open their lunch box:

- Strawberry Lady Bug: "Glue" a few mini chocolate chips on top of a halved strawberry with a dab of peanut butter and stick two pretzel rods into the top of the strawberry as antennae.

- Chocolate Spider: Stick 6 small "pretzel legs" into the white part of an Oreo and add 2 eyes on top of the Oreo with frosting or peanut butter.

- Cheesy Letters and Numbers: Using letter or number cookie cutters, cut letters and numbers out of a cheese slice. Make sure there are 1 or 2 treats in their lunch box with that same letter—*P*eanuts and *P*retzels, or *C*antaloupe and *C*orn.

- Gingerbread Waffles or Pancakes: During the holidays, use your gingerbread cookie cutter and cut waffles or pancakes into the shape of gingerbread men. Add some eyes and mouth, or leave plain. Use other cookie cutter shapes to make shapes out of the pancakes or waffles.

Hopefully these ideas will spur your creativity and you can add something cute and clever to your child's lunch box every now and then.

Also, it might be wise to buy a few extra lunch boxes when they are on deep discount in the middle or end of the school year. You'll be glad to have some backups for when they get lost, or too dirty to use anymore.

And finally, don't forget to slip an endearing note into your child's lunch box every few days. It can be something as simple as a smiley face on a napkin, or a "good luck on your test" note underneath their wrap or sandwich. Perhaps you could include a reminder of what's on the plan for afternoon snack time (that is if you are that far ahead of yourself and know what's on the menu!). If your child is old enough to get some criticism from friends when you send a note, but you know your child still appreciates the loving gesture, sneak the note or just a smiley face somewhere in their lunch box, where only they will see it and can smile on the inside.

Lunch at Home

I spent six years of my adult life living in the Dominican Republic. As a Latin culture, they celebrate and practice the Siesta Hour. Starting around 10 A.M., I'd start to smell the garlic, then the beans, and finally the chicken being fried for the Siesta meal. Moms, grandmas, and great-grandmas would gather in the kitchen in the mid-morning to start preparing for Siesta. Chances are they were out earlier that morning at the farmers' market, getting the necessary meat or vegetables for that day's feast. From noon to 2 P.M. every day, my little town would shut down and everyone would go home to enjoy a feast and quick nap. I think that the Spanish and Latin cultures are on to something here.

Being a stay-at-home turned work-at-home mom, I usually can spare a few extra minutes to prepare lunch. Most days, it's more of a grab and eat or leftovers and reheat situation, but it is nice to get out some different ingredients every now and again, and put together a new wrap, or make up a new salad dressing for my salads.

I also like to use the time that I have with the boys at the table to create teachable moments. It's a great time for counting practice, playing with words using the magnetic letters on the fridge, or doing phonemic awareness practice with the pretzels as they make different letters with each bite. As they get older, we'll do more advanced math skills with measuring and counting, along with reading recipes and talking about nutrition and how food fuels our body. Being intentional with what I teach them is important to me, and something that is easy to work in while I set out pretzels, sliced apples, almonds, and a Peanut Butter, Honey, and Banana Roll Up (see page 197) onto their plates for lunch.

If you are feeling especially uninspired one day, jump out of the "sandwich and salads box" and serve pancakes and scrambled eggs for lunch. Breakfast for lunch is an easy way to mix up the lunch hour routine.

The slow cooker can also be used for lunch, using those recipes that only take 3 to 5 hours to cook. If you can get a meal into the slow cooker by 7 or 8 A.M., you'll just have to dish it up to serve lunch that day. This would be a great way to enjoy some chili or soup on a cold winter's day.

Another idea for those who are home most of the day is to pull out the shelf-stable ingredients for dinner and set the meat or chicken in the refrigerator to thaw, if you haven't yet. I have found that if a few of the ingredients are sitting on the countertop, then I'll see them as I whip through the kitchen and out the backdoor to watch the kids play outside. It keeps dinner prep at the front of my mind. Depending on the rest of the afternoon's work and play schedule, I can mentally figure out the best plan for dinner preparation. The name of the game is thinking ahead to the next meal and staying one step ahead of yourself. (See, I said it again.)

Summertime Lunches

When school gets out, take advantage of the newfound freedom in your family's schedule and enjoy picnics at the park, or in the backyard. Take the time to teach the kids how to pack a lunch, what should go into a lunch, the importance of healthy eating. Have the kids each pack their own backpack with their lunch and give them the responsibility to get their lunch to the car, or out to the blanket in the backyard. With older kids, take a hike at a nearby park and stop for lunch somewhere along the way.

If you are eating at home for lunch, fire up the grill and cook some chicken or burgers. While you've got the grill on, throw on a few extras and get some batch grilling done. Have that chicken or those burgers for dinner the following night. You could also store some in the freezer and use during the cooler winter months so you don't have to stand outside shivering while you grill up some chicken for a meal.

Make good use of that grill and those warm beautiful days when the schedule is light and you can slow down long enough to enjoy making lunch.

Lunch Time Cleanup

In my efforts to make the most out of each minute in the day, I have adopted what I call the "One Touch Rule." I apply this rule to my in-box, the dishes in my sink, batch cooking in the kitchen, and cleaning up after meals.

Here's what it looks like in the kitchen:

- Don't rinse the dish and put it into the sink, and then load it into the dishwasher later. Touch it once and rinse it and put it straight into the dishwasher. This goes for the dishes that you dirty during your batch cooking time, as well as for the dirty lunch boxes that come home from school.

- Teach your children to unload their lunch boxes from their backpacks right next to the sink. While they are having their afternoon snack, rinse or clean out the lunch boxes or lunch bags and set them aside to dry. When it comes time to pack their lunch boxes after dinner, or in the morning, there are no dirty surprises and you don't have to spend time cleaning out or drying off their lunch box. Minutes . . . whatever it takes to save those precious, precious minutes.

Having a cleanup routine for your lunch boxes and lunch dishes will help streamline your time and efficiency in working in the kitchen. Remember the "One Touch Rule."

Before we move on to the recipe chapters, I wanted to share some solutions to some of the irritating issues surrounding lunchtime.

Lunch-Hour Frustrations

I asked the $5 Dinners online community to share their greatest lunchtime woes. Below you will find the most common complaints from people concerning lunch, along with some workable solutions to getting past those frustrations and enjoying a peaceful lunch.

"The Lunch Meal is so difficult to plan."

Solution: Yes, yes it is. Like I mentioned above, I have trouble planning lunch meals as well. I tend to have a wide variety of ingredients on hand and just throw together a sandwich, wrap, salad, or leftovers. Because it's so easy to get into a rut when it comes to lunches, I encourage you to plan at least one or two meals each week that will keep the menu balanced, fresh, and exciting.

"I'm tired of only sandwiches and salads—It gets old!"

Solution: Try a wrap, or a hot soup in the winter or a cold soup in the summer. Make a pasta salad at the beginning of the week and serve a cupful with each lunch. One way to keep pasta salads tasting fresh is to mix up the pasta, chicken, veggies, and other ingredients in a bowl, and the dressing in another plastic container. Toss the dressing with the pasta salad just before serving it or packing it into your lunch box. The recipes that follow in this chapter will hopefully help you get out of the "sandwiches and salads" rut.

"I always succumb to coworker peer pressure and end up going out to lunch instead of eating what I brought to the office."

Solution: It's like the middle school lunchroom all over again, just fast forward a decade or so—the cool kids are going out to eat and I can't not go with them. Be sensible, or should I say "centsible." If you find yourself going out for lunch a few times a week, commit to staying home for dinner and avoid going out for multiple meals. You could always go home and have a light sandwich dinner on those days you went out to eat with colleagues. Another option would be to set up the cash allowance system that I mentioned on page 148. Strike the balance that works for you, your workplace situation, and your finances.

"I loathe soggy sandwiches."

Solution: Me too. I have always packed my lettuce and tomato apart from the meat, cheese, and bread. I can quickly assemble the sandwich just before eating it, and don't have to worry about gooey bread. Also, I have found that the thicker all-natural peanut butters and thick jellies don't cause as much sogginess to PBJ sandwiches, as those ingredients have less moisture.

"My family has 4 different lunch schedules during the week."

Solution: I have found with our family's different lunch schedules that it's best to have a variety of ingredients on hand to quickly put together lunch boxes or brown bags for each family member, as they head in different directions. Be sure to reconnect after a busy week and eat lunch together on the weekends. And remember that while it can get old and monotonous, packing lunches for your children and your spouse is a labor of love.

"I'm bored with eating the same thing all the time . . . but I still need a routine."

Solution: This is the endless cycle that has plagued the noon meal for decades. While it may feel like eating sandwiches or salads is boring, others may need the routine. I recommend creating a solid "prep hour" routine that will help those with

Type A tendencies, and then varying the foods that you prepare so you are not eating the same thing all the time.

"There is just no time to get lunch ready."

Solution: As I mentioned in the introduction, it will take "time" to get lunch food. That time could be spent waiting in the line at the drive-through, or waiting in the line in the deli in your office building, or walking down the street to your favorite downtown street vendor for a gyro, or finally, the hour it might take to prepare your breakfast and lunch foods each week.

Getting food together and eating lunch will take some time out of your day, no matter what the situation. It's up to you to decide how to spend that time, and ultimately how to spend your money. You could spend 10 minutes waiting for someone else to prepare, bag, and hand you some food for lunch. Or you could spend anywhere from 30 seconds to 5 minutes getting a lunch together in the morning.

In the end it comes down to being prepared and staying ahead of yourself. If your priority is to spend less money on food and groceries, then you'll figure out how to spend a few minutes in the morning getting lunch ready, so you don't have to stand in line (wasting time) waiting for take out (wasting money.)

"I don't want to have to spend another hour in the kitchen every day."

Solution: You certainly don't need to spend an hour in the kitchen every day preparing lunch, but you might prefer to spend an hour once a week in the kitchen preparing the food you need for lunch that week.

"Eating from plastic containers at the office every day gets old."

Solution: Get creative with your lunch layout. Bring a lightweight tablecloth and some easy to wash plastic plates and forks to the office and keep them in your desk. Come lunchtime, throw the tablecloth over your desk (and computer if it's large enough!) and have yourself a desk picnic. When you're finished, take a minute to clean and dry your dishes in the office lunchroom. No more plastic containers!

"My lunch was eaten by a coworker."

Solution: Don't store your food in the office lunchroom's refrigerator. If your food must be kept cold, the get a thermal-style lunch bag and pack a blue ice pack wrapped in a dishcloth inside. If this is a common problem in your workplace, I suggest speaking with your boss about the situation. And finally, I'm really sorry if this has ever happened to anyone. The nerve of some people!

While there will probably always be something frustrating about the lunch hour, at least there is something you can do about it, or a new way you can think about that frustration. For me, that frustration is the planning part of lunch. So my personal solution is to have enough food on hand to throw something together, and to use it as the meal to eat up the leftovers. It works for us. Many of the other frustrations can be avoided when you keep ahead of yourself and are always thinking of the next meal or snack.

Conclusion

When you have family members flying in all different directions at lunchtime, you have to come up with a system and routine that works for your family without losing your mind, or spending half of your paycheck at the grocery store. Set up a prep hour; work in some batch cooking when you're working on other meals in the kitchen. Get into a routine that will help streamline your time in the kitchen, reduce the frustrations of not having quick and easy homemade convenience foods, or spending too much on convenience foods at the grocery store.

And without further ado, here are 88 new lunch recipes that are sure to bring creativity and spark back into your lunch hour.

FIVE

Sandwiches, Wraps, Quesadillas, and More

Fruity Chicken Salad Sandwiches

2 cups finely shredded, cooked chicken ($1.50)
½ cup mayonnaise ($.20)
1 can (8 ounces) pineapple tidbits, drained ($.69)

1 cup grapes, halved ($.50)
¼ cup sliced or slivered almonds ($.37)
1 celery stalk, finely chopped ($.10)
Salt and pepper
8 slices whole wheat bread ($.60)

Fresh fruit ($.50)

Add all the ingredients, except the bread, to a medium mixing bowl and stir until well combined.

Divide the chicken salad evenly among four slices of whole wheat bread and top with the other four slices of whole wheat bread.

Serve Fruity Chicken Salad Sandwiches with favorite Fresh Fruit.

Makes 4 sandwiches

Cost $4.46

FRUGAL FACT: *Make the chicken salad and then wrap it up in tortillas. Freeze the wraps for a quick-and-easy, to-go lunch.*

Mandarin Chicken Salad Sandwiches

2 cups finely shredded, cooked chicken ($1.50)

½ cup mayonnaise ($.20)

1 can (8 ounces) mandarin oranges, juice reserved ($.69)

1 celery stalk, finely chopped ($.10)

1 tablespoon sesame seeds ($.20)

1 teaspoon ground ginger ($.05)

1 teaspoon garlic powder ($.05)

Salt and pepper

8 slices whole wheat bread ($.60)

Pineapple Coleslaw (page 247) ($1.16

Add all the ingredients (except the bread) plus 2 tablespoons of the reserved juice from the mandarin oranges to a medium mixing bowl and stir until well combined.

Divide chicken salad evenly among four slices of whole wheat bread and top with the other four slices of whole wheat bread.

For improved flavor, toast the sesame seeds for 1 to 2 minutes in a skillet before adding them to the chicken salad.

Serve Mandarin Chicken Salad Sandwiches with Pineapple Coleslaw.

Makes 4 sandwiches

Cost $4.55

FRUGAL FACT: *Stock up on canned fruit when you see the 15-ounce cans for less than $1 and the 8-ounce cans for less than $.75.*

Curried Chicken Salad Sandwiches

2 cups finely shredded, cooked chicken ($1.50)

½ cup mayonnaise ($.20)

½ cup raisins ($.37)

1 celery stalk, finely chopped ($.10)

1 teaspoon curry powder ($.10)

Salt and pepper

8 slices whole wheat bread ($.60)

Spinach ("Green") Smoothies (page 277) ($1.20)

Add all the ingredients, except the bread, to a medium mixing bowl and stir until well combined.

Divide chicken salad evenly among four slices of whole wheat bread and top with the other four slices of whole wheat bread.

Serve Curried Chicken Salad Sandwiches with Spinach ("Green") Smoothies.

Makes 4 sandwiches

Cost $4.07

FRUGAL FACT: *Purchase curry powder and other ethnic ingredients for less at international grocery stores in your area.*

Waldorf Chicken Salad Sandwiches

2 cups finely shredded, cooked chicken ($1.50)

½ cup mayonnaise ($.20)

2 Granny Smith apples, peeled, cored, and diced ($.50)

1 celery stalk, finely chopped ($.10)

½ cup walnuts, chopped ($.37)

Salt and pepper

8 slices whole wheat bread ($.60)

Cinnamon–Sweet Potato Fries (page 250) ($1.43)

Add all the ingredients, except the bread, to a medium mixing bowl, and stir until well combined.

Divide chicken salad evenly among four slices of whole wheat bread and top with the other four slices of whole wheat bread.

Serve Waldorf Chicken Salad Sandwiches with Cinnamon–Sweet Potato Fries.

Makes 4 sandwiches

Cost $4.70

FRUGAL FACT: *My "never-pay-more-than" price for a loaf of whole wheat bread is $1.50.*

Cranberry Turkey Salad Sandwiches

2 cups leftover turkey meat, shredded ($1.50)

1 cup leftover cranberry sauce ($.50)

½ cup mayonnaise ($.20)

2 tablespoons apple juice ($.02)

Salt and pepper

8 slices whole wheat bread ($.60)

Mustard Potato Salad (page 244) ($.80)

Add all the ingredients, except the bread, to a medium mixing bowl, and stir until well combined.

Divide turkey salad evenly among four slices of whole wheat bread and top with the other four slices of whole wheat bread.

Serve Cranberry Turkey Salad Sandwiches with Mustard Potato Salad.

Makes 4 sandwiches

Cost $3.62

FRUGAL FACT: *The perfect post-Thanksgiving Day lunch.*

Crunchy Tuna Sandwiches

....

2 cans (6 ounces each) tuna, drained ($1)

½ cup mayonnaise ($.20)

2 tablespoons pickle relish ($.10)

½ cup chopped celery ($.10)

Large handful potato chips, crushed ($.20)

Salt and pepper

8 slices whole wheat bread ($.60)

Fruit Salad with Yogurt Dressing (page 243) ($2.38

Add all the ingredients, except the bread, to a medium mixing bowl, and stir until well combined.

Divide tuna salad evenly among four slices of whole wheat bread and top with the other four slices of whole wheat bread.

TO-GO OPTION

Place the bread, tuna salad, and potato chips in different containers and assemble the sandwich just before serving.

Serve Crunchy Tuna Sandwiches with Fruit Salad with Yogurt Dressing.

Makes 4 sandwiches

Cost $4.58

FRUGAL FACT: *My "never-pay-more-than" price for a 6-ounce can of tuna is $.50.*

Tuna Parmesan Sandwiches

2 cans (6 ounces each) tuna, drained ($1)

½ cup mayonnaise ($.20)

½ cup grated Parmesan cheese ($.50)

1 tablespoon Dijon mustard ($.05)

1 teaspoon lemon juice ($.01)

1 teaspoon garlic powder ($.05)

Salt and pepper

8 slices whole wheat bread ($.60)

Succotash Summer Salad (page 256) ($1.43)

Add all the ingredients, except the bread, to a medium mixing bowl and stir until well combined.

Divide tuna salad evenly among four slices of whole wheat bread and top with the other four slices of whole wheat bread.

Serve Tuna Parmesan Sandwiches with Succotash Summer Salad.

Makes 4 sandwiches

Cost $3.84

FRUGAL FACT: *A quick "pantry lunch" that you can whip up in minutes for home or for the road.*

Swiss Tuna Melts

2 cans (6 ounces each) tuna, drained ($1)
½ cup mayonnaise ($.20)
2 tablespoons pickle relish ($.10)
1 tablespoon Dijon mustard ($.05)

1 teaspoon lemon juice ($.01)
1 teaspoon garlic powder ($.05)
Salt and pepper
8 slices whole wheat bread ($.60)
4 slices Swiss cheese ($.75)

Fresh fruit ($.50)

Add all the ingredients, except the bread and cheese, to a medium mixing bowl. Stir until well combined.

Preheat an electric griddle to 300 degrees or preheat a large skillet on the stovetop over medium-low heat. Lightly coat the griddle or skillet with nonstick cooking spray. Place ½ cup tuna salad and 1 slice of Swiss cheese between two slices of the bread and repeat with the remaining ingredients to make 4 sandwiches. Toast both sides of each sandwich, long enough melt the cheese.

Serve Swiss Tuna Melts with Fresh Fruit.

Makes 4 sandwich melts

Cost $3.26

FRUGAL FACT: *Sliced cheese does not freeze well, but can last 2 to 3 weeks in the refrigerator. It is one of those products that is difficult to stockpile, but with sale prices and regularly released coupons, you can keep a steady supply without paying full price for it on "off sale" weeks.*

Honey Mustard Ham and Cheese Melts

4 tablespoons honey mustard ($.25)
8 slices whole wheat bread ($.60)
4 slices leftover holiday ham or thick-
   carved deli meat ($2)

4 slices Swiss or cheddar cheese
   ($.75)

Mint Cucumber Onion Salad (page 254) ($1.40)

Spread the honey mustard sauce on one side of each slice of bread. Place the ham and cheese between the bread slices. Repeat with the remaining ingredients to make 4 sandwiches.

Preheat an electric griddle to 300 degrees or preheat a large skillet on the stovetop over medium-low heat. Lightly coat the griddle or skillet with nonstick cooking spray. Toast both sides of each sandwich, long enough to melt the cheese.

Serve Honey Mustard Ham and Cheese Melts with Mint Cucumber Onion Salad.

Makes 4 sandwich melts

Cost $5.00

FRUGAL FACT: *Use "reduced-for-quick-sale" bread in your freezer and make melts and other sandwiches on breads other than "sandwich" bread.*

Swiss BLT Melts

8 bacon slices ($.67)

4 tablespoons mayonnaise ($.10)

8 slices whole wheat bread ($.60)

1 large tomato, sliced ($.75)

4 large lettuce leaves ($.15)

4 slices Swiss cheese ($.75)

Fresh fruit ($.50)

Place the bacon slices on a microwave-safe plate lined with 2 paper towels. Cover with another paper towel. Microwave on high for 5 to 7 minutes, or until crisp. If you prefer, cook the bacon in a skillet over medium-high heat until crisp. Transfer to clean paper towels and let cool before adding to sandwiches.

Spread the mayonnaise onto the "insides" of each slice of bread. Place the tomato slices, lettuce, cheese slices, and cooled, cooked bacon between the slices of bread, making 4 sandwiches.

Preheat an electric griddle to 300 degrees, or preheat a large skillet on the stovetop over medium-low heat. Lightly coat the griddle or skillet with nonstick cooking spray. Toast both sides of each sandwich, long enough to melt the cheese.

Serve Swiss BLT Melts with Fresh Fruit.

Makes 4 sandwiches

Cost $3.52

FRUGAL FACT: *Many bread manufacturers release coupons for their bread products. Don't be brand particular—match coupons with the different breads that are on sale each week.*

Turkey and Provolone Sandwiches

2 tablespoons sandwich spread ($.10)
2 tablespoons Dijon mustard ($.10)
8 slices whole wheat bread ($.60)
8 ounces sliced deli turkey meat ($2)

4 slices provolone cheese ($.75)
4 large lettuce leaves ($.15)
1 large tomato, sliced ($.75)

Fresh fruit ($.50)

Spread the sandwich spread and Dijon mustard on on one side of each slice of bread. Place the sliced turkey meat, cheese, lettuce, and tomato slices between the bread slices, making 4 sandwiches.

TO-GO OPTION

To prevent the lettuce and tomato from causing a soggy sandwich mess, pack them in separate containers and assemble the sandwich just before eating.

Serve Turkey and Provolone Sandwiches with Fresh Fruit.

Makes 4 sandwiches

Cost $4.95

FRUGAL FACT: *My "never-pay-more-than" price for a half-pound package of deli meat is $2.*

Chicken Pesto Sandwiches

PESTO MAYONNAISE

⅓ cup pine nuts ($.75)

3 tablespoons extra-virgin olive oil ($.30)

2 cups fresh spinach leaves ($.50)

1 cup fresh basil leaves ($.50)

Salt and pepper

¼ cup mayonnaise ($.10)

1 garlic clove ($.05)

SANDWICHES

2 cooked chicken breasts, thinly sliced ($1.66)

8 slices whole wheat bread ($.60)

Fresh fruit ($.50)

Place the pine nuts, olive oil, spinach leaves, basil leaves, garlic cloves, and salt and pepper in a blender or food processor and purée. Stir the purée into the mayonnaise. Use immediately or store in the refrigerator and use within 3 days.

Spread the pesto mayonnaise on the bread slices and fill with sliced chicken and lettuce, making 4 sandwiches.

Serve Chicken Pesto Sandwiches with Fresh Fruit.

Makes 4 sandwiches

Cost $4.96

FRUGAL FACT: *Substitute deli chicken meat for the slices of chicken breast. This would also be great on bagels or croissants.*

Chicken-and-Tomato Bagel Sandwiches

4 ounces cream cheese, softened ($.50)

1 garlic clove, crushed ($.05)

1 teaspoon Italian seasoning ($.05)

Salt and pepper

2 cooked chicken breasts, sliced ($1.66)

1 large tomato, sliced ($.75)

4 large bagels, toasted (optional) ($.80)

Fresh fruit ($.50)

Place the softened cream cheese in small mixing bowl and stir in the crushed garlic clove and Italian seasonings. Season with salt and pepper to taste.

Spread the cream cheese onto the bagels and add the sliced chicken and tomato.

Serve Chicken-and-Tomato Bagel Sandwiches with Fresh Fruit.

Makes 4 bagel sandwiches

Cost $4.31

FRUGAL FACT: *During the summer months, grill 20 to 30 boneless, skinless chicken breasts at one time (page 142). Slice half of the grilled chicken breasts, and dice the other half. Place the sliced and diced chicken into plastic freezer bags. Then you have grilled chicken ready in a flash for sandwiches, salads, and summer pasta dishes.*

Deviled Egg Salad Sandwiches

....

8 large eggs ($.10)
½ cup sandwich spread ($.25)
1 celery stalk, finely chopped ($.10)
1 teaspoon paprika ($.10)

1 tablespoon fresh chives, chopped
   ($.25)
Salt and pepper
8 slices whole wheat bread ($.60)

Four Bean Salad (page 253) ($1.12)

In a medium saucepan, boil the eggs for 12 minutes and then remove from the heat. Let sit for 10 minutes, and then drain the hot water. Place the eggs into a bowl of cold water for 15 to 20 minutes.

Peel the eggs and place them into a mixing bowl. Cut the eggs using a pastry blender, two knives, or a large fork. Once the eggs are cut, add the sandwich spread, chopped celery, paprika, chives, and salt and pepper to taste.

Serve Deviled Egg Salad Sandwiches with Four Bean Salad.

Makes 4 sandwiches

Cost $2.52

FRUGAL FACT: *Substitute ½ cup of mayonnaise plus ½ teaspoon cider vinegar for the sandwich spread.*

Cucumber-Dill Sandwiches

....

4 ounces cream cheese ($.50)
2 garlic cloves, crushed ($.10)
2 teaspoons fresh or dried dill ($.10)

Salt and pepper
1 cucumber, thinly sliced ($.75)
8 slices whole wheat bread ($.60)

Chickpea Summer Salad (page 253) ($1.47)

Place the softened cream cheese in a small mixing bowl and stir in the crushed garlic and dill. Season to taste with salt and pepper.

Spread the cream cheese onto the bread and top with the thinly sliced cucumber, making 4 sandwiches.

Serve Cucumber-Dill Sandwiches with Chickpea Summer Salad.

Makes 4 sandwiches

Cost $3.52

FRUGAL FACT: *My "never-pay-more-than" price for cucumbers is $.75, although they can be found for as little as $.50 through the summer.*

Turkey and Hummus Sandwiches

¼ cup Roasted Garlic Hummus
   (page 271) ($.50)
8 slices whole wheat bread ($.60)

8 ounces sliced deli turkey meat ($2)
4 slices provolone cheese ($.75)
1 large tomato, sliced ($.75)

4 hard-boiled eggs ($.40)

Spread the hummus on both sides of the bread slices. Add the turkey meat, cheese, and tomato slices, making 4 sandwiches.

TO-GO OPTION

Place the hummus and tomato slices in separate containers and spread onto the bread just before serving, to prevent the sandwich from getting soggy.

Serve Turkey and Hummus Sandwiches with Hard-boiled Eggs.

Makes 4 sandwiches

Cost $5.00

FRUGAL FACT: *Use a tomato from the garden to reduce the overall cost of this lunch.*

Chicken Caesar Wraps

2 grilled boneless, skinless chicken breasts, sliced ($1.66)
¼ head romaine lettuce, chopped ($.25)
½ cup grated Parmesan cheese ($.50)

½ cup Caesar salad dressing ($.50)
4 burrito-size, whole wheat tortillas ($.67)

Parmesan Potato Wedges (page 249) ($1.40)

Place 3 slices of the grilled chicken breast, a handful of chopped lettuce, and a few sprinkles of grated Parmesan cheese onto each burrito-size tortilla. Drizzle each wrap with Caesar salad dressing and roll up. Cut the wraps in half on the diagonal.

Serve Chicken Caesar Wraps with Parmesan Potato Wedges.

Makes 4 burrito-size wraps

Cost $4.98

FRUGAL FACT: *My "never-pay-more-than" price for burrito-size tortillas is $1.29 for 8 tortillas.*

Balsamic Veggie Wraps

1 cucumber, halved, seeded, and sliced ($.75)

1 red bell pepper, seeded and sliced ($1)

1 green bell pepper, seeded and sliced ($.75)

¼ head romaine lettuce, chopped ($.25)

½ cup grated Parmesan cheese ($.50)

4 tablespoons store-bought balsamic vinaigrette dressing ($.25)

8 soft, taco-size, flour tortillas ($.67)

Fresh fruit ($.50)

Place the cucumber slices, red and green bell pepper slices, lettuce, and grated Parmesan cheese onto each of the soft, taco-size tortillas. Drizzle the dressing over each wrap and roll up. Cut the wraps in half on the diagonal.

Serve Balsamic Veggie Wraps with Fresh Fruit.

Makes 8 soft, taco-size wraps

Cost $4.67

FRUGAL FACT: *Stock up on store-bought salad dressings in the late spring, when sale prices are low and coupons are available.*

Pepper Turkey Wraps

8 ounces sliced deli turkey meat ($2)
¼ head romaine lettuce, chopped ($.25)
1 red bell pepper, seeded and sliced ($.75)
1 green bell pepper, seeded and sliced ($.75)

4 tablespoons homemade (below) or store-bought honey mustard dressing ($.20)
4 burrito-size, whole wheat tortillas ($.67)

Fresh fruit ($.50)

Place the turkey meat, lettuce, and red and green bell pepper slices onto the burrito-size tortillas. Drizzle the honey mustard dressing over each of the wraps and roll up. Cut the wraps in half on the diagonal.

Serve Pepper Turkey Wraps with Fresh Fruit.

Makes 4 burrito-size wraps

Cost $4.37

FRUGAL FACT: *Make your own honey mustard dressing by whisking equal amounts of honey, mustard, and mayonnaise. Store in an airtight container for 1 to 2 weeks in the refrigerator.*

Bacon, Lettuce, and Tomato Wraps

8 bacon slices ($.67)
2 cups chopped lettuce ($.25)
1 large tomato, sliced ($.75)

¼ cup store-bought ($.25) or Homemade
Ranch Dressing (page 227)
8 soft, taco-size flour tortillas ($.67)

Roasted Red Potato Salad (page 245) ($1.36)

Place the bacon slices on a microwave-safe plate lined with 2 paper towels. and cover with another paper towel. Microwave on high for 5 to 7 minutes, or until crisp. If you prefer, cook the bacon in a skillet over medium-high heat until crisp. Transfer to clean paper towels and let cool before adding to the wraps.

Place a slice of bacon, along with lettuce and a tomato slice, onto each of the soft, taco-size tortillas. Drizzle Ranch dressing over top and roll up.

Serve Bacon, Lettuce, and Tomato Wraps with Roasted Red Potato Salad.

Makes 8 soft, taco-size wraps

Cost $3.95

FRUGAL FACT: *My "never-pay-more-than" price for soft, taco-size tortillas is $2.19 for 20 tortillas.*

Grilled Chicken and Avocado Wraps

....

2 boneless, skinless chicken breasts, grilled and sliced ($1.66)
4 slices cheddar cheese, cut in half ($.75)
2 cups chopped lettuce ($.25)
1 avocado, sliced ($.68)

¼ cup store-bought ($.25) or Homemade Ranch Dressing (page 227)
4 burrito-size, whole wheat tortillas ($.67)

Fresh fruit ($.50)

Place 2 to 3 slices of grilled chicken, 2 cheese slice halves, lettuce, and 2 avocado slices onto each of the burrito-size tortillas. Drizzle each wrap with the Ranch dressing and roll up.

Serve Grilled Chicken and Avocado Wraps with Fresh Fruit.

Makes 4 large burrito-size wraps

Cost $4.76

FRUGAL FACT: *This is the perfect meal to use up the batch-cooked, grilled chicken slices (page 142) from the freezer.*

California Club Wraps

8 bacon slices ($.67)
4 slices cheddar cheese, cut in half ($.75)
2 cups chopped lettuce ($.25)
1 avocado, pitted and sliced ($.68)
4 hard-boiled eggs, sliced ($.40)

¼ cup store-bought ($.25) or Homemade
  Ranch Dressing (page 227)
4 burrito-size, whole wheat tortillas
  ($.67)

Oven Chili Fries (page 248) ($.76)

Place the bacon slices on a microwave-safe plate lined with 2 paper towels. Cover with another paper towel. Microwave on high for 5 to 7 minutes, or until crisp. If you prefer, cook the bacon in a skillet over medium-high heat until crisp. Transfer to clean paper towels and let cool before adding to the wraps.

Place a slice of bacon, 2 cheese slice halves, lettuce, avocado slices, and hard-boiled egg slices onto each of the burrito-size tortillas. Drizzle each wrap with Ranch dressing and roll up. Cut the wraps in half on the diagonal.

Serve California Club Wraps with Oven Chili Fries.

Makes 4 burrito-size wraps

Cost $4.43

FRUGAL FACT: *Use any variety of lettuce from the garden to cut costs on this meal.*

Caesar Tuna Wraps

2 (6 ounces each) cans tuna, drained ($1)

¼ head romaine lettuce, chopped ($.25)

½ cup grated Parmesan cheese ($.50)

½ cup Caesar salad dressing ($.50)

4 burrito-size, whole wheat tortillas ($.67)

Honey Ginger Citrus Salad (page 242) ($1.53)

Place the tuna, lettuce, and grated Parmesan cheese onto each of the burrito-size tortillas. Drizzle the Caesar salad dressing over each wrap and roll up. Cut the wraps in half on the diagonal.

Serve Caesar Tuna Wraps with Honey Ginger Citrus Salad.

Makes 4 burrito-size wraps

Cost $4.45

FRUGAL FACT: *Because there are rarely coupons for name-brand Parmesan cheeses, consider buying the store brand for grated and shredded Parmesan cheeses.*

Brown Rice and Red Bean Burritos

2 cups cooked red beans ($.40)
1 cup uncooked brown rice ($.40)
1 teaspoon ground cumin ($.05)
Salt and pepper
¼ cup sour cream ($.10)

2 tablespoons chopped fresh cilantro
($.20)
4 burrito-size, whole wheat tortillas
($.67)

Fresh fruit ($.50)

The beans can be cooked according to the batch-cooking directions on page 141. If in a time crunch, substitute two cans (15 ounces each) of red kidney beans, rinsed and drained.

Cook the brown rice according to the package directions.

In a large mixing bowl, stir together the cooked red beans, cooked brown rice, cumin, and salt and pepper to taste. Place about 1 cup of the beans and rice mixture, along with a few dollops of sour cream and chopped cilantro, onto each of the burrito-size tortillas. Roll up and serve warm.

Serve Brown Rice and Red Bean Burritos with Fresh Fruit.

Makes 4 burritos

Cost $2.32 (Note: The cost will change with the substitution of canned beans.)

FRUGAL FACT: *Serve extra rice and beans mixture for lunch the following day, topped with salsa and sour cream.*

FREEZER FRIENDLY

Spicy Black Bean Burritos

2 cups cooked black beans ($.40)
1 can (10 ounces) diced tomatoes with
   green chilies ($.59)
1 teaspoon ground cumin ($.05)

Salt and pepper
¼ cup sour cream ($.10)
8 soft, taco-size, flour tortillas ($.67)

Avocado, Corn, and Black Bean Salsa (page 255) ($1.14)

The beans can be cooked according to the batch-cooking directions on page 141. If in a time crunch, substitute two cans (15 ounces each) of black beans, rinsed and drained.

In a mixing bowl, add the cooked black beans and stir in the diced tomatoes with green chilies, cumin, and salt and pepper to taste. Place the black bean mixture onto the tortillas. Add a dollop or two of sour cream to each burrito. Roll up and serve warm.

Serve Spicy Black Bean Burritos with Avocado, Corn, and Black Bean Salsa.

Makes 8 mini burritos

Cost $2.95 (Note: The cost will change with the substitution of canned beans.)

FRUGAL FACT: *Stock up on cans of diced tomatoes with green chilies when they are on sale for $.60 or less. I typically pay less than $.25 per can by matching coupons with sale prices and store promotions.*

Peaches 'n Cream Oatmeal, *page 34*

Peach-Raspberry Breakfast Parfait, *page 52*

Pumpkin Nut Muffins, *page 116*

Maple Pecan Oatmeal, *page 31*

Huevos Rancheros, *page 54*

Hawaiian Ham-wiches, *page 135*

Chocolate Chip Raspberry Pancakes, *page 97*

Berry Breakfast Bread Pudding, *page 59*

California Club Wraps, *page 179*

Chicken and Broccoli Stir-Fry, *page 206*

Chickpea Summer Salad, *page 253*

Spaghetti Sauce Pitas, *page 185*

Minestrone Pasta Salad, *page 221*

Avocado and Tomato Salad with Cilantro-Lime Dressing, *page 239*

Pantry Trail Mix, *page 266*

Quick Caramel Popcorn, *page 282*

Black Bean, Pepper, and Onion Wraps

3 cups cooked black beans ($.60)
1 can (10 ounces) diced tomatoes and
   green chilies ($.59)
1 teaspoon ground cumin ($.05)
Salt and pepper

1 bag (12 ounces) frozen peppers and
   onions ($1)
1 tablespoon canola or vegetable oil
   ($.03)
8 soft, taco-size, flour tortillas ($.67)

Fresh fruit ($.50)

The beans can be cooked according to the batch-cooking directions on page 141. If in a time crunch, substitute three (15 ounces each) cans of black beans, rinsed and drained.

Place the cooked black beans, diced tomatoes and green chilies, cumin, and salt and pepper to taste into a blender. Add ¼ to ½ cup of water, depending on how thick you want the black beans. Purée the beans.

In a skillet, sauté the frozen peppers and onions in the oil for 5 to 7 minutes, or until cooked through and beginning to brown.

Place about ½ cup of the black bean puree onto each of the tortillas. Top with the sautéed peppers and onions, and roll up.

Serve Black Bean, Pepper, and Onion Wraps with Fresh Fruit.

Makes 4 soft taco-size wraps

Cost $3.43 (Note: The cost will change with the substitution of canned beans.)

FRUGAL FACT: *Double or triple this recipe using your stockpile of cooked black beans and cans of diced tomatoes and green chilies. Freeze for future lunches.*

Pepperoni Pizza Pitas

6 pita pockets ($.99)
1 cup store-bought ($.50) or Homemade
   Pizza Sauce (page 304) ($.42)
18 pepperoni slices ($.37)

½ cup grated Parmesan cheese ($.25)
1½ cups shredded mozzarella cheese
   ($1.13)

Fresh fruit ($.50)

Open the pita pockets and add about 2 tablespoons of pizza sauce to each pita, along with 3 pepperoni slices, a spoonful of Parmesan cheese, and handful of shredded mozzarella cheese.

Heat the pita pockets in the microwave on high for 2 minutes, or until the cheese has melted.

Serve Pepperoni Pizza Pitas with Fresh Fruit.

Makes 6 pita pockets

Cost $3.74 ($3.66 if using homemade sauce)

FRUGAL FACT: *It's more cost-effective to buy pita bread on sale from the store, rather than make it yourself.*

Spaghetti Sauce Pitas

6 pita pockets ($.99)
2 cups leftover store-bought ($1) or
    Homemade Spaghetti Sauce (page
    304) ($.69)

18 pepperoni slices ($.37)
½ cup grated Parmesan cheese ($.25)
1½ cups shredded mozzarella cheese
    ($1.13)

Fresh fruit ($.50)

Open the pita pockets and add about 2 tablespoons of spaghetti sauce to each pita, along with 3 pepperoni slices, a spoonful of the grated Parmesan cheese and a handful of the shredded mozzarella cheese.

Heat in the microwave on high for 2 minutes, or until cheese has melted.

Serve Spaghetti Sauce Pitas with Fresh Fruit.

Makes 6 pita pockets

Cost $4.24 ($3.32 if using homemade sauce)

FRUGAL FACT: *Keep an eye out for pita bread that's been marked down for quick sale. Pita bread freezes well.*

Tuna Pitas

2 cans (6 ounces each) tuna, drained ($1)
½ cup mayonnaise ($.20)
1 tablespoon Dijon mustard ($.05)
1 teaspoon lemon juice ($.01)
1 teaspoon garlic powder ($.05)
Salt and pepper
6 pita pockets ($.99)
1 cup chopped lettuce ($.13)

Sweet and Spicy Coleslaw (page 246) ($1.13)

In a mixing bowl, prepare the tuna salad by combining the tuna, mayonnaise, Dijon mustard, lemon juice, garlic powder, and salt and pepper to taste.

Spoon the tuna salad into the pita pockets and add the chopped lettuce.

Serve Tuna Pitas with Sweet and Spicy Coleslaw.

Makes 6 pita pockets

Cost $3.56

FRUGAL FACT: *To prevent the pitas from getting soggy in a lunch box, pack the pita pockets separate from the tuna and lettuce.*

Guacamole Veggie Pitas

1 avocado ($.68)
2 teaspoons lime juice ($.05)
1 teaspoon ground cumin ($.05)
1 teaspoon garlic powder ($.05)
Salt and pepper

6 pita pockets ($.99)
1 green bell pepper, seeded and sliced ($.50)
1 red bell pepper, seeded and sliced ($1)
6 slices Pepper Jack cheese ($1)

Fresh fruit ($.50)

Cut open the avocado lengthwise, remove the seed, and scoop out the flesh with a spoon. Put in a mixing bowl. Mash the avocado with the lime juice, cumin, garlic powder, and salt and pepper to taste.

Place a spoonful of guacamole into each pita and add the green and red pepper slices. Add a slice of pepper Jack cheese to each pita.

Heat the pita pockets in the microwave on high for 2 minutes, or until cheese has melted.

Serve Guacamole Veggie Pitas with Fresh Fruit.

Makes 6 pita pockets

Cost $4.82

FRUGAL FACT: *Guacamole can be frozen, sealed with plastic wrap to prevent browning, in a plastic freezer container. Press the plastic wrap directly on top of the guacamole and push out any air bubbles. Place the lid of the container on top and freeze.*

Chicken Caesar Pitas

2 grilled boneless, skinless chicken
   breasts, sliced ($1.66)
¼ head romaine lettuce, chopped ($.25)

½ cup grated Parmesan cheese ($.50)
¼ cup Caesar salad dressing ($.25)
6 pita pockets ($.99)

Fresh fruit ($.50)

Place 2 to 3 slices of the chicken breast, along with chopped lettuce, grated Parmesan cheese, and a drizzle of Caesar salad dressing into each of the pita pockets.

Serve Chicken Caesar Pitas with Fresh Fruit.

Makes 6 pita pockets

Cost $4.15

FRUGAL FACT: *Because store-bought salad dressing is shelf-stable, stock up when the price drops below $1 for a 16-ounce bottle.*

Chicken Quesadillas

2 cups shredded, cooked chicken ($1.50)

1 cup store-bought salsa ($.50) or Homemade Salsa Fresca (page 306)

2 cups shredded cheddar or Mexican blend cheese ($1.50)

4 teaspoons canola or vegetable oil ($.02)

4 burrito-size, whole wheat tortillas ($.67)

Fresh fruit ($.50)

In a large mixing bowl, combine the chicken, salsa, and shredded cheese.

Add 1 teaspoon of the oil to a skillet large enough to hold the tortilla flat. Once the oil is hot, add the tortilla and top with about a cup of the chicken mixture. Spread the mixture out evenly, and then fold the tortilla in half. Cook on high for another 1 to 2 minutes, on each side.

The quesadilla will cook quickly, so don't leave it unattended. Cook the other 3 quesadillas with the remaining ingredients. Let cool slightly before cutting into wedges and serving.

Serve Chicken Quesadillas with Fresh Fruit.

Makes 4 quesadillas

Cost $4.69

FRUGAL FACT: *Make quesadillas on a baking sheet in the oven, on the grill, on an indoor grill, or in a quesadilla maker.*

Bean Quesadillas

....

2 cups cooked black beans ($.40)
2 cups cooked red kidney beans
  ($.40)
1 cup store-bought salsa ($.50) or
  Homemade Salsa Fresca (page 306)

2 cups shredded cheddar or Mexican
  blend cheese ($1.50)
4 teaspoons canola or vegetable oil ($.02)
Salt and pepper
4 burrito-size, whole wheat tortillas ($.67)

Avocado, Corn, and Black Bean Salsa (page 255) ($1.14)

The beans can be cooked according to the batch-cooking directions on page 141. If in a time crunch, substitute one can (15 ounces) of black and red kidney beans, rinsed and drained.

In a mixing bowl, combine the cooked black and red kidney beans, salsa, and shredded cheese. Season with salt and pepper to taste.

Add 1 teaspoon of the oil to a skillet large enough to hold the tortilla flat. Once the oil is hot, add the tortilla and top with about a cup of the bean mixture. Spread the mixture out evenly, and then fold the tortilla in half. Cook on high for another 1 to 2 minutes, on each side.

The quesadilla will cook quickly, so don't leave it unattended. Cook the other 3 quesadillas with the remaining ingredients. Let cool slightly before cutting into wedges and serving.

Serve Bean Quesadillas with Avocado, Corn, and Black Bean Salsa.

Makes 4 quesadillas

Cost $4.63 (Note: The cost will change with the substitution of canned beans.)

FRUGAL FACT: *Eat any of these lunch recipes with leftover vegetables from the previous night's dinner to spend even less on the meal.*

Beef Taco Quesadillas

1 pound ground beef ($1.49)

1 can (6 ounces) tomato paste ($.19)

1 teaspoon ground cumin ($.05)

1 teaspoon chili powder ($.05)

1 teaspoon garlic powder ($.05)

1 teaspoon onion powder ($.05)

Salt and pepper

2 cups shredded cheddar or Mexican blend cheese ($1.50)

4 teaspoons of canola or vegetable oil ($.02)

4 burrito-size, whole wheat tortillas ($.67)

Oven Chili Fries (page 248) ($.76)

In a skillet, brown the ground beef. Drain the mixture and return it to the skillet. Stir in the tomato paste plus 1 tomato paste can of water. Stir in the seasonings and let simmer for 10 minutes.

In a mixing bowl, combine the cooked taco meat and shredded cheese.

Add 1 teaspoon of the oil to a skillet large enough to hold the tortilla flat. Once the oil is hot, add the tortilla and top with about a cup of the beef mixture. Spread the beef mixture evenly on the tortilla, and then fold the tortilla in half. Cook on high for another 1 to 2 minutes, on each side.

The quesadilla will cook quickly, so don't leave it unattended. Cook the other 3 quesadillas with the remaining ingredients. Let cool slightly before cutting into wedges and serving.

Serve Beef Taco Quesadillas with Oven Chili Fries.

Makes 4 quesadillas

Cost $4.83

FRUGAL FACT: *This recipe is a quick and easy way to use up leftover ground beef.*

Corn and Black Bean Quesadillas

2 cups cooked black beans ($.40)
2 cups frozen corn kernels ($1)
1 cup store-bought salsa ($.50) or
    Homemade Salsa Fresca (page 300)

2 cups shredded cheddar or Mexican
    blend cheese ($1.50)
Salt and pepper
4 teaspoons canola or vegetable oil ($.02)
4 burrito-size, whole wheat tortillas ($.67)

Fresh fruit ($.50)

The beans can be cooked according to the batch-cooking directions on page 141. If in a time crunch, substitute one can (15 ounces) of black beans, rinsed and drained.

Cook the corn kernels according to the package directions.

In a mixing bowl, combine the cooked black beans, corn, salsa, shredded cheese, and salt and pepper to taste.

Add 1 teaspoon of the oil to a skillet large enough to hold the tortilla flat. Once the oil is hot, add the tortilla and top with about a cup of the black bean mixture to the tortilla. Spread the mixture out evenly, and then fold the tortilla in half. Cook on high for another 1 to 2 minutes, on each side. The quesadilla will cook quickly, so don't leave it unattended. Cook the other 3 quesadillas with the remaining ingredients. Let cool slightly before cutting into wedges and serving.

Serve Corn and Black Bean Quesadillas with Fresh Fruit.

Makes 4 large quesadillas

Cost $4.59 (Note: The cost will change with the substitution of canned beans.)

FRUGAL FACT: *Freeze quesadillas by placing the mixture in between two whole tortillas and placing the full-circle quesadilla into a gallon-size freezer bag. To cook, remove the frozen quesadilla from the bag and place on a baking sheet and into an oven preheated to 350 degrees for 15 to 20 minutes, or until the cheese has melted. Let cool, then cut into wedges before serving.*

English Muffin Pizzas

6 English muffins ($.99)

1 cup store-bought ($.50) or Homemade
   Pizza Sauce (page 304) ($.42)

24 pepperoni slices ($.50)

¼ cup grated Parmesan cheese ($.25)

2 cups shredded mozzarella cheese
   ($1.50)

Fresh fruit ($.50)

Preheat the oven to 350 degrees.

Open up the English muffins and place on a baking sheet. Add about 2 tablespoons of pizza sauce to each muffin half. Place 2 pepperoni slices on each muffin and top with a pinch of grated Parmesan cheese and handful of shredded mozzarella cheese.

Place muffin pizzas in the preheated oven and bake for 10 to 15 minutes, or until the cheese has melted and is beginning to turn golden.

Serve English Muffin Pizzas with Fresh Fruit.

Makes 12 English Muffin Pizzas

Cost $4.24 ($3.16 if using homemade sauce)

FRUGAL FACT: *Store sliced pepperoni for up to 6 months in the freezer.*

FREEZER FRIENDLY

Pepperoni Calzones

....

Homemade Pizza Dough (page 81)
  ($1.28)

1 cup store-bought ($.50) or Homemade
  Pizza Sauce (page 304) ($.42)

About 40 pepperoni slices ($1)

2 cups shredded mozzarella cheese
  ($1.50)

1 tablespoon olive oil ($.10)

Garlic salt, for sprinkling ($.05)

Fresh fruit ($.50)

Prepare the pizza dough according to the directions on pages 81 and 82. Use store-bought pizza dough if in a time crunch.

Preheat the oven to 350 degrees. Lightly coat two large baking sheets with nonstick cooking spray.

Form the dough into 8 balls and roll out each ball from the center, into a rectangle approximately 5 inches by 8 inches, leaving the short ends slightly rounded. Place a spoonful of pizza sauce onto on half of the rectangle. Add a few pepperoni slices and some shredded mozzarella cheese to each calzone. Fold the dough over and press the edges together with a fork, sealing in the sauce, pepperoni, and cheese. Brush the top of each calzone with olive oil and sprinkle garlic salt on top.

Bake the calzones in the preheated oven for 10 to 15 minutes, or until golden brown on top. Let cool slightly before serving. Serve warm.

Serve Pepperoni Calzones with Fresh Fruit.

Makes 8 calzones

Cost $4.93 ($4.85 if using homemade sauce)

FRUGAL FACT: *These calzones are freezer friendly and would be great for batch cooking. Freeze after baking.*

Grilled Cheese Sandwiches with Creamy Tomato Soup

....

SOUP

1 tablespoon extra-virgin olive oil ($.10)

½ onion, chopped ($.15)

2 garlic cloves, crushed ($.10)

1 celery stalk, chopped ($.10)

1 can (28 ounces) crushed tomatoes
($1.59)

1 can (15 ounces) tomato sauce ($.59)

1 cup whole milk or cream ($.10)

2 tablespoons chopped, fresh basil ($.25)

1 tablespoon chopped, fresh parsley
($.15)

Salt and pepper

SANDWICHES

butter or margarine ($.20)

8 slices whole wheat bread ($.60)

4 slices sharp cheddar cheese ($.75)

Heat the olive oil in a large saucepan and add the chopped onions, chopped celery, and garlic cloves. Sauté over medium-high heat for 5 to 7 minutes, or until softened. Lower the heat to medium, add the crushed tomatoes and cream, and cook for 15 minutes. Stir in the fresh basil and parsley and cook for another 3 minutes.

Pour half of the soup into a blender and puree. Stir the pureed soup back into the chunky soup in the saucepan. (For a thinner soup, puree all of it in the blender.) Keep hot.

Spread the butter or margarine onto both sides of the bread. Place 1 slice of sharp cheddar cheese in between 2 buttered bread slices.

Preheat an electric griddle to 300 degrees or preheat a large skillet on the stovetop over medium-low heat. Toast each side of the cheese sandwich, long enough for the cheese to melt and the bread to brown.

Serve Grilled Cheese Sandwiches with Creamy Tomato Soup.

Makes 4 sandwiches and 4 soup servings

Cost $4.68

FRUGAL FACT: *Making your own tomato soup using canned tomatoes is both refreshing and delicious, and preservative free, too.*

Peanut Butter Surprise Sandwiches

SELECT THE BREAD

Whole wheat bread

Whole wheat tortillas, as roll ups or cut
as pinwheels

Flatbread

Pita bread

Bagels

Mini bagels

English muffins

Toasted bread

PEANUT BUTTER AND . . .

Jelly

Honey

Banana slices

Thinly sliced apples

Potato chips

Thin crackers

Mini chocolate chips

Granola

Broccoli-Raisin Salad (page 251) ($1.63)

Mix and match, and enjoy surprising your kiddos with fun variations of their favorite sandwiches.

Serve Peanut Butter Surprise Sandwiches with Broccoli-Raisin Salad.

Cost $3.63

FRUGAL FACT: *Get out of the PBJ sandwich rut and jazz up your kid's favorite sandwich. It's also a great way to use up the last apple in the fridge, or the potato chip crumbs in the bottom of the bag.*

SIX

Soups and Other Hot Lunches

Balsamic French Onion Soup

....

4 white onions ($1.20)
2 tablespoons extra-virgin olive oil ($.20)
2 garlic cloves, crushed ($.10)
¼ cup balsamic vinegar ($.25)
4 cups homemade (free) or store-bought beef broth ($1.49)

4 slices stale French bread ($.25)
½ cup grated Parmesan cheese ($.50)
Salt and pepper
4 slices Swiss cheese or 1 cup shredded Swiss cheese ($.75)

Slice the onions into 2-inch half-moons.

Heat the olive oil in a large saucepan. Add the sliced onions and crushed garlic and sauté over medium-high heat for 25 to 30 minutes. After about 15 minutes add the balsamic vinegar, so the onions will caramelize and take on the balsamic flavor.

Once the onions have caramelized, add the beef broth plus 1 cup of water and bring to a boil. Reduce the heat and let simmer for 5 to 10 minutes.

To serve, add about 2 cups of the soup to each oven proof bowl, then top with a slice of stale bread. Sprinkle a few pinches of Parmesan cheese. Season with salt and pepper to taste, and top with a slice of Swiss cheese, or ¼ cup shredded Swiss cheese. Place the soup bowls under the broiler for 10 minutes, or until the cheese is golden brown on top.

TO-GO DIRECTIONS

Place the warm soup into a thermos bowl. Place the slice of bread and slice of Swiss cheese in another container. When ready to eat, place the soup into a bowl, add the bread and cheese and microwave for 1 minute.

Serve Balsamic French Onion Soup.

Makes 4 lunch portions

Cost $4.74 ($3.24 if using homemade beef broth)

FRUGAL FACT: *Slice a loaf of "reduced-for-quick-sale" bread to use in this recipe. Or use frozen croutons (see page 84).*

Thyme Chicken Noodle Soup

4 cups homemade (free) or store-bought chicken broth ($1.49)

4 cups water

⅓ cup lime juice ($.25)

1 small yellow onion, finely chopped ($.30)

2 carrots, peeled and sliced ($.20)

2 celery stalks, sliced ($.20)

2 teaspoons dried thyme ($.25)

1 teaspoon garlic powder ($.05)

2 cups shredded, cooked chicken ($1.50)

½ pound angel hair pasta ($.48)

Salt and pepper

In a large saucepan, bring the chicken broth, water, and lime juice to a boil. Add the chopped onion, sliced carrots, sliced celery, thyme, and garlic powder, and return to a boil.

Add the shredded, cooked chicken and the angel hair pasta and cook at a gentle boil for 8 to 10 minutes. Season to taste with salt and pepper.

Serve Thyme Chicken Noodle Soup.

Makes 6 to 8 lunch portions

Cost $4.72

FRUGAL FACT: *Use homemade chicken broth to make this soup for just $3.23.*

SLOW-COOKER ADAPTABLE *(see page 142)*

Twice-Baked, Fully Loaded Baked Potato Soup

....

6 large or 8 medium russet potatoes ($.80)

2 tablespoons butter or margarine ($.20)

1 bunch scallions, sliced, white and green parts separated ($.50)

2 garlic cloves, crushed ($.10)

2 tablespoons all-purpose flour ($.02)

6 cups whole or 2 percent milk ($.60)

Salt and pepper

1 cup shredded sharp cheddar cheese ($.75)

4 cooked bacon slices, crumbled ($.75)

4 dollops sour cream ($.20)

Fresh fruit ($.50)

Preheat the oven to 400 degrees. Place the potatoes into a 9 × 13-inch glass baking dish with about 1 cup of water. Cover with aluminum foil and steam-bake in the preheated oven for 45 to 50 minutes. Once the potatoes have cooked through, remove them from the dish and cut into chunks; let cool as you prepare the soup.

In a large saucepan over medium heat, melt the butter or margarine. Add the white parts of the scallion and the crushed garlic and sauté for 2 to 3 minutes. Add the baked potato chunks and sauté for another 2 to 3 minutes. (Reserve the green portions of the scallions for garnish.)

Vigorously whisk the flour and the milk into the sautéed vegetables. Let cook over high heat until the mixture bubbles and begins to thicken. Season to taste with salt and pepper. Stir in the shredded cheese. Let simmer for 10 to 15 minutes, or until it reaches desired consistency.

To each serving bowl, add a pinch of crumbled bacon, a pinch of the sliced scallion tops, and a dollop of sour cream.

Serve Twice-Baked, Fully Loaded Baked Potato Soup with Fresh Fruit.

Makes 4 to 6 lunch portions

Cost $4.42

FRUGAL FACT: *Bake extra potatoes for dinner, and make this soup for lunch the next day.*

SLOW-COOKER ADAPTABLE *(see page 142)*

Baked Parmesan Chicken Fingers

....

1 package chicken tenderloins (about
   1½ pounds) ($2.63)
½ cup fine yellow cornmeal ($.25)
½ cup grated Parmesan cheese ($.50)
1 teaspoon garlic powder ($.05)
½ teaspoon salt

½ teaspoon pepper
1 large egg ($.10)
2 tablespoons milk ($.01)
1 cup spaghetti or marinara sauce, for
   dipping ($.25)

Spinach ("Green") Smoothies (page 277) ($1.20)

Preheat the oven to 350 degrees. Lightly coat a 9 × 13-inch glass baking dish with nonstick cooking spray.

Rinse the chicken tenderloins and pat dry with paper towels.

In a small mixing bowl, toss together the cornmeal, Parmesan cheese, garlic powder, salt, and pepper.

In another small mixing bowl, whisk together the egg and milk.

Dip each chicken tenderloin into the egg-milk mixture and then coat with the cornmeal mixture. Place the coated chicken tenderloins into the prepared baking dish.

Bake the chicken fingers in the preheated oven for 25 to 30 minutes, or until cooked through. The cooking time may vary depending on the thickness of the chicken tenderloins.

Serve Baked Parmesan Chicken Fingers with Marinara Dipping Sauce and Spinach ("Green") Smoothies.

Makes 8 to 10 chicken fingers

Cost $4.99

FRUGAL FACT: *Remember to stock up on chicken tenderloins and chicken breasts when their price falls below $1.99 per pound.*

SLOW-COOKER ADAPTABLE *(see page 142)*

Chicken and Broccoli Stir-Fry

1 cup uncooked brown rice ($.20)
2 large boneless, skinless chicken breasts
    ($2)
¼ cup soy sauce ($.40)
3 tablespoons canola oil ($.15)
2 heads broccoli, cut into florets ($.79)

1 small yellow onion, chopped ($.30)
3 garlic cloves, crushed ($.15)
1 teaspoon crushed red pepper flakes
    ($.10)
Salt and pepper

In a medium saucepan, cook the rice according to the package directions.

Dice the chicken breast into ½-inch pieces. Toss the diced chicken pieces with the soy sauce and let marinate in the refrigerator for at least 30 minutes.

In a large skillet or wok, heat the canola oil and add the marinated chicken pieces. Cook over high heat for 7 to 9 minutes, or until the chicken pieces have cooked through. The cooking time may vary depending on thickness of the chicken pieces. Stir the chicken often while it cooks.

Once the chicken is cooked through, add the broccoli, chopped onion, crushed garlic cloves, red pepper flakes, and salt and pepper to taste. Saute for 5 to 7 minutes. Serve warm.

Serve Chicken and Broccoli Stir-Fry over Brown Rice.

Makes 4 to 6 lunch portions

Cost $4.09

FRUGAL FACT: *If you don't have soy sauce on hand, but you do have teriyaki sauce, you can substitute it for the soy sauce in this recipe to make Teriyaki Chicken and Broccoli Stir-Fry.*

Lasagna Roll Ups

12 lasagna noodles ($.99)
¾ pound ground beef ($1.04)
½ small yellow onion, chopped ($.15)
2 cups store-bought ($1) or Homemade
   Spaghetti Sauce (page 304) ($.84)
1 cup chopped, fresh spinach ($.25)

2 tablespoons Italian seasoning ($.15)
1 teaspoon garlic powder ($.05)
Salt and pepper
1 cup ricotta cheese ($.99)
4 slices provolone cheese ($.75)

Preheat the oven to 350 degrees. Lightly coat a 9 × 13-inch glass baking dish with nonstick cooking spray.

In a large saucepan, boil the lasagna noodles according to the package directions. Drain and pat dry. Set aside.

In a skillet over medium-high heat, brown the ground beef with the chopped onion. Drain the mixture and return to the skillet. Stir in the spaghetti sauce and chopped spinach. Add the Italian seasoning, garlic powder, and salt and pepper to taste. Simmer for 5 to 10 minutes.

Remove the ground beef mixture from the heat and let cool for 5 minutes. Stir in the ricotta cheese.

Place one of the lasagna noodles in the prepared baking dish. Add about ½ cup of the meat mixture and roll the lasagna noodle around the mixture. Place the roll ups in the prepared baking dish. Repeat using all 12 lasagna noodles. Tear the slices of provolone cheese and spread them over the tops of the roll ups.

Bake the roll ups in the preheated oven for 10 to 15 minutes, or until the cheese has melted and golden on top.

Makes 4 lunch portions

Cost $5.37 ($5.21 if using homemade sauce.)

FRUGAL FACT: *Substitute 1 cup shredded mozzarella cheese for the provolone cheese. With the right coupon matchup and sale price, shredded cheese can cost as little as $.49 per cup.*

Italian Stuffed Shells

1 box (12 ounces) jumbo pasta shells ($1.99)

1 box (10 ounces) frozen spinach, chopped ($.50)

¾ pound ground beef ($1.04)

1 cup chopped onion ($.10)

1 jar or can (26 ounces) spaghetti sauce ($1)

Salt and pepper

1 large egg ($.10)

¼ cup grated Parmesan cheese ($.25)

In a large saucepan, cook the pasta shells according to the package directions. Drain and pat dry. Set aside.

Cook the spinach as directed on the package. Drain and squeeze dry.

In a large skillet over medium-high heat, brown the ground beef with the chopped onion. Drain the mixture and return to the skillet. Stir in the spaghetti sauce and season with salt and pepper to taste. Whisk in the egg and Parmesan cheese. Let cook over medium-high heat until bubbling, and the egg has cooked. Spoon the ground beef mixture into the shells.

Serve Italian Stuffed Shells.

Makes 6 to 8 lunch portions

Cost $4.98

FRUGAL FACT: *My "never-pay-more-than" price for a box of frozen spinach is $.50, by matching up a coupon with a sale price.*

Chuckwagon Chili

....

2 cups cooked red kidney beans ($.40)
1 pound ground beef ($1.49)
1 small yellow onion, chopped ($.30)
2 garlic cloves, crushed ($.10)
1 can (15 ounces) diced tomatoes ($.59)
1 can (6 ounces) tomato paste ($.19)

1 tablespoon garlic powder ($.15)
3 tablespoons chili powder ($.25)
Salt and pepper
½ pound rotelle (wagon-wheel) pasta ($.48)
1 cup shredded cheddar cheese ($.75)

The beans can be cooked according to the batch-cooking direction on page 141. If in a time crunch, substitute 2 15-ounce cans of red kidney beans, rinsed and drained.

In a medium saucepan, brown the ground beef with the chopped onion and crushed garlic. Once cooked, drain and return to the sauce pan. Add the diced tomatoes and the tomato paste, plus 4 tomato paste cans full of water. Stir in the garlic powder and chili powder and let simmer over for 10 to 15 minutes. Season to taste with salt and pepper.

In a large pot, prepare the pasta according to package directions. Drain the pasta and then stir into the chili. Spoon the hot chili into bowls and top with the shredded cheese.

Serve Chuckwagon Chili with Shredded Cheddar Cheese.

Makes 4 to 6 lunch portions

Cost $4.70 (Note: The cost will change with the substitution of canned beans.)

FRUGAL FACT: *Use a rice pasta for a gluten-free version of this chili.*

SLOW-COOKER ADAPTABLE *(see page 142)*

Cincinnati-Style Chili

1 pound ground beef chuck ($1.79)
½ yellow onion, chopped ($.15)
2 garlic cloves, crushed ($.10)
1 can (15 ounces) crushed tomatoes ($.59)
1 teaspoon ground cinnamon ($.05)
1 teaspoon ground allspice ($.05)
½ teaspoon ground cloves

1 tablespoon unsweetened cocoa powder ($.05)
1 tablespoon sugar ($.01)
1 tablespoon white vinegar ($.05)
Salt and pepper
½ pound spaghetti ($.48)
1 cup shredded cheddar cheese (optional)

Fresh fruit ($.50)

In a large skillet over medium-high heat, brown the ground chuck with the chopped onion and crushed garlic. Drain the mixture and return it to skillet. Reduce the heat to medium, add the crushed tomatoes, and stir through. Mix in the cinnamon, allspice, ground cloves, cocoa powder, sugar, and white vinegar. Season to taste with salt and pepper. Cover and let simmer for 10 to 15 minutes while the pasta cooks.

In a large pot, cook the spaghetti according to the package directions.

Serve Cincinnati-Style Chili over Spaghetti with Fresh Fruit. Optional: Top with shredded cheddar cheese.

Makes 8 lunch portions

Cost $3.82

FRUGAL FACT: *Double the meat sauce part of this recipe and freeze half the meat portion for future lunches. Thaw, reheat, and then serve the meat sauce with leftover spaghetti from another meal.*

SLOW-COOKER ADAPTABLE *(see page 142)*

White Bean Chili

1 tablespoon extra-virgin olive oil ($.10)
2 garlic cloves, crushed ($.10)
1 green bell pepper, seeded and diced ($.75)
1 cup chopped red onion ($.25)
1 can (15 ounces) diced tomatoes with jalapeños (don't drain) ($.59)

1 can (6 ounces) tomato paste ($.19)
1 tablespoon chili powder ($.15)
6 cups cooked great northern beans ($1)
Salt and pepper

Fresh fruit ($.50)

In a large saucepan, heat the oil over medium-high heat. Add the crushed garlic, diced bell pepper, and chopped red onion and sauté for 4 to 6 minutes, or until the onions begin to turn translucent.

Reduce the heat to medium and add the diced tomatoes with jalapeños and the tomato paste, plus 3 tomato paste cans full of water. Stir to combine. Whisk in the chili powder and then stir in the cooked beans. Bring to a boil, reduce the heat, and simmer for 10 to 15 minutes. Season to taste with salt and pepper.

Serve White Bean Chili with Fresh Fruit.

Makes 8 lunch portions

Cost $3.63

FRUGAL FACT: *Plan a cool day to cook up several packages of dried beans at once. Once the beans have cooked and cooled, they can be frozen in 2-cup portions.*

SLOW-COOKER ADAPTABLE *(see page 142)*

Spicy Sloppy Joes

1 pound ground beef chuck ($1.79)
1 small yellow onion, chopped ($.30)
2 garlic cloves, crushed ($.10)
1 can (4 ounces) green chilies, drained
 ($.59)
1 cup ketchup ($.50)
¼ cup water

2 tablespoons prepared mustard ($.05)
2 tablespoons brown sugar ($.03)
Salt and pepper
1 teaspoon crushed red pepper flakes
 (optional)
8 store-bought ($1) or Homemade
 Hamburger Buns (page 305) ($.90)

Fresh fruit ($.50)

In a large skillet, brown the ground beef with the chopped onions and crushed garlic. Drain the mixture and return to the skillet. Stir in the green chilies, ketchup, water, mustard, brown sugar, and salt and pepper to taste. Stir in the crushed red pepper flakes, if using. Let simmer over medium-low heat for 5 to 10 minutes. Serve on buns.

Serve Spicy Sloppy Joes with Fresh Fruit.

Makes 8 lunch portions

Cost $4.91 ($4.81 with homemade buns)

FRUGAL FACT: *Stock up on nearly free mustard at the start of grilling season in May. Match coupons with sale prices to get free or nearly free bottles of mustard.*

Salsa and Black Bean Chicken

1 package (1 pound) boneless, skinless chicken breasts or chicken tenderloins ($1.99)

1½ cups store-bought salsa ($.75) or Homemade Salsa Fresca (page 306)

2 cups cooked black beans ($.40)

1 teaspoon ground cumin ($.05)

1 teaspoon garlic powder ($.05)

Salt and pepper

Leftover cooked rice or 8 burrito-size, whole-wheat tortillas ($1)

Fresh fruit ($.50)

Preheat the oven to 350 degrees.

The beans can be cooked according to the batch-cooking directions on page 141. If in a time crunch, substitute 1 15-ounce can of black beans, washed and drained.

Dice the chicken into 1-inch cubes, or smaller. Place the cubes into an 8 × 8-inch glass baking dish.

In a large mixing bowl, combine the salsa, cooked black beans, cumin, and garlic powder. Season to taste with salt and pepper. Pour the mixture over the diced chicken in the baking dish and gently stir together.

Bake the chicken in the preheated oven for 35 to 30 minutes, or until all the chicken pieces are cooked through. The cooking time may vary depending on the thickness of the chicken pieces.

Serve Salsa and Black Bean Chicken over Rice, or as a Burrito, with Fresh Fruit.

Makes 8 lunch portions

Cost $4.99 (Note: The cost will change with the substitution of canned beans.)

FRUGAL FACT: Serve this as is on the first day and repurposed as a burrito the next day, for lunch.

SLOW COOKER ADAPTABLE *(see page 142)*

Beef and Zucchini Tacos

1 pound ground beef ($1.49)
2 cups zucchini, diced ($.25)
½ yellow onion, chopped ($.15)
1 teaspoon garlic powder ($.05)
1 teaspoon onion powder ($.05)
1 teaspoon chili powder ($.05)

1 teaspoon ground cumin ($.05)
Salt and pepper
1 cup chopped iceberg lettuce ($.20)
1 cup shredded cheddar cheese ($.75)
8 hard-shell corn tacos or 8 burrito-size,
   whole wheat tortillas ($1.19)

Fresh fruit ($.50)

In a large skillet, brown the ground beef with the diced zucchini and chopped onion. Drain the mixture and return it to the skillet. Stir in the garlic powder, onion powder, chili powder and cumin. Season to taste with salt and pepper, and simmer for 4 to 5 minutes.

Meanwhile, chop the iceberg lettuce with a plastic lettuce knife to prevent browning of the edges.

Prepare the tacos by adding the meat mixture, chopped lettuce, and shredded cheese to the taco shells or tortillas.

Serve Beef and Zucchini Tacos with Fresh Fruit.

Makes 8 lunch-size tacos or burritos

Cost $4.73

FRUGAL FACT: *Just as zucchini can be shredded and frozen, it can also be diced and then frozen for use in recipes such as this one.*

Coconut Rice and Beans

1 can (15 ounces) of coconut milk ($1.39)
1 can (15 ounces) of pineapple slices, juices reserved ($.75)
1 cup uncooked brown rice ($.40)

2 cups cooked pinto beans (page 141) ($.40)
Salt and pepper

In a medium saucepan, bring the coconut milk, the reserved pineapple juice, plus 1 cup of water to a boil. Stir in the brown rice and return to a boil. Cover the pan, reduce heat to medium, and cook for 45 to 50 minutes, or until the rice has cooked through.

Fluff the rice with a fork and then stir in the cooked pinto beans. Season to taste with salt and pepper.

Serve Coconut Rice and Beans with Pineapple Slices.

Makes 4 lunch portions

Cost $2.94

FRUGAL FACT: *Keep an eye out for coupons for coconut milk and canned pineapple.*

Cilantro Black Beans and Rice

2 tablespoons lime juice ($.05)

1 tablespoon extra-virgin olive oil ($.10)

1 cup uncooked brown rice ($.40)

3 fresh cilantro sprigs, chopped ($.75)

2 cups cooked black beans (page 141) ($.40)

1 teaspoon garlic powder ($.05)

Salt and pepper

Fresh fruit ($.50)

To a medium saucepan, add 2½ cups of water, the lime juice, and the olive oil and bring to a boil. Add the brown rice and return to a boil. Cover the pan, reduce the heat to medium, and let cook for 45 minutes.

Once the rice has cooked, add the chopped cilantro, cooked black beans, and garlic powder. Season to taste with salt and pepper.

Serve Cilantro Black Beans and Rice with Fresh Fruit.

Makes 6 to 8 lunch portions

Cost $2.25

FRUGAL FACT: *Wrap up leftover black beans and rice in tortillas, and send in lunch boxes the next day.*

Meatless Shepherd's Pie

2 large baking potatoes, such as russet, well scrubbed ($.60)
¼ cup butter ($.40)
½ to ¾ cups milk ($.08)
¼ cup grated Parmesan cheese ($.25)
Salt and pepper

1 bag (12 ounces) frozen mixed vegetables ($1)
1 teaspoon Italian seasoning ($.05)
1 cup shredded mozzarella cheese ($.75)
Ketchup or BBQ sauce ($.25)

Pumpkin Smoothies (page 276) ($1.25)

Preheat the oven to 350 degrees. Lightly coat an 8 × 8-inch glass baking dish with nonstick cooking spray.

Wash and peel the potatoes. Cut them into quarters and boil in water to cover a large saucepan for 10 to 15 minutes, or until tender. Drain the potatoes and return them to the saucepan. Add the butter, milk, grated Parmesan cheese, and salt and pepper to taste. Mash the potatoes, adding more milk as needed to reach the desired consistency.

Meanwhile, cook the frozen mixed vegetables according to the package directions. Place the cooked mixed vegetables into the bottom of the prepared baking dish, and sprinkle with the Italian seasoning. Spoon the mashed potatoes over the mixed vegetables and spread evenly to fill the baking dish. Top with the shredded mozzarella cheese.

Bake the pie in the preheated oven for 15 to 20 minutes, or until the cheese has melted and beginning to turn golden. Let cool before slicing and serving.

Serve Meatless Shepherd's Pie with ketchup or BBQ sauce and Pumpkin Smoothies.

Makes 4 lunch portions

Cost $4.63

FRUGAL FACT: *This recipe can be easily doubled in a 9 × 13-inch baking dish and will make 10 to 12 lunch portions.*

SEVEN

Pasta Salads and Garden Salads

Macaroni Salad

1 package (16 ounces) elbow macaroni ($.97)

½ cup mayonnaise ($.20)

2 tablespoons lemon juice ($.10)

2 teaspoons vinegar ($.10)

2 teaspoons sugar ($.05)

2 carrots, peeled and diced ($.20)

2 green bell peppers, seeded and diced ($1.50)

½ large red onion, chopped ($.30)

Salt and pepper

Fresh fruit ($.50)

In a large saucepan, cook the pasta according to the package directions. Drain and rinse with cool water.

In a small bowl, whisk together the mayonnaise, lemon juice, vinegar, and sugar.

In a large mixing bowl, toss together the cooked pasta, diced carrots, diced bell peppers, chopped red onion, and dressing. Season to taste with salt and pepper. Chill the salad at least 2 hours before serving.

Serve Macaroni Salad with Fresh Fruit.

Makes 8 lunch portions

Cost $3.89

FRUGAL FACT: *Making your own pasta salad and dressing is quick and simple, and costs dollars less than what you would pay for a salad at the grocery store's deli.*

Minestrone Pasta Salad

1 package (16 ounces) elbow macaroni ($.97)

4 cups cooked red kidney beans ($.80)

2 carrots, peeled and chopped ($.40)

2 celery stalks, chopped ($.20)

2 cans (15 ounces each) diced tomatoes, drained ($1.18)

1 tablespoon Italian seasoning ($.10)

1 teaspoon garlic powder ($.05)

1 cup grated Parmesan cheese ($1)

Salt and pepper

In a large saucepan, cook the pasta according to the package directions. Drain and rinse with cool water.

The beans can be cooked according to the batch-cooking direction on page 141. If in a time crunch, substitute 2 15-ounce cans red kidney beans.

In a large mixing bowl, toss together the cooked pasta, cooked red kidney beans, chopped carrots and celery, diced tomatoes, Italian seasoning, garlic powder, grated Parmesan cheese, and salt and pepper to taste. Chill the salad at least 2 hours before serving.

Serve Minestrone Pasta Salad.

Makes 8 lunch portions

Cost $4.70 (Note: The cost will change with the substitution of canned beans.)

FRUGAL FACT: *Make this meal for less by stocking up on cans of diced tomatoes when they are on sale for less than $.50, or for less than $.25 when you match with a coupon.*

Southwest Pasta Salad

1 package (16 ounces) small shell pasta ($.97)
2 cups cooked black beans ($.40)
1 cup frozen corn kernels ($.40)
1 can (10 ounces) diced tomatoes with green chilies, drained ($.59)

1 cup shredded Mexican blend cheese ($.99)
1 teaspoon ground cumin ($.05)
1 teaspoon garlic powder ($.05)
Salt and pepper

Fresh fruit ($.50)

In a large saucepan, cook the pasta according to the package directions. Drain and rinse with cool water.

The beans can be cooked according to the batch-cooking directions on page 141. If in a time crunch, substitute a 15-ounce can of black beans.

Cook the frozen corn kernels as directed on the package.

In a large mixing bowl, toss together the cooked pasta, cooked black beans, drained, diced tomatoes with green chilies, cooked corn kernels, shredded cheese, cumin, garlic powder, and salt and pepper to taste.

Serve the salad warm, or refrigerate for at least 2 hours and serve chilled.

Serve Southwest Pasta Salad with Fresh Fruit.

Makes 4 to 6 lunch portions

Cost $3.95 (Note: The cost will change with the substitution of canned beans.)

FRUGAL FACT: *Stock up on those canned vegetables when you see them on sale near the $.50-per-can price mark. You can substitute 1 can of corn, drained, for the frozen corn kernels in this recipe.*

Chicken with Asparagus Pasta Salad

1 package (16 ounces) penne or rotini pasta ($.97)

¼ cup extra-virgin olive oil ($.40)

1 tablespoon red wine vinegar ($.10)

Salt and pepper

2 cups shredded, cooked chicken ($1.50)

1 can (15 ounces) diced tomatoes, drained ($.59)

½ pound cooked asparagus, cut into 1-inch pieces ($.50)

2 garlic cloves, crushed ($.10)

½ cup grated Parmesan cheese ($.50)

In a large saucepan, cook the pasta according to package directions. Drain and rinse with cool water.

In a small plastic container, combine the olive oil and the vinegar with some salt and pepper to taste. Shake vigorously.

In a large mixing bowl, toss together the pasta, shredded chicken, drained, diced tomatoes, asparagus pieces, and crushed garlic. Pour the vinaigrette dressing over the pasta and chicken and toss until evenly coated. Stir in the Parmesan cheese. Season to taste with additional salt and pepper if needed.

Serve the salad warm, or refrigerate for at least 2 hours and serve chilled.

Serve Chicken with Asparagus Pasta Salad.

Makes 8 lunch portions

Cost $4.66

FRUGAL FACT: *Use leftover asparagus from dinner and make this pasta salad just after cleaning up the dinner dishes. Refrigerate and enjoy for lunch the following day!*

Summer Squash Pasta Salad

....

1 package (16 ounces) spaghetti ($.97)
3 tablespoons extra-virgin olive oil ($.30)
2 garlic cloves, crushed ($.10)
2 tablespoons red wine vinegar ($.20)
1 yellow summer squash, sliced ($.79)
1 small zucchini, sliced ($.79)

About 10 cherry tomatoes, halved ($1)
2 tablespoons chopped, fresh basil leaves ($.10)
2 tablespoons chopped, fresh parsley leaves ($.10)
Salt and pepper

Fresh fruit ($.50)

In a large saucepan, cook the pasta according to the package directions. Drain and rinse with cool water.

Place the pasta in a large mixing bowl and toss with 1 tablespoon of the olive oil.

In a large skillet, sauté the garlic cloves in the remaining 2 tablespoons olive oil for 2 to 3 minutes, or until golden. Add the vinegar, sliced yellow squash, and sliced zucchini and sauté for 5 to 6 minutes. Once the zucchini begins to turn translucent, add the halved cherry tomatoes, and the fresh basil and parsley. Sauté all together for another 4 to 5 minutes, or until the cherry tomatoes begin to pop. Add to the spaghetti and toss to combine. Season with salt and pepper to taste.

Serve the salad warm, or refrigerate for at least 2 hours and serve chilled.

Serve Summer Squash Pasta Salad with Fresh Fruit.

Makes 8 lunch portions

Cost $4.85

FRUGAL FACT: *Grow a few pots of your favorite herbs on your patio. Basil, parsley, rosemary, oregano, and mint all grow very easily in small containers.*

Chicken Spinach Pesto Pasta Salad

....

1 package (16 ounces) penne pasta ($.97)
2 chicken breasts ($1.66)

Salt and pepper
1 tablespoon extra-virgin olive oil ($.10)

PESTO

2 cups fresh spinach leaves ($.50)
1 cup fresh basil leaves ($.50)
2 tablespoons fresh mint leaves ($.10)
⅓ cup pine nuts ($.75)

3 to 4 tablespoons extra-virgin olive oil ($.30)
Salt and pepper

In a large saucepan, cook the pasta according to package directions. Drain and rinse with cool water.

Dice the chicken breasts and season to taste with salt and pepper. In a skillet, sauté the chicken pieces in the olive oil for 7 to 10 minutes, or until cooked through. Set aside to cool.

In a food processor or blender, blend together the spinach, basil, mint, pine nuts, olive oil, and salt and pepper to taste.

In a large mixing bowl, toss together the cooked pasta, cooled, cooked chicken, and pesto sauce.

Serve the salad warm, or refrigerate for at least 2 hours and serve chilled.

Serve Chicken Spinach Pesto Pasta Salad.

Makes 6 to 8 lunch portions

Cost $4.88

FRUGAL FACT: *Grow spinach and basil leaves in the garden and use to make this pesto sauce. Pesto can be frozen in plastic containers or plastic bags if you have an overabundance of spinach and pesto sauce that you can't use right away.*

Chicken Caesar Pasta Salad

1 package (16 ounces) penne pasta ($.97)
1 tablespoon extra-virgin olive oil ($.10)
6 chicken tenderloins (about ¾ pound) ($1.50)

1 teaspoon garlic powder ($.05)
Salt and pepper
½ small onion, finely chopped ($.15)
⅓ cup grated Parmesan cheese ($.33)
⅔ cup Caesar salad dressing ($.50)

In a large saucepan, cook the pasta according to the package directions. Drain and rinse with cool water.

Heat the oil in a medium skillet. Season the chicken tenderloins with garlic powder and salt and pepper. Sauté in the olive oil for 6 to 8 minutes, or until chicken has cooked through. Remove the chicken from the skillet and dice into ½-inch pieces. Let cool for 10 to 15 minutes.

In a large mixing bowl, toss together the cooked pasta, cooled, diced chicken, chopped onion, Parmesan cheese, and Caesar salad dressing. Chill the salad at least 2 hours before serving.

Serve Chicken Caesar Pasta Salad.

Makes 6 to 8 lunch portions

Cost $3.60

FRUGAL FACT: *Buy the store-brand salad dressing, or match a coupon for your favorite brand to get the best deal. Salad dressing is one of those products where sometimes the store brand is the less expensive option.*

Ranch BLT Pasta Salad

1 package (16 ounces) small shell pasta ($.97)

8 bacon slices ($1.50)

2 small plum tomatoes, seeded and diced ($1)

2 cups romaine lettuce, chopped ($.25)

½ cup mayonnaise ($.20)

¼ cup milk ($.03)

½ teaspoon lemon juice ($.01)

2 tablespoons chopped, fresh parsley ($.20)

1 teaspoon dried dill ($.05)

2 garlic cloves, crushed ($.10)

Salt and pepper

Fresh fruit ($.50)

In a large saucepan, cook the pasta according to the package directions. Drain and rinse with cool water.

Place the bacon slices on a microwave-safe plate lined with 2 paper towels. Cover with another paper towel. Microwave on high for 5 to 7 minutes, or until crisp. If you prefer, cook the bacon in a skillet over medium-high heat until brown and crisp. Transfer to clean paper towels and let cool, then crumble into little bacon bits.

Seed and dice the tomatoes and cut the lettuce into smaller-than-bite-size pieces.

In a small bowl, whisk together the mayonnaise, milk, lemon juice, chopped parsley, dill, and crushed garlic cloves. Season to taste with salt and pepper.

In a large mixing bowl, toss together the cooked pasta, bacon bits, diced tomatoes, and cut lettuce. Pour the dressing over the top and toss to coat.

Serve the salad warm, or refrigerate for at least 2 hours and serve chilled.

Serve Ranch BLT Pasta Salad with Fresh Fruit.

Makes 6 to 8 lunch portions

Cost $4.81

FRUGAL FACT: *Use rice pasta for inexpensive gluten-free pasta salads.*

Tuna with Lemon and Dill Pasta Salad

1 package (16 ounces) farfalle pasta ($.97)

½ cup mayonnaise ($.20)

Juice from 1 lemon (about 2 tablespoons) ($.10)

½ teaspoon grated lemon zest ($.01)

2 teaspoons fresh or dried dill ($.25)

2 garlic cloves, crushed ($.10)

2 cups frozen peas ($.80)

2 cans (6 ounces each) tuna in water, drained ($1)

Salt and pepper

Spinach ("Green") Smoothies (page 277) ($1.20)

In a large saucepan, cook the pasta according to the package directions. Drain and rinse with cool water.

In a small bowl, whisk together the mayonnaise, lemon juice, lemon zest, dill, and crushed garlic. Set the dressing aside.

Cook the frozen peas as directed on the package.

In a large mixing bowl, toss the cooked pasta with the lemon-dill dressing, cooked peas, and drained tuna, and salt and pepper to taste. Chill the salad at least 2 hours before serving.

Serve Tuna with Lemon and Dill Pasta Salad with Spinach ("Green") Smoothies.

Makes 6 to 8 lunch portions

Cost $4.63

FRUGAL FACT: *By matching coupons with sale prices, you can often purchase tuna cans and tuna pouches for free. My "never-pay-more-than" price for a can or pouch of tuna is $.50.*

Spinach Orzo Pasta Salad

1 package (16 ounces) orzo pasta ($1.49)

3 tablespoons extra-virgin olive oil ($.30)

2 garlic cloves, crushed ($.10)

2 cups fresh spinach leaves, chopped ($.50)

1 can (15 ounces) diced tomatoes, drained ($.59)

2 tablespoons chopped, fresh basil leaves ($.10)

1 tablespoon rice wine vinegar ($.10)

½ cup grated Parmesan cheese ($.50)

Salt and pepper

Fresh fruit ($.50)

In a large saucepan, cook the pasta according to the package directions. Drain and rinse with cool water.

Heat 2 tablespoons of the olive oil in a skillet over medium heat. Add the crushed garlic and sauté for 2 to 3 minutes. Then add the chopped spinach leaves, the drained canned tomatoes, and the chopped basil leaves. Sauté for another 3 to 4 minutes, or until the spinach begins to wilt.

In a large mixing bowl, toss together the cooked orzo, sautéed spinach mixture, the remaining 1 tablespoon olive oil, and the vinegar. Mix in the Parmesan cheese. Season to taste with salt and pepper.

Serve the salad warm, or refrigerate for at least 2 hours and serve chilled.

Serve Spinach Orzo Pasta Salad with Fresh Fruit.

Makes 8 lunch portions

Cost $4.18

FRUGAL FACT: *Add 2 cups cooked and shredded chicken ($1.50) for some extra protein in this pasta salad.*

Summer Squash and Lentil Salad

1 cup green lentils ($.40)
1 small zucchini, diced ($.79)
1 small yellow squash, diced ($.79)
1 teaspoon plus 3 tablespoons extra-
    virgin olive oil ($.33)
½ cup red onion, finely chopped ($.40)

1 cucumber, seeded and diced ($.75)
1 can (15 ounces) petite diced tomatoes,
    drained ($.59)
2 tablespoons lemon juice ($.04)
Salt and pepper

Cook the lentils according to the package directions. Drain excess cooking liquids.

Wash and dice the zucchini and yellow squash. Heat the 1 teaspoon of olive oil in a medium skillet over medium-high heat. Add the diced squash and the chopped red onion and sauté in the olive oil for 5 to 7 minutes, or until the vegetables turn translucent.

In a large mixing bowl, toss together the cooked lentils, sautéed squash and onion, diced cucumber, drained diced tomatoes, the remaining 3 tablespoons olive oil, lemon juice, and salt and pepper to taste.

Serve Summer Squash and Lentil Salad.

Makes 8 servings

Cost $4.09

FRUGAL FACT: *Fresh cucumber prices fluctuate throughout the summer months. Watch for prices between $.50 and $1; or better yet, grow some in your garden.*

Sesame Chicken Salad

SALAD

2 chicken breasts ($1.66)
1 tablespoon extra-virgin olive oil ($.10)
1 tablespoon soy sauce ($.05)
Black pepper

1 can (15 ounces) mandarin orange
  slices, drained ($.50)
½ head romaine lettuce ($.49)

SESAME DRESSING

¼ cup canola or vegetable oil ($.10)
2 tablespoons sesame oil ($.25)
1 tablespoon soy sauce ($.05)
2 tablespoons white vinegar ($.10)

1 teaspoon sugar ($.01)
1 teaspoon ground ginger ($.05)
1 teaspoon garlic powder ($.05)

Bread slices ($.50)

Cut the chicken breasts into ½-inch cubes. Heat the olive oil in a skillet over medium-high heat. Add the chicken cubes and sauté in the olive oil for 6 to 8 minutes, or until no longer pink in the middle. Add the soy sauce and cook a few minutes more. Sprinkle with a little pepper. Remove the chicken from skillet and set aside to cool for a few minutes.

Wash, and then tear or cut the lettuce with a plastic lettuce knife into bite-size pieces.

In a small plastic container with a lid, combine the ingredients for the dressing. Shake vigorously.

In a large bowl, toss together the cooled, cooked chicken, the drained mandarin orange slices, and the lettuce. Pour over the dressing, and toss to coat evenly.

Serve Sesame Chicken Salad with Homemade or Store-bought Bread.

Makes 4 lunch portions

Cost $3.91

FRUGAL FACT: *Combine a great sale price with a newspaper or Internet coupon and stock up on canned fruit.*

Taco Salad

SALAD

½ pound ground beef ($.95)
½ onion, finely chopped ($.15)
1 can (6 ounces) tomato paste ($.50)
1 tablespoon ground cumin ($.10)
1 tablespoon chili powder ($.10)
1 tablespoon garlic powder ($.10)

Salt and pepper
2 cups frozen corn kernels ($.80)
1 avocado ($.68)
1 teaspoon lime juice ($.02)
½ head iceberg lettuce ($.44)

DRESSING

¼ cup extra-virgin olive oil ($.40)
3 tablespoons lime juice ($.10)

½ teaspoon ground cumin ($.02)
Salt and pepper

Tortilla chips for serving ($.50)

In a skillet, brown the ground beef with the chopped onion. Drain the mixture and return it to the skillet. Stir in the tomato paste plus 2 tomato paste cans full of water. Mix in the ground cumin, chili powder, and garlic powder. Simmer on low heat for 10 minutes. Season to taste with salt and pepper.

Cook the frozen corn kernels as directed on the package.

Cut open the avocado lengthwise and remove the seed. Slice the avocado into ½-inch chunks and remove with a spoon. Place the avocado in a small bowl with the lime juice and toss together; the lime juice will prevent the avocado from browning.

Wash, and then tear or cut the lettuce with a plastic lettuce knife into bite-size pieces.

In a small plastic container with a lid, combine the ingredients for the dressing. Shake vigorously.

In a large bowl, toss together the lettuce, corn, avocado, and meat mixture with the dressing.

Serve Taco Salad with Tortilla Chips.

Makes 4 lunch portions

Cost $4.86

FRUGAL FACT: *Use leftover taco meat to make this salad for lunch the next day.*

Cucumber and Orange Salad

SALAD

2 cucumbers, seeded and diced ($1)
4 cups Bibb lettuce ($1)

4 clementines, peeled and separated ($1)

ORANGE HONEY DRESSING

½ cup extra-virgin olive oil ($.80)
3 tablespoons white vinegar ($.15)
3 tablespoons orange juice ($.05)

2 tablespoon honey ($.20)
Salt and pepper

Bread slices, butter, and honey for serving ($.75)

Tear or cut the lettuce with a plastic lettuce knife into bite-size pieces. Slice the cucumber lengthwise and scoop out the seeds with a spoon. Dice the cucumber. Peel the clementines and separate into segments.

In a small plastic container with a lid, combine the ingredients for the dressing. Shake vigorously.

In a large bowl, toss the lettuce, diced cucumbers, and clementine segments with the dressing, tossing to evenly coat.

Butter the bread slices and drizzle honey over the top.

Serve Cucumber and Orange Salad with Honey-Drizzled Bread.

Makes 4 lunch portions

Cost $4.95

FRUGAL FACT: *Use newspaper and Internet coupons when buying bags or boxes of clementines.*

Bacon, Egg, and Tomato Salad

SALAD

8 bacon slices ($1.50)
4 hard-boiled eggs ($.40)
2 small plum tomatoes, seeded and
   diced ($1)

1 head romaine lettuce ($.99)

RANCH DRESSING

½ cup mayonnaise ($.20)
2 tablespoons milk ($.01)
½ teaspoon lemon juice ($.01)
2 tablespoons chopped, fresh parsley
   ($.20)

1 teaspoon dried dill ($.05)
2 garlic cloves, crushed ($.10)
Salt and pepper

Bread slices ($.50)

Place the bacon slices on a microwave-safe plate, lined with 2 paper towels. Cover with another paper towel. Microwave on high for 5 to 7 minutes, or until crisp. If you prefer, cook the bacon in a skillet over medium-high heat until crisp. Transfer the bacon to clean paper towels and let cool, then crumble into little bacon bits.

Peel the hard-boiled eggs and cut the eggs with a pastry blender or two knives into ¼-inch pieces.

Seed and dice the tomatoes, and cut the lettuce into bite-size pieces using a plastic lettuce knife.

In a small bowl, whisk together the mayonnaise, milk, lemon juice, chopped parsley, dill, and crushed garlic cloves. Season to taste with salt and pepper.

In a large bowl, toss together the bacon bits, hard-boiled eggs, diced tomatoes, and lettuce. Pour the dressing over the top and toss.

Serve Bacon, Egg, and Tomato Salad with Homemade or Store-bought Bread.

Makes 4 lunch portions

Cost $4.96

FRUGAL FACT: *Romaine lettuce can last up to 3 weeks if stored in a reduced-humidity drawer in the refrigerator. When on sale for $1 or less, be sure to buy 2 or 3 extra heads.*

Autumn Salad

SALAD

½ head romaine lettuce ($.49)
2 sweet apples, such as Golden Delicious
($1)

1 Anjou pear ($.67)
1 cup raisins ($.75)

APPLE VINAIGRETTE DRESSING

½ cup extra-virgin olive oil ($.80)
¼ cup white vinegar ($.20)
¼ cup apple juice ($.10)

1 tablespoon sugar ($.02)
Salt and pepper

Bread slices and butter ($.60)

Tear or cut the lettuce with a plastic lettuce knife into bite-size pieces. Dice the apples and the pear into ¼-inch pieces.

In a large bowl, toss together the lettuce, diced apples, diced pears, and raisins.

In a small plastic container with a lid, combine the ingredients for the dressing. Shake vigorously and pour over the salad.

Serve Autumn Salad with Homemade or Store-bought Bread and Butter.

Makes 4 lunch portions

Cost $4.63

FRUGAL FACT: *Make this delicious and refreshing salad during the fall and winter months when pear and apple prices are at their best.*

Avocado and Tomato Salad
with Cilantro-Lime Dressing

SALAD

½ head romaine lettuce ($.49)   1 pint cherry tomatoes ($2)
1 avocado ($.68)

CILANTRO-LIME DRESSING

½ cup canola or vegetable oil ($.20)   ½ teaspoon ground cumin ($.03)
¼ cup lime juice ($.10)   1 teaspoon salt
3 sprigs cilantro, chopped ($.75)   1 teaspoon pepper

4 burrito-size, flour tortillas ($.50)

Tear or cut the lettuce with a plastic lettuce knife into bite-size pieces. Cut open the avocado lengthwise and remove the seed. Cut the flesh into cubes and scoop out with a spoon. Halve the cherry tomatoes.

In a large bowl, toss together the lettuce, diced avocado, and tomato halves.

In a small plastic container with a lid, combine the ingredients for the dressing. Shake vigorously.

Pour the dressing over the salad in the bowl, using enough to coat evenly.

Warm the tortillas and roll up for serving. If there is any leftover Cilantro-Lime dressing, use it as a dip for the tortillas.

Serve Avocado and Tomato Salad with Cilantro-Lime Dressing and Rolled Tortillas.

Makes 4 lunch portions

Cost $4.75

FRUGAL FACT: *Maintain the pantry staples list (Appendix A, page 303) and you'll be able to make your own salad dressings, using oils and vinegars from your pantry.*

EIGHT

Side Salads and Side Dishes
for Lunch

Honey Ginger Citrus Salad

2 small red grapefruits ($1)
4 navel oranges or 6 tangerines or
    clementines ($1.50)
¼ cup honey ($.40)

1 tablespoon lime juice ($.02)
½ teaspoon ground ginger ($.10)
¼ teaspoon ground cinnamon ($.03)

Using a sharp knife, cut off the tops and bottoms of the oranges and grapefruits. Peel or slice away the remaining skin. Slice along the white membranes between each segment and gently pull the segments apart from the white connective membranes. Remove any seeds. Place the orange slices and grapefruit segments into a serving bowl.

In a small bowl, whisk together the honey, lime juice, ground ginger and ground cinnamon. Pour the mixture into the bowl with the fruit slices. Gently toss with the citrus segments.

Serve immediately or chill for an hour.

Serve Honey Ginger Citrus Salad as a breakfast or lunch side dish.

Makes 8 to 10 side-dish servings

Cost $3.05

FRUGAL FACT: *Make this delicious fruit salad in the winter months when prices on citrus fruits are at their lowest.*

Fruit Salad with Yogurt Dressing

FRUIT SALAD

4 cups mixed fresh fruit pieces, choose from: cantaloupe, apples, bananas, strawberries, mangoes, peaches, pears, orange slices, pineapple, grapes, and blueberries. ($2)

1 teaspoon lemon juice ($.02)

YOGURT DRESSING

½ cup yogurt ($.15)
2 tablespoons honey ($.20)

½ teaspoon lemon juice ($.01)

Cut the larger fruits into 1-inch pieces and place in a large mixing bowl, along with the grapes and blueberries, if using.

In a small bowl, stir together the yogurt, lime juice, and honey. Toss with the fruit pieces.

If using apples, peaches, or pears, toss the diced fruit with lemon juice before adding them to the mixing bowl to prevent browning.

Serve Fruit Salad with Yogurt Dressing as a breakfast or lunch side dish.

Makes four 1-cup servings

Cost $2.38

FRUGAL FACT: *Get the best yogurt price by compare the unit prices of small yogurt containers and the larger "bulk" yogurt containers. Sometimes a sale price on the smaller containers is cheaper than buying the larger container.*

Mustard Potato Salad

....

2 large eggs ($.20)
6 medium potatoes ($.80)
1 small onion ($.15)
1 dill pickle plus 2 tablespoons pickle
   juice ($.10)
2 garlic cloves, crushed ($.05)

½ cup mayonnaise ($.20)
3 tablespoons prepared yellow or Dijon-
   style mustard ($.10)
Salt and pepper

In a medium saucepan, boil the eggs for 12 minutes and then remove from the heat. Let sit for 10 minutes, and then drain the hot water. Place the eggs into a bowl of cold water for 15 to 20 minutes. Chop the eggs with a pastry blender or two knives.

Scrub and peel the potatoes and cut into ½-inch dice, or smaller.

In a medium saucepan, boil the diced potatoes for 8 to 10 minutes. When the potatoes have softened, drain them and rinse with cool water.

Meanwhile, chop the onion and dill pickle. Place them into a large mixing bowl along with the crushed garlic. Add the diced potatoes and the cooked and chopped hard-boiled eggs.

In a small bowl, whisk together the pickle juice, mayonnaise, and mustard. Toss the mayonnaise dressing with the potatoes and eggs in the mixing bowl. Season to taste with salt and pepper.

Serve Mustard Potato Salad as a lunch side dish.

Makes 8 to 10 side-dish servings

Cost $1.60

FRUGAL FACT: *Condiments can often be purchased for free or nearly free by matching coupons with sale prices.*

Roasted Red Potato Salad

12 small, well-scrubbed red potatoes (about 1 pound) ($1.99)
3 sprigs rosemary ($.30)
Olive oil for drizzling ($.10)

Salt and pepper
½ cup mayonnaise ($.20)
½ cup milk ($.05)
2 tablespoons Dijon mustard ($.07)

Preheat the oven to 400 degrees. Lightly coat a 9 × 13-inch glass baking dish with nonstick cooking spray.

Cut the red potatoes into quarters. Place the quartered potatoes into the prepared baking dish.

Wash the rosemary sprigs and pat dry with a towel. Pull away the rosemary leaves from the stem and run a knife through them, gently chopping them to release the flavors and fragrant oils from the leaves. Sprinkle the chopped rosemary over the quartered red potatoes. Drizzle olive oil over the potatoes and sprinkle with salt and pepper to taste.

Roast the red potatoes and rosemary in the preheated oven for 30 to 35 minutes. When the potatoes have softened and turned golden brown, remove from the oven and let cool. Place the potatoes and rosemary in a mixing bowl.

Meanwhile, in a small mixing bowl, whisk together the mayonnaise, milk, and Dijon mustard. Pour over the potatoes in the bowl and toss gently. Taste and add more salt and pepper, if needed.

Serve the salad warm, or place in the refrigerator for at least 2 hours and serve chilled.

Serve Roasted Red Potato Salad as a lunch side dish.

Makes 8 to 10 side-dish servings

Cost $2.71

FRUGAL FACT: *Look for a sale price of $1.99 per pound or less on red potatoes.*

Sweet and Spicy Coleslaw

1 bag (14 ounces) coleslaw mix ($1.49)
1 cup mayonnaise ($.40)
2 to 3 tablespoons hot sauce ($.25)
¼ cup sugar ($.02)

1 teaspoon lemon juice ($.02)
1 teaspoon cider vinegar ($.02)
1 teaspoon garlic powder ($.05)
Salt and pepper

Place the coleslaw mix into a large mixing bowl.

In a small mixing bowl, whisk together the mayonnaise, hot sauce, sugar, lemon juice, vinegar, and garlic powder. Pour over the coleslaw mix and toss. Season to taste with salt and pepper.

Serve Sweet and Spicy Coleslaw as a lunch side dish.

Makes 8 side-dish servings

Cost $2.25

FRUGAL FACT: *Keep a large bottle of lemon juice in the refrigerator to use for making your own side dish salads, dressings, and marinades.*

Pineapple Coleslaw

1 bag (14 ounces) coleslaw mix ($1.49)
1 cup crushed pineapple, drained, juices
   reserved ($.50)
½ cup mayonnaise ($.20)

1 tablespoon lime juice ($.05)
2 tablespoons sugar ($.02)
Salt and pepper

Place the coleslaw mix into a mixing bowl. Toss the crushed pineapple with the coleslaw mix.

In a small mixing bowl, whisk together the mayonnaise, lime juice, 4 tablespoons of the reserved pineapple juice, and the sugar. Pour the dressing over the coleslaw mix and toss. Season to taste with salt and pepper.

Serve Pineapple Coleslaw as a lunch side dish.

Makes 8 side-dish servings

Cost $2.31

FRUGAL FACT: *Be sure to incorporate coleslaws into your summer meal plans, as prepared coleslaw mix can be purchased for as little as $1 during the summer months.*

Oven Chili Fries

4 large potatoes, such as russets ($.60)
1 tablespoon vegetable or canola oil
   ($.05)

1 tablespoon chili powder ($.10)
1 teaspoon kosher salt ($.01)
Black pepper

Preheat the oven to 350 degrees. Line a baking sheet with aluminum foil and coat lightly with nonstick cooking spray.

Wash and peel the potatoes and cut into ¼-inch-thick strips. Place the potatoes into a large bowl and toss with the canola oil, chili powder, and kosher salt.

Place the potato strips onto the foil-lined baking sheet in a single layer. Bake the fries in the preheated oven for 15 to 20 minutes. Remove the fries from the oven and turn with a spatula. Return to oven and bake for another 10 to 15 minutes, or until golden brown and crispy. Season with black pepper to taste.

Serve Oven Chili Fries as a lunch side dish.

Makes 4 to 6 side-dish servings

Cost $0.76

FRUGAL FACT: *Make your own French fries throughout the year, especially during the "rock-bottom-potato-price" months of January and February.*

Parmesan Potato Wedges

4 large baking potatoes, such as russets ($.80)

2 tablespoons vegetable or canola oil ($.10)

¼ cup grated Parmesan cheese ($.25)

2 tablespoons chopped fresh rosemary ($.25)

Salt and pepper

Preheat the oven to 400 degrees. Line a baking sheet with aluminum foil and lightly coat with nonstick cooking spray.

Wash potatoes thoroughly and pat dry. Slice the potatoes lengthwise into 3-inch-long wedges, about ¾-inch thick at the skin side. Place the wedges in a large mixing bowl and toss with the oil, Parmesan cheese, and chopped rosemary, and sprinkle with salt and pepper.

Place the Parmesan potato wedges on the foil-lined baking sheet in a single layer. Bake the wedges in the preheated oven for 15 to 20 minutes. Remove the wedges from the oven and turn with a spatula. Return to oven and bake for another 10 to 15 minutes, or until golden brown and crispy.

Serve Parmesan Potato Wedges as a lunch side dish.

Makes 4 side-dish servings

Cost $1.40

FRUGAL FACT: *Rosemary is a perennial herb that grows easily in the garden or in a small pot outside your kitchen window.*

Cinnamon–Sweet Potato Fries

2 large sweet potatoes, peeled and cut into strips ($1.25)

2 tablespoons vegetable or canola oil ($.10)

1 tablespoon packed brown sugar ($.03)

1 teaspoon ground cinnamon ($.05)

salt and pepper

Preheat the oven to 350 degrees. Line a baking sheet with aluminum foil and lightly coat with nonstick cooking spray.

Wash and peel the sweet potatoes. Cut into ¼-inch-thick strips. Rinse the sweet potato strips and pat dry with a towel.

Place the strips into a large bowl and toss with the oil, brown sugar, and cinnamon, and sprinkle with salt and pepper.

Place the sweet potato strips onto the foil-lined baking sheet in a single layer. Bake the fries in the preheated oven for 15 to 20 minutes. Remove the fries from the oven and turn with a spatula. Return to oven and bake for another 10 to 15 minutes, or until golden brown and crispy.

Serve Cinnamon–Sweet Potato Fries as a lunch side dish.

Makes 4 to 6 side-dish servings

Cost $1.43

FRUGAL FACT: *Sweet potatoes can last as long as a month in your cupboard if stored in a dry, cool place, so grab a few extra when you see them on sale for $.79 per pound or less.*

Broccoli-Raisin Salad

1 bunch broccoli, about 4 broccoli heads
  ($1.78)
½ cup mayonnaise ($.20)
2 tablespoons milk ($.02)

1 tablespoon sugar ($.01)
1 cup raisins ($.75)
Salt and pepper
½ cup chopped peanuts ($.50)

Wash the broccoli and remove the stems, leaving the florets.

Steam the florets in a stovetop steamer for 2 to 3 minutes, or place the florets in a microwave-safe bowl with ¼ cup of water and cover with plastic wrap. Microwave on high for 2 to 3 minutes. Drain the partially steamed florets in a colander and rinse with cool water. Pat dry with a towel and add to a large mixing bowl.

In a small mixing bowl, whisk together the mayonnaise, milk, and sugar. Toss the mayonnaise dressing with the broccoli florets and raisins in the mixing bowl, and add salt and pepper to taste. Chill the salad for at least 2 hours in the refrigerator.

Stir in the chopped peanuts just before serving.

Serve Broccoli-Raisin Salad as a lunch side dish.

Makes 8 side-dish servings

Cost $3.26

FRUGAL FACT: *Save on peanuts by using newspaper or Internet coupons, and if those coupons are unavailable, buy the store brand.*

Four Bean Salad

....

2 cups fresh or frozen green beans ($.75)

2 cups cooked great northern beans ($.40)

2 cups cooked black beans ($.40)

2 cups cooked red beans ($.40)

2 tablespoons extra-virgin olive oil ($.20)

2 tablespoons lemon juice ($.04)

½ teaspoon garlic powder ($.03)

½ teaspoon onion powder ($.03)

4 tablespoons chopped, fresh parsley ($.05)

½ teaspoon salt

½ teaspoon pepper

Cook green beans as directed on package if frozen, or steam in a stovetop steamer if fresh.

The beans can be cooked according to the batch-cooking direction on page 141. If in a time crunch, substitute one 15-ounce can great northern beans, one 15-ounce black beans, and one 15-ounce can red beans, rinsed and drained.

In a small mixing bowl, whisk together the olive oil, lemon juice, garlic powder, onion powder, and chopped fresh parsley. Season to taste with salt and pepper. Pour over the beans in the mixing bowl. Chill the salad at least 2 hours in the refrigerator before serving.

Serve Four Bean Salad as a lunch side dish.

Makes 8 to 10 side-dish servings

Cost $2.30 (Note: The cost will change with the substitution of canned beans.)

FRUGAL FACT: *Use fresh green beans from your garden to make an even less expensive side dish.*

Chickpea Summer Salad

1 cup dried chickpeas ($.50)

1 red bell pepper, seeded and diced ($.75)

1 cucumber, seeded and diced ($.75)

½ cup red onion, finely chopped ($.40)

2 tablespoons extra-virgin olive oil ($.20)

1 tablespoon vinegar ($.05)

½ teaspoon garlic powder ($.03)

Salt and pepper

Soak and cook chickpeas in a saucepan according to the package directions. When softened and cooked through, drain and rinse with cool water.

Add the drained, cooked chickpeas to a mixing bowl. Add the diced bell pepper, diced cucumber, and chopped red onion.

In a small bowl, whisk together the olive oil, vinegar, and garlic powder. Toss the dressing with chickpeas and diced vegetables. Season to taste with salt and pepper. Chill the salad for at least 2 hours in the refrigerator before serving.

Serve Chickpea Summer Salad as a lunch side dish.

Makes 8 side-dish servings

Cost $2.68

FRUGAL FACT: *If you are in a time crunch, substitute 2 cans (15 ounces each) of chickpeas for the cooked, dried chickpeas.*

Mint Cucumber Onion Salad

2 cucumbers, sliced into rounds ($1.50)
½ large red onion, finely sliced into
  circles ($.80)
½ cup cider vinegar ($.40)
2 tablespoons sugar ($.03)

1 tablespoon, fresh or dried mint ($.10)
1 teaspoon fresh or dried dill ($.10)
1 teaspoon salt
½ teaspoon pepper

Place the sliced cucumbers and onions into a large mixing bowl.

In a small mixing bowl, whisk together the vinegar, white sugar, mint, dill, and salt and pepper. Pour the vinegar dressing over the cucumbers and red onions. Chill the salad at least 2 hours in the refrigerator. For best results, chill overnight and serve the following day.

Serve Mint Cucumber Onion Salad as a lunch side dish.

Makes 8 to 10 side-dish servings

Cost $2.93

FRUGAL FACT: *Mint grows easily in the garden. Use fresh mint in this refreshing cucumber onion salad.*

Avocado, Corn, and Black Bean Salsa

2 cups cooked black beans ($.40)
1 bag (12 ounces) frozen corn kernels
    ($.80)
1 avocado ($.75)
1 teaspoon lime juice ($.02)

¼ cup store-bought salsa ($.13) or
    Homemade Salsa Fresca (page 306)
1 teaspoon ground cumin ($.10)
Salt and pepper

Cook the beans according to the batch-cooking direction on page 141. If in a time crunch substitute 1 15-ounce can of black beans, drained and rinsed.

Cook the corn according to the package directions. Drain and rinse with cool water.

Cut open the avocado lengthwise and remove the seed. Slice the avocado into ½-inch chunks and remove with spoon. Place in a small bowl with the lime juice and toss; the lime juice will prevent the avocado from browning.

In a large mixing bowl, combine the corn, black beans, diced avocado, and salsa. Stir in the ground cumin and season to taste with salt and pepper. Serve chilled.

Serve Avocado, Corn, and Black Bean Salsa as a lunch side dish.

Makes 6 to 8 side-dish servings

Cost $2.20 (Note: The cost will change with the substitution of canned beans.)

FRUGAL FACT: *Use garden tomatoes, peppers, and hot peppers to make homemade salsa.*

Succotash Summer Salad

1 bag (12 ounces) frozen corn kernels ($.80)

1 bag (12 ounces) frozen baby lima beans ($.80)

1 can (15 ounces) petite diced tomatoes, drained ($.59)

½ cup red onion, finely chopped ($.40)

2 tablespoon extra-virgin olive oil ($.20)

1 tablespoon cider vinegar ($.05)

½ teaspoon garlic powder ($.03)

Salt and pepper

Cook the frozen corn kernels and frozen baby lima beans according to the package directions. Drain in a colander and run under cool water.

In a large mixing bowl, toss the cooled corn and baby lima beans, diced tomatoes, chopped red onion, olive oil, cider vinegar, garlic powder, and salt and pepper to taste.

Serve Succotash Summer Salad as a lunch side dish.

Makes 8 to 10 side-dish servings

Cost $2.87

FRUGAL FACT: *Frozen vegetable prices are lowest during the months of February and March.*

PART III

Snacks — Tasty Between-Meal Treats that Fill You Up and Keep You on Your Budget

With the time constraints that so many of us face these days, it is so tempting to just grab a piece (or three) of candy, or drive through and get an order of fries or a frostie. Working healthy snacks into our shrinking grocery budgets and ever-expanding family schedules seems like an impossibility. But what if you were armed with a handful of grab-and-go ideas? Or if you had a list on the refrigerator door of some creative snacking options to keep you out of the crackers-and-cheese rut?

Sensible Snacking

Sensible snacking can be difficult with all the different convenience-food options that are so readily available and so easy to drop into the grocery cart. Many of the convenience foods and prepackaged snacks are not sensible for a healthy lifestyle. When it comes to sensible snacking, think about what your body needs to get through the rest of the day. How does that handful of candy make you feel thirty minutes after eating it? Do you feel like crashing after the sugar rush ends? Do those fries leave you feeling more hungry, or like a greaseball landed in your stomach? Or maybe they leave you craving a burger to go with them?

Sensible snacking is about giving your body the necessary fuel to finish strong and get through until dinner. A healthy afternoon snack will provide the necessary nutrients and vitamins to fill you up and keep you full. Munching on whole grains, fiber-filled, and protein-rich foods will leave you satisfied until dinnertime.

When choosing a sensible snack, also look for raw and wholesome ingredients, like nuts, fruits, and vegetables. Keep a stash of cut raw veggies in your refrigerator, for a quick grab-and-go snack. Keep a plastic container in the freezer with your favorite frozen fruit bites, like frozen grapes, frozen blackberries, or other frozen berries. Every two or three days cut up some fresh fruit and mix up a simple fruit salad to keep in the refrigerator for when you get hit with a sweet snack craving. This fruit salad can also be used in a lunch box or with a muffin for breakfast.

When baking a snack from scratch, use half whole wheat flour and half white flour, replace some or all of the oil with applesauce, and reduce the amount of sugar in the recipe to ½ cup. Mix in some chopped nuts or dried fruits to give more dimension, protein, and fiber to your baked goods.

Need a visual reminder for your sensible snacking? Keep a bowl of fresh fruit on the countertop, or as a centerpiece on your dining table. Keep some whole almonds, walnuts, or other nut mixes in a clear decorative container on the counter or on your desk at the office. A few handfuls is all it takes to keep your tummy satisfied and your energy level up.

Grazing or Scheduled Snacks

Speaking of grabbing a handful . . . that leads to a very important question about snacking. Is it better to graze on a variety of healthy snacks, or stick to a rigid time schedule for snacking? I believe that the answer to that question varies from person to person.

A grazing schedule would work well for someone who is in tune with their body signals for hunger and thirst and who has the self-control to not turn every grazing snack session into a full-blown meal.

Scheduled snacks work best for young kids and those who might lack the self-control needed to keep snacks small and simple. Your body will know what to expect when it comes to eating and snacking when you settle into a snacking routine.

As long as you are listening to your body, eating sensible foods, and not gaining weight, either of these snacking options will provide you with the necessary fuel to get from meal to meal.

Changing Your Snack Habits

When it comes to making changes to your snack habits, start by taking a look at what you are bringing home from the grocery store. If you bring home a bag of chocolate every week and other sweet treats that will only give you about 20 minutes worth of energy, then you'll find yourself crashing after every snack session. Changing your snack habits and starting the journey to healthy snacking starts with what you put into your cart at the grocery store. Trade that bag of chocolate goodies for a bag of whole wheat pita chips or crackers and some fresh produce.

Still need to satisfy that chocolate craving? Buy some dark chocolate chunk candies and mix them into a trail mix. That will appease your sweet tooth, while filling up your tummy with other nutrient-dense foods like nuts and dried fruits (see Pantry Trail Mix on page 266). Or you could bake some Black Bean Coconut Brownies (page 296) . . . but more on those in a minute.

Time- and Money-Saving Tips for Healthy Snacks

Saving time and money on snacks seems to be a constant balancing act. Many of the wholesome and nutrient-dense foods, like nuts, can be more expensive than the prepackaged convenience foods. Of course, if you are not buying the processed foods, and instead using that money to get wholesome ingredients, the overall cost won't be that different. I recommend keeping a few convenience snacks on hand, like pretzels, whole wheat crackers, and blue corn tortilla chips.

By making your own snacks from scratch, you are sure to save money. Take popcorn, for example. Popping the kernels in your air popper or on the stovetop and adding some of your own seasonings is much cheaper and healthier than popping the butter- and salt-laden pre-packaged bags of popcorn.

"Batch chopping," which I mentioned in the Batch Cooking section of the Breakfast At Home and On-the-Go chapter, is essential for saving time on those fresh veggie snacks. You are far more likely to grab a handful of celery sticks or pepper strips if you have already sliced them. Eat them raw or with a favorite dip and you've got a quick and simple snack that won't cause you to crash a half hour later.

Meal-Planning Tips

Meal planning for snacks can be more difficult than for other meals. Snacks seem to be more tied to the emotions and the fact that I *"feel like having . . ."* I have found the key to successfully planning snacks is to have an arsenal of healthy grab-and-go snacks, ready at all times. This is especially true if there are little people around. I like to offer the boys a choice of two different snack options and let them decide what they want to enjoy.

Also, snack time can be a time to come up with very creative and unique food combinations. Try a thin slice of apple with some peanut butter or sliced bananas, maybe with a sprinkle of cinnamon or honey. What about a saltier creation like a slice of cheese and salsa atop a plain rice cake? Or maybe some pistachios sprinkled over a cup of chocolate pudding. Be creative with the different fresh and raw ingredients that you have on hand and come up with a new favorite snack.

Portion Control

While every person's caloric needs are different, and even vary as the years go by, it's important to keep the snack portion small yet nutrient dense. Mothers with nursing infants have a much higher caloric intake requirement than their neighbor without kids, and they may need to eat a few extra snacks each day. Naturally athletic children who never stop moving will have a slightly higher caloric need than their friends who enjoy reading and just hanging out. Husbands training for a marathon (like mine!) will need a hefty snack after work, even if dinner is just thirty minutes away.

Don't let your snacking get out of control by letting snack time turn into small meal time. Keep snack time simple and small, and short and sweet.

Snack Time Presentation

Whether you are trying to impress the little people in your life, or trying to trick yourself into wanting a healthy snack, you might want to experiment with the presentation. While being creative in the presentation may take a few extra minutes, the adorable look of disbelief on your little one's face, or the fact that they actually try a new food if its presented in the right way is totally worth it!

Here are a few ideas for you:

• Kebabs: Skewer some small veggies like cherry tomatoes or diced red bell peppers with rolled, deli meat slices and rolled cheese slices and dip in

Homemade Ranch Dressing (page 227); or make Fruit Kebabs with Yogurt Dip (page 269).

- Funny-Shaped Sandwiches: Use cookie cutters on sandwiches or cut the sandwiches into different letters and do phonemic awareness with young children.

- Treasure Hunt: Bury some fresh fruit or granola in some yogurt and "go hunting."

- Sailboat: Make blue jello in a shallow bowl. When it sets, add a canned peach as the boat and a cheese slice on a toothpick as the sail.

- Go Tropical: Add umbrellas or silly straws to your smoothies.

- A Stick Sandwich: Wrap sliced turkey and cheese around thick pretzel rods, and dip in honey mustard sauce.

Clever presentation of snack foods will change the way you and your family enjoy an afternoon snack.

Snack Recipes

In developing these snack recipes, my goal was to provide a variety of snack options, both sweet and salty, that anyone would enjoy. With the baked goods, I tried to limit the amount of sugar to ½ cup per recipe. I used applesauce for a portion of the oil in as many recipes as I could. I have not done much experimenting with sugar substitutes, but from what I have read Sucanat substitutes well on a 1:1 basis for sugar. Splenda can be substituted, but the substitution ratio varies depending on the recipe type. Also I like to give baked goods and smoothies a boost of omega-3s by adding ground flaxseed to the recipe.

A quick note about the Black Bean Coconut Brownies (page 296) . . . they contain an *obscene* amount of sugar. If you are watching your sugar intake, I'm sorry. I couldn't *not* share this recipe . . . they are not to be kept secret. So I'm including the recipe with this "obscene sugar disclaimer." It's easy to justify that the pureed black beans that replace the eggs and oil make it OK for it to have that much sugar in the recipe. At least that's what I tell myself every time I make a batch. These brownies are also great for families dealing with food allergies. They do not contain eggs or nuts. For those on a gluten-free diet, I have made them using rice flour instead of regular flour and they are just as delicious. Also, the milk in the recipe can be substituted with rice or almond milk without dramatically affecting the outcome of the recipe.

And finally, each of these snacks is "little-person approved," thanks to my little taste-test team!

So let's move on to the recipes for tasty between-meal treats that will fill you up and keep you within your grocery budget. Smoothies, popcorns, homemade popsicles, muffins, cookies, and of course the Black Bean Coconut Brownies . . . read on . . .

NINE

Morning, Afternoon, and Midnight
Snack Recipes

Pantry Trail Mix

1 CUP EACH, YOUR CHOICE OF 6 OF THE FOLLOWING INGREDIENTS:

Raisins

Dried fruit—cranberries, apricots

Almonds—slivered, sliced, or whole

Walnuts

Cashews

Pecans

Peanuts

Pretzels

Dry cereal

Coconut flakes

Chocolate chips

White chocolate chips

Butterscotch chips

Toffee chips

M&Ms

In a large bowl, combine the various ingredients for your pantry trail mix.

Store in an airtight container or a sealed plastic bag.

Munch, munch, munch!

Makes 6 cups of pantry trail mix

Cost $2.50 to $3, varies depending on the mixture

FRUGAL FACT: *Making trail mix is a great way to use up the leftover nuts, dried fruit, and baking chips from the holiday season. Raid the pantry and start mixing up some different trail mixes. Trail mixes are also a great addition to lunch boxes.*

Dehydrated Fruits

....

4 cups fruit (apples, peaches, bananas, pears, apricots, plums, mangoes, pineapple, strawberries, or other favorite fruit), sliced into ⅛-inch-thick pieces ($2)

2 tablespoons lemon juice ($.10)
½ teaspoon ground cinnamon ($.02)

Slice the fruit into thin strips. In a mixing bowl, toss the fruit with the lemon juice and cinnamon.

Lay the fruit slices in a single layer in the food dehydrator. Turn on the dehydrator and let run for several hours. Dehydration times will vary by the type of fruit, the thickness of the fruit, and the dehydrator itself.

Serve Dehydrated Fruits at snack time.

Will wary by fruit, how long it was dried, and how much water was removed.

Cost $2.12

FRUGAL FACT: *During the summer months, dehydrate your favorite fruits for a snacks. Dehydrated fruit can be frozen and saved for the winter months, too.*

Muffin Pan Snacks

FILL UP THE 6 OR 12 WELLS OF A MUFFIN PAN WITH A SELECTION OF THE FOLLOWING:

Almonds

Raisins

Dried fruit

Grapes

Pretzels

Cheerios

Goldfish crackers

Mandarin orange slices

Cheese cubes

Carrot sticks

Crackers

Cut fruit (cantaloupe, strawberries, pineapple)

Popcorn

Prepare the above finger-type foods and place them into the wells of a muffin pan.

Serve to hungry children.

Fills six to twelve wells of a muffin pan.

Cost $3 to $4, depending on food choices and type of pan

FRUGAL FACT: *Throw together this easy snack after a long afternoon of errands, or even use it for lunch when getting home late from a morning appointment.*

Fruit Kebabs with Yogurt Dipping Sauce

KEBABS

4 skewers ($.25)
24 pieces of fruit (cantaloupe chunks, watermelon chunks, whole berries, pineapple slices, apple pieces, grapes, peach slices, pear slices) ($2)

YOGURT DIP

1 cup plain or vanilla yogurt ($.25)
2 tablespoons honey ($.20)
½ teaspoon lemon juice ($.01)
½ teaspoon vanilla extract ($.03)

Place the cut fruit in random patterns onto bamboo or metal skewers.

Prepare the yogurt dip by whisking together the yogurt, honey, lemon juice, and vanilla in a small bowl.

Serve Fruit Kebabs with Yogurt Dip.

Makes 4 Fruit Kebabs and 1¼ cup Yogurt Dipping Sauce

Cost $2.74

FRUGAL FACT: *This is a perfect way to use up the last bit of a mixed fruit salad.*

Pumpkin Applesauce

2 cups applesauce ($.50)
1 cup canned 100 percent pure pumpkin
    puree ($.67)

1 cup plain or vanilla yogurt ($.25)
1 teaspoon pumpkin pie spice ($.05)
½ teaspoon ground cinnamon ($.03)

In a small mixing bowl, stir together all the ingredients.

Serve Pumpkin Applesauce to hungry children.

Makes four 1-cup servings

Cost $1.50

FRUGAL FACT: *This simple variation of applesauce is sure to be a crowd-pleaser. Use the remaining pumpkin from making Pumpkin Chocolate Chip Muffins (page 289) or Pumpkin Smoothies (page 276) to make this applesauce.*

Roasted Garlic Hummus

1 head garlic ($.33)
Extra-virgin olive oil for drizzling plus 2
    tablespoons ($.25)
Salt and pepper
2 cups cooked chickpeas ($.50)

¼ cup lemon juice ($.20)
½ cup water
Crackers, crudités, and/or pita chips for
    serving ($1)

Preheat the oven to 400 degrees.

Slice off the top of the head of garlic, exposing the cloves. Place the garlic into a small roasting pan and drizzle a bit of olive oil over the top. Sprinkle salt and pepper onto the garlic.

Roast the garlic in the preheated oven for 20 to 25 minutes. Set aside until cool enough to handle.

Cook 1 cup of chickpeas according to the package instructions, yielding 2 cups of cooked chickpeas. Place the cooked chickpeas into a blender or food processor with the 2 tablespoons olive oil, lemon juice, water and a dash of salt and pepper. Squeeze the roasted garlic pulp into the blender or food processor. Blend the ingredients for 1 to 2 minutes, or until smooth, streaming in additional water as needed until the hummus reaches the desired consistency. The blending time may vary on the blender or processor.

Scoop out the hummus into a serving bowl. Season with salt and pepper to taste.

Serve Roasted Garlic Hummus with Crackers, Crudités, or Pita Chips.

Makes 3 cups hummus

Cost $2.28

FRUGAL FACT: *In a time crunch, substitute 1 can (15 ounces) canned chickpeas for the 2 cups of cooked chickpeas. Drain and rinse the canned beans before using in the recipe.*

Creamy Garlic and White Bean Dip

3 large garlic cloves ($.15)

2 cups cooked white beans, such as great northern, rinsed and drained ($.40)

1 small white or yellow onion, chopped ($.20)

1 tablespoon extra-virgin olive oil ($.10)

½ cup milk ($.05)

¼ cup lemon juice ($.20)

Salt and pepper

Crackers, crudités, and/or pita chips for serving ($1)

In a blender or food processor, blend together the garlic cloves, cooked white beans, chopped onion, olive oil, milk, and lemon juice until smooth.

Season to taste with salt and pepper.

Serve Creamy Garlic and White Bean Dip with Crackers, Crudités, or Pita Chips.

Makes 3 cups of bean dip.

Cost $2.10

FRUGAL FACT: *Cook an entire bag of dried white beans at once and then freeze the cooked white beans in 2-cup portions. Saves time, money, and dish soap!*

Strawberry-Banana Smoothies

....

1 banana ($.20)
1 cup strawberries ($.99)
1 cup milk ($.10)
1 cup plain or vanilla yogurt ($.25)

2 tablespoons sweetener (honey, sugar,
   or agave nectar) ($.10)
2 tablespoons ground flaxseed ($.10)

Peel the banana. Wash the strawberries and remove the stems.

In a blender, blend the banana, strawberries, milk, yogurt, sweetener, and ground flaxseed until smooth.

Serve Strawberry-Banana Smoothies.

Makes four 1-cup servings

Cost $1.74

FRUGAL FACT: *Every few months, bananas will go on sale for less than half their normal price. When this happens, buy a few extra bunches to freeze. Peel the bananas and place them in a single layer on a cookie sheet. Freeze. Once frozen, transfer the bananas to freezer bags for storage.*

Mango-Raspberry Smoothies

....

1 mango, or 1 cup frozen mango ($.50)
1 cup raspberries ($.99)
1 cup milk ($.10)
1 cup plain or vanilla yogurt ($.25)

2 tablespoons sweetener (honey, sugar, or agave nectar) ($.10)
2 tablespoons ground flaxseed ($.10)

Peel the mango and cut the fruit off the seed. Rinse the raspberries and pat dry.

In a blender, blend the mango, raspberries, milk, yogurt, sweetener, and ground flaxseed until smooth.

Serve Mango-Raspberry Smoothies.

Makes four 1-cup servings

Cost $2.04

FRUGAL FACT: *Look for a price of $1.99 per pint or less for raspberries. When you see them for less than $1.49 per pint, buy a few extra pints and quick freeze the berries according to the directions on page 21.*

Blueberry Smoothies

2 bananas ($.40)
1 cup blueberries ($.99)
1 cup milk ($.10)
1 cup apple juice ($.20)

2 tablespoons sweetener (honey, sugar,
   or agave nectar) ($.10)
2 tablespoons ground flaxseed ($.10)

Peel the banana. Rinse and stem the blueberries and pat dry.

In a blender, blend the banana, blueberries, milk, apple juice, sweetener, and ground flaxseed until smooth.

Serve Blueberry Smoothies.

Makes four 1-cup servings

Cost $1.89

FRUGAL FACT: *Blueberries can be quick frozen in the same way as raspberries. When you see a great price, grab a few extra boxes and quick freeze (page 21) them too.*

Pumpkin Smoothies

....

1 banana ($.20)

1 cup canned 100 percent pure pumpkin
   puree ($.67)

1 cup milk or plain yogurt ($.10)

1 teaspoon pumpkin pie spice ($.05)

2 tablespoons sweetener (honey, sugar,
   or agave nectar) ($.10)

½ teaspoon vanilla extract ($.03)

2 tablespoons ground flaxseed ($.10)

Peel the banana.

In a blender, blend the banana, pumpkin, milk or yogurt, pumpkin pie spice, sweetener, vanilla, and ground flaxseed until smooth.

Serve Pumpkin Smoothies.

Makes four 1-cup servings

Cost $1.25

FRUGAL FACT: *This smoothie is the perfect way to use up any extra canned pumpkin from other recipes.*

Spinach "Green" Smoothies

1 banana ($.20)

1 cup baby spinach, about 1 large handful ($.50)

1 cup milk or plain yogurt ($.10)

1 cup apple juice ($.20)

1 cup water or ice

2 tablespoons sweetener (honey, sugar, or agave nectar) ($.10)

2 tablespoons ground flaxseed ($.10)

Peel the banana. Wash and dry baby spinach, if necessary.

In a blender, blend the banana, baby spinach, milk or yogurt, apple juice, sweetener, and ground flaxseed until smooth.

Serve Spinach "Green" Smoothies.

Makes four 1-cup servings

Cost $1.20

FRUGAL FACT: *A wide variety of nutrients in one glass—this smoothie makes for a quick and healthy breakfast on the go!*

Peach-Strawberry Smoothies

1 cup strawberries ($.99)
1 banana ($.20)
1 cup frozen peaches ($.75)
1 cup milk or yogurt ($.10)

1 cup water or ice
2 tablespoons sweetener (honey, sugar, or agave nectar) ($.10)
2 tablespoon ground flaxseed ($.10)

Wash strawberries and remove stems. Peel the banana.

In a blender, blend the strawberries, banana, frozen peaches, milk or yogurt, water or ice, sweetener, and ground flaxseed until smooth.

Serve Peach Strawberry Smoothies.

Makes four 1-cup servings

Cost $2.24

FRUGAL FACT: *When peaches are on sale during the mid to late summer, buy extra to quick freeze (page 21).*

Piña Colada Popsicles

1 banana ($.20)
3 cups fresh pineapple chunks ($.75)
½ can pure coconut milk (about 7.5 ounces) ($.75)

2 tablespoons sweetener (honey, sugar, or agave nectar) ($.10)
About 1 cup water

Add all the ingredients to a blender and puree until smooth.

Pour the mixture into a popsicle mold and freeze.

Serve Piña Colada Popsicles on a hot summer afternoon.

Makes 4 to 8 popsicles, depending on size of your popsicle mold

Cost $1.80

FRUGAL FACT: *Purchase the generic brand of coconut milk if there are no coupons available for the name brands.*

Creamy Mango Tropical Popsicles

1 banana ($.20)
2 ripe mangoes, peeled and seed
removed ($1)
½ can pure coconut milk (about 7.5
ounces) ($.75)

2 tablespoons sweetener (honey, sugar,
or agave nectar) ($.10)
About 1 cup water

Add all the ingredients to a blender and puree until smooth.

Pour the mixture into a popsicle mold and freeze.

Serve Creamy Mango Tropical Popsicles on a hot summer afternoon.

Makes 4 to 8 popsicles, depending on size of your popsicle mold

Cost $2.05

FRUGAL FACT: *Look for prices of $.50 per mango or less during the summer months. Mangoes can also be sliced and the mango pulp frozen using the quick-freeze method (page 21).*

Cajun Popcorn

¼ cup butter or margarine, melted ($.40)

½ teaspoon lemon-pepper seasoning ($.05)

2 teaspoon Cajun seasoning ($.10)

8 cups popped popcorn ($.25)

In a small bowl, stir together the melted butter or margarine, lemon-pepper seasoning, and Cajun seasonings, until well blended.

Toss the popped popcorn with the butter-seasoning mixture in a large bowl. Store in an airtight container.

Munch, munch, munch on Cajun Popcorn.

Makes 8 cups

Cost $.80

FRUGAL FACT: *Purchase a large bag of popcorn kernels and store them in an airtight container. Pop them in an air popper, or in a pot on the stovetop. To pop on the stovetop, put 2 tablespoons of canola or vegetable oil into a large pot. Heat the oil on high for 1 minute, then add ½ to 1 cup of kernels, depending on the size of the pot. Cover tightly. Cook until the popcorn kernels slow down to one pop every 3 seconds, frequently shaking the pot to move the kernels around in the oil and get them all popped. Remove from heat immediately. The popped popcorn is ready for seasoning.*

Quick Caramel Popcorn

1 cup firmly packed brown sugar ($.25)
½ cup butter or margarine ($.80)
1 teaspoon vanilla extract ($.05)

¼ teaspoon salt
10 cups popped popcorn ($.33)

In a small microwave-safe glass bowl, combine the brown sugar, butter or margarine, vanilla, and salt. Microwave on high for 2 minutes. Stir until well blended. Microwave another 2 minutes.

Put the popped popcorn into a large plastic microwave-safe bowl. Pour the syrup over the popcorn and stir until the syrup coats the popcorn.

Place the bowl and the caramel popcorn into the microwave and cook on high for 1 minute. Remove carefully, and stir the contents again.

Place the caramel popcorn onto wax or parchment paper and let cool. Store in an airtight container.

Munch, munch, munch on Quick Caramel Popcorn.

Makes 10 cups

Cost $1.43

FRUGAL FACT: *Match margarine coupons with sale prices to get inexpensive tubs of margarine.*

Pizza Popcorn

....

2 tablespoons grated Parmesan cheese ($.15)

1 teaspoon Italian seasoning ($.05)

1 teaspoon garlic powder ($.05)

¼ teaspoon salt

½ teaspoon pepper

8 cups popped popcorn ($.25)

In a blender or mini food processor, blend the Parmesan cheese, Italian seasoning, garlic powder, and salt and pepper for 1 minute.

Add freshly popped popcorn to a large bowl and sprinkle the cheese-herb mixture over the top. Toss until the popcorn is evenly coated. Store in an airtight container.

Munch, munch, munch on Pizza Popcorn.

Makes 8 cups

Cost $.50

FRUGAL FACT: *Save time by blending two or four times the cheese and seasoning mixture. Store the seasoning mix in the refrigerator for up to a week or in the freezer, for longer. Then when you want pizza popcorn again, you've got the seasoning mix ready to go.*

Lemon Coconut Mini Loaves

¾ cup sugar ($.08)

4 tablespoon butter or margarine ($.40)

2 tablespoons canola or vegetable oil ($.03)

2 tablespoons applesauce ($.05)

2 large eggs ($.20)

1 teaspoon vanilla extract ($.05)

1 teaspoon lemon extract ($.10)

2 teaspoon lemon juice ($.02)

2½ cups all-purpose flour ($.50)

1 tablespoon baking powder ($.15)

1 teaspoon salt

1 cup sweetened coconut flakes ($.67)

Preheat the oven to 350 degrees. Lightly coat 8 mini loaf pans, or 1 large 9 × 5-inch loaf pan, with nonstick cooking spray.

In the bowl of a stand mixer or in a large mixing bowl, stir the sugar, butter or margarine, oil, applesauce, eggs, vanilla and lemon extracts, and the lemon juice until smooth.

In a small mixing bowl, whisk together the flour, baking powder, and salt. Add the dry ingredients to the wet ingredients in the bowl. Stir until a batter forms.

Stir in the coconut flakes. Spoon the batter into the prepared mini loaf pan, or large loaf pan.

Bake in the preheated oven for 20 to 22 minutes for the mini loaves, or for 45 to 55 minutes for the large loaf, or until a knife or toothpick inserted in the center of the loaves comes out clean. Let cool on a wire rack before serving.

Serve Lemon Coconut Mini Loaves.

Makes 8 mini loaves or 1 large loaf

Cost $2.25

FRUGAL FACT: *Coconut flakes can be stored in the freezer for up to a year.*

FREEZER FRIENDLY

Pumpkin Coconut Bread

....

3 large eggs ($.30)
1⅓ cups firmly packed brown sugar
   ($.37)
1⅓ cups granulated sugar ($.13)
½ cup canola or vegetable oil ($.20)
½ cup applesauce ($.12)
½ cup milk ($.05)
1 can (15 ounces) 100 percent pure
   pumpkin purée ($1.29)

1 cup unsweetened coconut flakes ($.67)
2½ cups whole wheat flour ($.70)
1 cup all-purpose flour ($.20)
2 teaspoon baking soda ($.06)
1 teaspoon ground nutmeg ($.05)
1½ teaspoons ground cinnamon ($.03)
1 cup walnuts (optional)

Preheat the oven to 350 degrees. Lightly coat 2 large loaf pans, or 1 loaf pan and 8 mini loaf pans, with nonstick cooking spray.

In the bowl of a stand mixer or in a large mixing bowl, mix together the eggs, brown sugar, granulated sugar, oil, applesauce, milk, pumpkin puree, and coconut flakes until well blended. Add the whole wheat and all-purpose flours, baking soda, nutmeg, and cinnamon and mix into the wet ingredients for 2 to 3 minutes.

Fold in walnuts, if desired. Pour the batter into the prepared pans.

Bake the bread in the preheated oven for 50 to 55 minutes, if using large loaf pans. For mini loaf pans, bake for 22 to 24 minutes, or until a knife inserted into the center of the loaves comes out clean. Let cool on rack before serving.

Serve Pumpkin Coconut Bread.

Makes 2 large loaves

Cost $4.17

FRUGAL FACT: *Stock up on canned pumpkin during the holiday feast sales and specials.*

FREEZER FRIENDLY

Blackberry Mini Muffins

....

½ cup butter or margarine ($.80)
½ cup sugar ($.05)
2 large eggs ($.20)
2 teaspoons vanilla extract ($.10)
1 cup milk ($.10)
2 cups all-purpose flour ($.40)

1 teaspoon baking soda ($.03)
½ teaspoon salt
2 cups blackberries, halved ($1)
2 tablespoons lemon juice ($.10)
2 tablespoons sugar ($.01)

Preheat the oven to 350 degrees. Lightly coat 24 wells of mini muffin pans with non-stick cooking spray, or line with paper liners.

In the bowl of a stand mixer or a large mixing bowl, cream the butter or margarine and the sugar. Mix in the eggs, vanilla, and milk for 1 to 2 minutes, or until well blended. Turn off the mixer.

To the mixing bowl, add the flour, baking soda, and salt. Stir for 2 to 3 minutes, or until batter is smooth.

In a small mixing bowl, toss the halved blackberries with the lemon juice and sugar.

Spoon the batter into the prepared muffin wells, only filling up about one-fourth of the well. Once all the wells have been filled with batter, add 2 sugar-coated blackberries on top of the batter. After all the wells have blackberries, spoon the remaining batter over the blackberries.

Bake the muffins in the preheated oven for 14 to 16 minutes, or until a toothpick inserted in the centers of the muffins comes out clean.

Serve Blackberry Mini Muffins.

Makes 24 mini muffins

Cost $2.79

FRUGAL FACT: *The stock-up price for blackberries is $1 per pint. Blackberries can be frozen by placing them on a cookie sheet and quick freezing them, and then adding the frozen blackberries to a plastic freezer bag (page 21).*

Chocolate Chocolate Chip Muffins

2 large eggs ($.20)
1 ripe banana ($.20)
½ cup canola or vegetable oil ($.25)
½ cup applesauce ($.10)
1 cup sugar ($.15)
1 cup buttermilk ($.10)
1 teaspoon vanilla extract ($.05)

1 cup all-purpose flour ($.20)
1 cup whole wheat flour ($.28)
4 tablespoons unsweetened cocoa
    powder ($.15)
1 teaspoon baking soda ($.05)
¼ teaspoon salt
1 cup mini chocolate chips ($.50)

Preheat the oven to 350 degrees. Lightly coat 18 wells of regular-size muffin pans with nonstick cooking spray, or line with paper liners.

In the bowl of a stand mixer or in a large mixing bowl, combine the eggs, banana, oil, applesauce, sugar, buttermilk, and vanilla. Mix in the stand mixer or with a hand mixer for 1 to 2 minutes, or until well blended. Turn off the mixer.

To the mixing bowl, add the all-purpose and whole wheat flours, cocoa powder, baking soda, and salt. Mix the dry ingredients for 2 to 3 minutes, or until the batter is smooth. Fold in the mini chocolate chips.

Pour the batter into the prepared muffin pans.

Bake the muffins in the preheated oven for 16 to 18 minutes, or until a toothpick inserted in the centers of the muffins comes out clean. Let cool on a wire rack before serving.

Serve Chocolate Chocolate Chip Muffins.

Makes 18 muffins

Cost $2.23

FRUGAL FACT: *Don't have buttermilk on hand? Add 1 teaspoon of vinegar to a 1-cup measuring cup and then fill up the remainder of the measuring cup with regular milk. The "buttermilk" is now ready to use in this recipe.*

FREEZER FRIENDLY

Pumpkin Chocolate Chip Muffins

2 large eggs ($.20)
¼ cup oil ($.13)
¼ cup applesauce ($.05)
½ cup sugar ($.08)
¼ cup milk ($.03)
¾ cup canned 100 percent pure
    pumpkin purée (about half a
    15-ounce can) ($.75)

1 cup all-purpose flour ($.20)
½ cup whole wheat flour ($.14)
1 teaspoon baking powder ($.05)
½ teaspoon baking soda ($.03)
1 teaspoon pumpkin pie spice ($.10)
½ teaspoon salt
1 cup mini or regular-size chocolate
    chips ($.50)

Preheat the oven to 350 degrees. Lightly coat 18 wells of regular-size muffin pans with nonstick cooking spray, or line with paper liners.

In the bowl of a stand mixer or in a large mixing bowl, add the eggs, banana, oil, applesauce, sugar, milk, and canned pumpkin. Mix in the stand mixer or with a hand mixer for 1 to 2 minutes, or until well blended. Turn off the mixer.

To the mixing bowl, add the all-purpose and wheat flours, baking powder, baking soda, pumpkin pie spice, and salt. Mix the dry ingredients for 2 to 3 minutes, or until the batter is smooth. Fold in the chocolate chips.

Pour the batter into the prepared muffin pans.

Bake the muffins in the preheated oven for 16 to 18 minutes, or until toothpick in the centers of the muffins comes out clean. Let cool on a wire rack before serving.

Serve Pumpkin Chocolate Chip Muffins.

Makes 18 muffins

Cost $2.26

FRUGAL FACT: *Not sure what to do with the other half of the canned pumpkin? Double this recipe and freeze the extra muffins for a quick snack later in the week.*

FREEZER FRIENDLY

Butterscotch Muffins

2 large eggs ($.20)
¾ cup sugar ($.08)
2 ripe bananas, mashed ($.40)
½ cup canola or vegetable oil ($.20)
¼ cup milk ($.03)
1 teaspoon vanilla extract ($.05)

2 cups whole wheat flour ($.56)
1 teaspoon baking powder ($.05)
½ teaspoon baking soda ($.02)
½ teaspoon salt
1 cup butterscotch chips ($.75)

Preheat the oven to 350 degrees. Lightly coat 12 wells of a regular-size muffin pan with nonstick cooking spray, or line with paper liners.

In the bowl of a stand mixer or in a large mixing bowl, add the eggs, sugar, bananas, oil, milk, and vanilla. Mix in the stand mixer or with a hand mixer for 1 to 2 minutes, or until well blended. Turn off the mixer.

To the mixing bowl, add the wheat flour, baking powder, baking soda, and salt. Mix the dry ingredients for 2 to 3 minutes or until the batter is smooth. Fold in the butterscotch chips.

Pour the batter into the prepared muffin pans.

Bake the muffins in the preheated oven for 16 to 18 minutes, or until a toothpick inserted in the center of the muffins comes out clean. Let cool on a wire rack before serving.

Serve Butterscotch Muffins.

Makes 12 muffins

Cost $2.34

FRUGAL FRIDAY: *My "never-pay-more-than" price for a bag of baking chips is $1.49.*

FREEZER FRIENDLY

Peanut Butter Chocolate Muffins

....

BATTER

2 large eggs ($.20)

1 cup milk ($.10)

1 cup plain or vanilla yogurt ($.25)

½ cup canola or vegetable oil ($.20)

1 teaspoon vanilla extract ($.05)

2 cups sugar ($.20)

2 cups all-purpose flour ($.40)

½ cup unsweetened cocoa powder ($.30)

1 teaspoon baking powder ($.05)

1 teaspoon salt

PEANUT BUTTER FILLING

4 ounces cream cheese, softened ($.50)

½ cup natural peanut butter, softened ($.28)

3 tablespoons sugar ($.03)

Preheat the oven to 350 degrees. Lightly coat 24 wells of two regular-size muffin pans with nonstick cooking spray, or line with paper liners.

In the bowl of a stand mixer or in a large mixing bowl, stir together the eggs, milk, yogurt, oil, vanilla, and sugar until smooth. Add the flour, cocoa powder, baking powder, and salt. Stir together until a smooth batter forms.

In a small mixing bowl, stir together the softened cream cheese, the softened peanut butter, and the sugar.

Spoon the batter into the prepared muffin wells, filling them halfway. Add a ¼-inch ball of the peanut butter filling. Then cover the peanut butter filling with more chocolate batter, filling the well three-quarters full.

Bake the muffins in the preheated oven for 22 to 25 minutes, or until toothpick inserted in the center of the muffins comes out clean. Let cool on a wire rack before serving.

Serve Peanut Butter Chocolate Muffins.

Makes 24 muffins

Cost $2.56

FRUGAL FACT: *Add your favorite chocolate frosting to turn these muffins into cupcakes!*

FREEZER FRIENDLY

Chocolate-Covered Bananas

8 bananas, peeled ($1.60)

¼ cup plus 2 tablespoons unsweetened cocoa powder ($.20)

¾ cup firmly packed brown sugar ($.20)

2 tablespoons all-purpose flour ($.02)

½ can evaporated milk (about 6 ounces) ($.49)

1½ teaspoons vanilla extract ($.07)

1 tablespoon butter or margarine ($.10)

1 teaspoon cornstarch ($.02)

1 cup chopped walnuts ($.75)

In a small saucepan, combine the cocoa powder, sugar, flour, evaporated milk, vanilla, butter or margarine, and cornstarch. Turn on the heat and, stirring constantly, bring to a rolling boil, then remove from the heat.

Once the chocolate sauce stops bubbling, dip one end of each banana into the sauce, covering as much of the banana as you can. Then roll the chocolate-covered portion of the banana in the chopped walnuts. Place the chocolate-covered banana onto a sheet wax paper. Let cool for a few minutes on the wax paper before slicing and serving.

Serve Chocolate-Covered Bananas.

Makes 8 bananas

Cost $3.45

FRUGAL FACT: *Use the leftover chocolate sauce for dipping pretzels and strawberries. Extra chocolate sauce can also be stored in an airtight container in the refrigerator for 3 to 4 days.*

Peanut Butter Walnut No-Bake Cookies

1 cup sugar ($.15)

½ cup butter or margarine ($.33)

¼ cup unsweetened cocoa powder ($.15)

½ cup milk ($.05)

½ teaspoon vanilla extract ($.03)

Pinch of salt

½ cup all-natural peanut butter ($.28)

3½ cups oats, old-fashioned or
   quick-cooking ($.42)

½ cup chopped walnuts ($.50)

Add the sugar, butter or margarine, cocoa powder, milk, vanilla, and salt to a saucepan. Bring to a boil and cook at a rolling boil for 1 minute, stirring continuously.

Stir in the peanut butter until it melts into the sauce. Stir in the chopped walnuts.

Add the oats and stir until a "dough" forms.

Spoon the no-bake "dough" onto a sheet of wax paper and let cool for at least 30 minutes.

Serve Peanut Butter Walnut No-Bake Cookies.

Makes 12 no-bake cookies

Cost $1.91

FRUGAL FACT: *Watch for great sale prices on oats at the national drugstore chains. Match with a coupon from the newspaper for an even better deal.*

Double Chocolate Brownies

¾ cup butter or margarine ($.67)
4 ounces unsweetened chocolate squares ($.99)
1 cup granulated sugar ($.10)
1 cup firmly packed brown sugar ($.25)
3 large eggs ($.30)

1 teaspoon vanilla extract ($.05)
1⅔ cups all-purpose flour ($.33)
½ teaspoon salt
1 cup chopped walnuts ($.75)
1 cup chocolate chips, any variety ($.50)

Preheat the oven to 350 degrees. Lightly coat a 9×13-inch glass baking dish with nonstick cooking spray.

In a microwave-safe bowl, add the butter or margarine and the unsweetened chocolate squares. Microwave for 1½ to 2 minutes until melted. Stir together with spoon until smooth.

In the bowl of a stand mixer or in a large mixing bowl, combine the granulated sugar, brown sugar, eggs, and vanilla. Stir until smooth. Then add the melted butter and chocolate. Stir again until smooth.

Stir in the flour and salt to the wet ingredients. Fold in the walnuts and chocolate chips. Pour the batter into the prepared baking dish.

Bake the brownies in the preheated oven for 25 to 30 minutes, or until toothpick inserted in the center comes out clean. Let cool on a wire rack before cutting and serving.

Serve Double Chocolate Brownies.

Makes 16 to 20 brownies

Cost $3.94

FRUGAL FACT: *Because unsweetened chocolate squares have a long shelf life, buy an extra box when you see them on sale.*

Black Bean Coconut Brownies

....

3 cups cooked black beans (page 141)
($.60)

2 cups sugar ($.20)

½ cup milk ($.05)

1 teaspoon vanilla extract ($.05)

1½ cups all-purpose flour ($.30)

½ cup unsweetened cocoa powder
($.30)

1 tablespoon baking powder ($.15)

1 teaspoon baking soda ($.03)

1 teaspoon salt

1 cup unsweetened shredded
coconut ($.50)

2 cups semisweet chocolate chips ($1)

Preheat the oven to 350 degrees. Lightly coat a 9 × 13-inch glass baking dish with nonstick cooking spray.

Puree the cooked black beans, with about ½ cup water, into a smoothie-like consistency. If you are in a time crunch you can substitute two cans (15 ounces each) of black beans for the 3 cups of cooked black beans. Drain and rinse the canned beans well before pureeing.

In a the bowl of stand mixer or in a large mixing bowl, combine the black bean puree, sugar, milk, and vanilla until smooth. Add the flour, cocoa powder, baking powder, baking soda, and salt and mix until a smooth batter forms. Stir in the shredded coconut and chocolate chips. Pour the batter into the prepared baking dish.

Bake the brownies in the preheated oven for 45 to 55 minutes, or until toothpick inserted in the center comes out clean. Let cool on a wire rack before cutting and serving.

Serve Black Bean Coconut Brownies.

Makes 24 brownies

Cost $3.18 (Note: The cost will change with the substitution of canned beans.)

FRUGAL FACT: *Make these gluten-free and casein-free brownies by substituting rice flour or gluten-free baking mix for the white flour and almond or rice milk for the regular.*

FREEZER FRIENDLY

Oatmeal-Cranberry Cookies

1 cup butter or margarine ($.80)
1 cup granulated sugar ($.10)
¾ cup firmly packed brown sugar ($.20)
2 large eggs ($.20)
1 teaspoon vanilla extract ($.05)
1 cup all-purpose flour ($.20)
¾ cup whole wheat flour ($.21)

1 teaspoon baking powder ($.05)
1 teaspoon baking soda ($.03)
1 teaspoon salt
3 cups quick-cooking or old-fashioned oats ($.36)
1 cup dried cranberries ($.75)

Preheat the oven to 350 degrees.

In a stand mixer or in a large mixing bowl, combine the butter or margarine, granulated and brown sugars, eggs, and vanilla. Mix in the stand mixer or with a hand mixer for 1 to 2 minutes, or until well blended. Turn off the mixer.

In a small mixing bowl, whisk together the all-purpose and whole wheat flours, baking powder, baking soda, and salt. Add to the wet ingredients in the stand mixer or mixing bowl. Stir until a batter forms. Stir in the quick cooking or old-fashioned oats. Then stir in the dried cranberries.

Spoon about 2 tablespoons of cookie dough at a time onto the prepared baking sheet. Bake in the preheated oven for 9 to 11 minutes. Let cool on a wire rack before serving.

Serve Oatmeal Cranberry Cookies.

Makes 3 dozen cookies

Cost $2.95

FRUGAL FACT: *Look for great sale prices on dried cranberries at the national drugstore chains.*

FREEZER FRIENDLY

AFTERWORD

A Practical Look:
Putting It All Together

Now that you've got all the recipes and have read my basic rules, let's review everything, set some goals, and get on the path to spending less on that weekly food budget!

Striking the Balance

Remember the importance of balancing the use of convenience and from-scratch foods. When looking for convenience-type snacks, look for raw and wholesome foods like nuts, dried fruits, and other natural foods. Stock up when you find them on sale and you can quickly assemble a pantry trail mix, or bake some cookies or muffins.

With all things in life, balance is essential. If you are especially stressed or busy one week, then by all means, grab a few extra convenience items at the store that week. Then when life settles a bit and you can get back into your routine and manage a little more time in the kitchen, get caught up on some of the batch cooking and food preparation that is essential for saving time and spending less at the grocery store.

Make it a goal to maintain a freezer full of homemade convenience foods, including snacks, breakfast, lunch, and dinner meals for those days when you are away from home all day or need to grab something for the road. When it comes time to spend extra time in the car shuffling kids from one game to the next practice, you'll have an arsenal ready and you won't have to stress about making food, or spending more money on takeout and the drive-through.

Planning Your Breakfast, Lunches, and Snacks

Making a plan for dinner is easy. Adding in a plan for breakfast, lunch, and snacks can seem daunting, to say the least. But it should be done.

No, it must be done!

Not knowing what to fix for dinner can be frustrating, but not knowing what to have for lunch is worse. Or what snacks to give the kids after school . . . ugh! Imagine not knowing what to eat for every meal. I might as well commit myself to the looney bin. Because that would make me looney! And I imagine it would make you looney, too.

Save yourself the troubles (and the ticket to the looney bin) and make a plan at the start of each week. Even if the plan is a short list of snacks; or a list of the batch cooking that you'd like to accomplish and which afternoon or evening you can incorporate that into the cooking plan.

Get a magnetic calendar and write on the refrigerator what's for breakfast, lunch, and dinner each day with a special section for snack options. The whole family knows what to expect at each meal.

If you don't accomplish any other goals on this list, at least do this one—for sanity's sake!

Grocery List and Budget

As you get more efficient with your planning, making your grocery list and budget each month, you'll likely find that you are spending less and less at the store. Keep track of your weekly and monthly expenses and find that "magic" number that works for your family. For our family, that magic number has been $60 a week for two years now. While it fluctuates above and below $60 from week to week, on average we hit the $60 per week mark each month. Finding that magic number and setting the goal to stay within budget keeps your pocketbook and bank account happy!

Prep Work

Look at each week and decide how much prep time you have to work with, whether on the weekend or during the evening. Remember that good, wholesome, healthy meals will take a few minutes to get together; but keeping one step ahead of yourself will save you time and a few shreds of sanity. And once your prep work is complete, you'll have both time and mental freedom as you go about your busy week. And of course, money will be saved from not going out to eat or not grabbing a triple-priced snack from the convenience store or the vending machine.

As you get more efficient with your prep work, set goals to spend a little less time in the kitchen preparing the food for the week, and more time with your family!

Challenge Weeks

Once you have mastered the concept of shopping at sales only and your stockpile is growing and growing, set the goal to only spend $20 at the store that week on milk and produce. Schedule a Pantry Challenge Week, or perhaps a No Cold Cereal Challenge Week (see page 13). Maybe you over-prepped and have more muffins or pancakes in your freezer than you know what to do with. Incorporate that into your weekly or monthly meal plan and set up one of these challenge weeks at least once a quarter, if not more often.

Being successful on a challenge week only adds to the joy of spending less money at the store and less time in the kitchen!

Now Go Get 'Em!

Now that you've got some goals in place and the tools you need to spend less time and money on breakfast, lunch, and snacks, get over to the grocery store, then spend a few minutes in the kitchen getting ready for the week. The days of feeling behind or guilty about another PBJ for lunch are over!

It's time to get ahead, stay ahead, and beat breakfast, lunch, and snacks at their own game*! Go get 'em!*

APPENDIX A
Pantry Staples List

Another aspect of saving money and time when planning and making meals is having an organized and fully stocked kitchen.

Below are my recommendations for the "must haves" in the freezer, refrigerator, pantry, and other cooking and baking supplies.

First up, I'm including four recipes from *The $5 Dinner Mom Cookbook* that you'll need to complete some of the recipes in this book.

Homemade Pizza Sauce

1 can (15 ounces) tomato sauce ($.59)
1 teaspoon dried oregano ($.05)
1 teaspoon dried basil ($.05)

1 teaspoon garlic powder ($.05)
1 teaspoon onion powder ($.05)
2 teaspoons extra-virgin olive oil ($.05)

In a small saucepan or skillet, whisk the tomato sauce with the spices and olive oil. Simmer for 6 to 8 minutes.

This recipe makes 2 cups of pizza sauce.

Cost $.84

Homemade Spaghetti Sauce

1 can (28 ounces) crushed tomatoes ($.79)
2 garlic cloves, crushed ($.10)
1 tablespoon dried basil ($.10)

1 tablespoon dried oregano ($.10)
1 tablespoon dried rosemary ($.10)
1 tablespoons extra-virgin olive oil ($.10)
salt and pepper

To a medium saucepan, add the crushed tomatoes, crushed garlic, basil, oregano, rosemary, olive oil, and salt and pepper to taste.

Simmer the sauce for 15 minutes, to allow the herbs and flavors to infuse.

The sauce can be stored for a week in the refrigerator, 6 months in the freezer, or indefinitely if canned.

Cost $1.39 for 4 cups

FRUGAL FACT: *Grow one pot of "Spaghetti Sauce Herbs" with basil, oregano, and rosemary. Don't let extra herbs go to waste—make a large batch of sauce and freeze in 2- or 3-cup portions.*

Homemade Hamburger Buns

1 cup hot water
2 cups white flour ($.28)
1 cup whole wheat flour ($.20)
1 tablespoon or package active dry yeast
   ($.25)

1 teaspoon sugar ($.02)
1 teaspoon salt
1 tablespoon canola oil ($.05)
1 tablespoon butter, melted ($.10)

BY HAND DIRECTIONS

In a mixing bowl, combine the hot water with 1 cup of the white flour. Add the yeast, sugar, salt, and oil. Whisk together to make a "spongy" dough. Let sit for 10 to 15 minutes.

Add other 1 cup of white flour plus 1 cup of wheat flour to the spongy dough and stir with a wooden spoon. When the dough becomes thick enough, knead it for 6 to 8 minutes on a floured surface or in a floured bowl, until it reaches the consistency of soft baby skin. Place the dough in a floured or greased bowl and let rise for 45 minutes to 1 hour.

Once the dough has risen and doubled in size, the dough is ready to be formed. Grease a baking sheet. Divide the dough ball in half, and then divide the 2 dough balls into thirds. Form smaller dough balls into bun shapes. Remember the dough will rise again, so "flat" buns are okay. Place the buns on the greased baking sheet. Set aside and let the buns rise for at least 30 minutes in a warm place. Preheat the oven to 350 degrees.

Bake the buns in the preheated oven for 20 to 25 minutes, until slightly golden on top. Remove the buns from the oven, brush the tops with melted butter, and return to oven for 2 minutes. Remove and let cool on a rack. Cool slightly before slicing.

BREAD MACHINE DIRECTIONS

Place the ingredients in the order listed, *except for the melted butter*, into a bread machine bowl. Set the machine to the dough cycle.

Once the dough cycle is complete, flour your fingers, remove the dough and place it on a floured surface. Shape into hamburger bun–sizes. Place the buns on the greased baking sheet. Set aside and let the buns rise for at least 30 minutes in a warm place. Preheat the oven to 350 degrees.

Bake the buns in the preheated oven for 20 to 25 minutes, until slightly golden on top. Remove the buns from the oven, brush the tops with melted butter, and return to the oven for 2 minutes. Remove and let cool on a rack. Cool slightly before slicing.

Cost $.90 for 8 to 10 buns

FRUGAL FACT: *Yeast can be stored for up to 1 year in the freezer.*

Homemade Salsa Fresca (Fresh Salsa)

6 large tomatoes ($2)
2 serrano chiles ($.79)
3 garlic cloves, crushed ($.15)

½ onion, quartered ($.15)
2 teaspoons olive oil ($.05)

Quarter the tomatoes and place in a food processor or blender.

Cut the stems off the chiles. Remove some seeds if you prefer a milder salsa. Add chiles, crushed garlic, quartered onions, and olive oil to the food processor or blender.

Blend or puree until the salsa reaches the desired consistency.

Serve the salsa with chips, or use when cooking or in recipes that call for salsa.

Makes 2 to 3 cups of salsa

Cost $3.04

FRUGAL FACT: *If you don't have space for a garden, consider growing a hot pepper plant in a medium pot on an outdoor table.*

Freezer

Chicken breasts
Ground beef
Ground turkey
Fresh or frozen fish
Shrimp
Any favorite meat cuts that are reduced
for quick sale and not to be used
immediately

Frozen vegetables
Frozen fruit
Breads that are reduced for quick sale
and not to be used immediately
Homemade beef, chicken, or vegetable
broth

Refrigerator

Milk
Eggs
Cheese (sliced, bar, shredded, grated*)
Deli meats
Butter or margarine
Yogurt
Fresh fruits
Fresh vegetables
Ketchup

Mustard
Mayonnaise
Sandwich spread
Vinegar (white, cider, balsamic,
red wine, white wine)
Natural peanut butter
Natural (sugarless) jelly
Pickles

Baking

All-purpose flour
Whole wheat flour
Baking powder
Baking soda
Salt
Unsweetened cocoa powder
Granulated sugar
Brown sugar

Confectioners' sugar
Honey
Stevia
Shortening (solid vegetable)
Oil (vegetable, canola, extra-virgin olive
oil, pure olive oil)
Flavored extracts, including vanilla
Flaxseed*

*Notes freezer-friendly food

Pantry/Cupboard

Breads (sandwich bread, bagels, English muffins, pita bread, French bread, hamburger buns*)
Tortillas (flour, corn, whole wheat*)
Dried beans
Variety of canned beans, to substitute for cooked dried beans
White rice
Brown rice
Variety of pasta (white and whole Wheat)

Pasta sauces
Tomato sauce
Tomato paste
Variety of canned diced tomatoes
Jarred or canned salsa
Canned green chilies
Canned tuna, packed in water
Beef, chicken, vegetable broth, if not making homemade

Herbs and Spices

Kosher salt
black pepper
Crushed red pepper flakes
Basil
Oregano
Thyme
Rosemary
Italian seasoning
Minced onion
Garlic powder
Garlic salt
Onion powder

Ground cumin
Chili powder
Ground ginger
Ground cloves
Ground allspice
Nutmeg
Pumpkin pie spice
Poultry seasoning
Dill
Paprika
Lemon-pepper seasoning
Seafood seasonings

Other Cooking Supplies

Aluminum foil
Plastic wrap
Airtight freezer containers

Plastic freezer bags
Napkins
Paper towels

APPENDIX B

Essential Kitchen Gadgets

By utilizing certain electronic kitchen appliances and kitchen gadgets, you will save time and reduce frustrations when preparing breakfast and lunch meals. By having "the basic" ingredients in my stockpile, I don't find myself thinking "I just don't have anything to cook today," and grabbing the keys and heading out for a fast-food lunch.

Below are my recommendations for "must-haves" in the kitchen and on the countertop.

Small Appliances

Slow cooker
Bread machine
Blender or food processor

Mini chopper
Stand mixer or hand mixer

Baking Essentials

Mixing bowls
Measuring cups and spoons
Mixing and serving spoons
Spatulas
Plastic spatulas

Baking sheets
Square and rectangular glass baking
   dishes (8 × 8 inches, 9 × 13 inches)
Muffin pans; miniature to jumbo
Pizza pan or stone

For the Stovetop

Large Dutch oven or stockpot
Small, medium, and large saucepans

Skillet
Stove-top steamer

Handy Gadgets

Cheese grater
Garlic press
Slotted serving spoons
Wooden spoons

Kitchen shears
Chef's knife
Paring knife
Plastic and wood cutting boards

APPENDIX C

Online Resources

Today there exist hundreds, if not thousands, of resources on the Internet that help consumers save money, including the Web site $5 Dinners.com or www.5dollardinners.com. The site is updated on a daily basis with resources for meal planning, couponing, and strategic grocery shopping.

Below is a list of Web sites where coupons can be printed directly from the site, as well as information on how to find a blogger in your area who shares coupon match-ups for your store, plus where to find details on recommended daily food requirements.

Couponing Resources

www.coupons.com

www.smartsource.com

www.redplum.com

www.mambosprouts.com/coupons (for organic coupons)

www.hotcouponworld.com

www.slickdeals.net

www.couponmom.com

Grocery Store Coupon Matchups

Also, hundreds of bloggers post coupon matchups each week for hundreds of different stores across the country. To find a blogger in your area who offers this free service, simply Google your city's name and the phrase "grocery store coupon matchups."

By taking the time to explore these great online resources and make grocery lists and meal plans based on the sale items and coupon matchups, you are sure to start reducing your weekly grocery bill.

Portion Sizes and Recommended Daily Food Requirements

http://www.mypyramid.gov/mypyramid/index.aspx

INDEX

apples
  Apple Bars, 104
  Apple Cinnamon Oatmeal, 30
  Apple Cinnamon Pancakes, 93
  Baked Apple Brown Rice Pudding, 48
  Caramel Apple Breakfast Casserole, 77
  Cranberry-Apple Breakfast Casserole, 76
  Pumpkin Applesauce, 270
  Sausage, Apple, and Egg Casserole, 72
  Waldorf Chicken Salad Sandwiches, 161
  Whole Wheat Apple Waffles, 89
Autumn Salad, 238
avocados
  Avocado and Tomato Salad with Cilantro-Lime
    Dressing, 239–40
  Avocado, Corn, and Black Bean Salsa, 255
  Bacon, Avocado, and Cheese Breakfast Taco, 131
  Egg in a Nest with Avocado Circle Sandwiches,
    83–84
  Grilled Chicken and Avocado Wraps, 178
  Guacamole Veggie Pitas, 187

bacon
  Bacon, Avocado, and Cheese Breakfast Taco,
    131
  Bacon, Egg, and Cheese Bagel Melts, 136
  Bacon, Lettuce, and Tomato Wraps, 177
  Bacon and Egg Breakfast Pizza, 81–82
  Bacon and Egg Quesadillas, 55
  Bacon and Tomato Omelet, 78
  Bacon-Spinach Frittata, 65–66
  California Club Wraps, 179
  Ranch BLT Pasta Salad, 227
  Swiss BLT Melts, 167
bagels
  Bacon, Egg, and Cheese Bagel Melts, 136
  Bagel Toppings, 125
  Chicken-and-Tomato Bagel Sandwiches,
    170
Baked Apple Brown Rice Pudding, 48
Baked Oatmeal with Pecans, 39
Baked Parmesan Chicken Fingers, 204–5
Baked Walnut French Toast, 71

baking mixes, making-ahead, 19–20
Balsamic French Onion Soup, 199–200
Balsamic Veggie Wraps, 175
bananas
    Banana Blueberry Loaf Bread, 107
    Banana Nut Oatmeal, 33
    Banana Nut Waffles, 88
    Chocolate-Covered Bananas, 293
    Piña Colada Popsicles, 279
    Strawberry-Banana Smoothies, 273
bars
    Apple Bars, 104
    Protein-Packed Cereal Bars, 49
    Raspberry Cereal Bars, 50–51
batch cooking, 4
    money saving benefits, 18–19
    single ingredients, batch cooking for freezer, 20–21
    and stocking your freezer, 17
batch cooking (lunch hour), 140–42
batch cooking plans (breakfast), 22–25
    one hour prep: plan A, 22–23
    one hour prep: plan B, 23–24
    one hour prep: plan C, 24–25
    while prepping dinner: plan A, 25
    while prepping dinner: plan B, 25–26
beans
    Avocado, Corn, and Black Bean Salsa, 255
    Bean and Cheese Breakfast Tacos, 133
    Bean Quesadillas, 190
    Black Bean, Pepper, and Onion Wraps, 183
    Black Bean Coconut Brownies, 296–97
    Brown Rice and Red Bean Burritos, 181
    Chuckwagon Chili, 210
    Cilantro Black Beans and Rice, 217
    Cincinnati-Style Chili, 211
    Coconut Rice and Beans, 216
    Corn and Black Bean Quesadillas, 192
    Four Bean Salad, 252
    Salsa and Black Bean Chicken, 214
    Spicy Black Bean Burritos, 182
    Creamy Garlic and White Bean Dip, 272
    White Bean Chili, 212
beef
    Beef and Zucchini Tacos, 215
    Beef Taco Quesadillas, 191
    Chuckwagon Chili, 210
    Cincinnati-Style Chili, 211
    Spicy Sloppy Joes, 213
Berry Breakfast Bread Pudding, 59
biscuits
    Buttermilk Biscuits, 102
    Cheesy Drop Biscuits, 101
    Drop Biscuits with Cinnamon Butter, 99–100
    Sour Cream and Chive Drop Biscuits, 103
Black Bean, Pepper, and Onion Wraps, 183
Black Bean Coconut Brownies, 296–97
blueberries
    Banana Blueberry Loaf Bread, 107
    Blueberries and Cream Oatmeal make-ahead packet, 37–38
    Blueberry Baked Oatmeal, 40
    Blueberry Breakfast Bake, 73
    Blueberry Oat Muffins, 118–19
    Blueberry Smoothies, 275
    Lemon Blueberry Muffins, 114
bread
    Whole Wheat Toasting Bread, 108–9
    See also biscuits; breakfast breads; loaf bread; rolls; muffins
breakfast (at home and on-the-go), 9–28
    baking mixes, make-ahead, 19–20
    batch cooking, money saving benefits, 18–19
    batch cooking and stocking your freezer, 17
    breakfast breads (waffles, pancakes, muffins, and more), 86–125
    breakfast cereals (oatmeals, granolas, rice puddings, and more), 30–52
    breakfast ingredients, 15–16
    breakfast tacos and breakfast sandwiches, 127–36
    coffee, 16–17
    egg dishes (frittatas, breakfast casseroles, French toast bakes, and more), 54–84
    freezer-friendly foods, 21–22
    freezing and thawing foods, tips for, 26–28
    ingredients, 15–16
    meal planning, 12–15
    morning people vs. night owls, 10–11
    morning routines, 9–18
    planning, 300

breakfast *(continued)*
  sample batch cooking plans, 22–25
  single ingredients, batch cooking for freezer,
    20–21
  weekend breakfasts, 12
breakfast breads (waffles, pancakes, muffins, and
    more), 86–125
  Apple Bars, 104
  Apple Cinnamon Pancakes, 93
  Bagel Toppings, 125
  Banana Blueberry Loaf Bread, 107
  Banana Nut Waffles, 88
  Blueberry Oat Muffins, 118–19
  Buttermilk Biscuits, 102
  Buttermilk Waffles, 86
  Cheesy Drop Biscuits, 101
  Cheesy Sausage Muffins, 113
  Chocolate Chip Raspberry Pancakes, 97–98
  Cinnamon Butternut Squash Muffins,
    120–21
  Cranberry-Raisin Loaf Bread, 105–6
  Drop Biscuits with Cinnamon Butter, 99–100
  English Muffins Toppings, 124
  Ginger Maple Pancakes, 96
  Half Whole Wheat Pancakes, 91
  Lemon Blueberry Muffins, 114
  Maple Pecan Pancakes, 94
  Oatmeal Pancakes, 92
  Pumpkin Nut Muffins, 116–17
  Pumpkin Chocolate Chip Waffles, 90
  Pumpkin Pancakes, 95
  Sour Cream and Chive Drop Biscuits, 103
  Southwest Sausage Muffins, 112
  Spiced Pumpkin Waffles, 87
  Sweet Bran Muffins, 122–23
  Whole Wheat Apple Waffles, 89
  Whole Wheat Cinnamon Rolls with Flaxseed,
    110–11
  Whole Wheat Toasting Bread, 108–9
  Zucchini-Carrot Muffins, 115
breakfast casseroles
  Caramel Apple Breakfast Casserole, 77
  Cranberry-Apple Breakfast Casserole, 76
  Egg Tortilla Casserole, 56
  Fiesta Breakfast Casserole, 74
  Sausage, Apple, and Egg Casserole, 72

breakfast cereals (oatmeals, granolas, rice
    puddings, and more), 30–52
  Apple Cinnamon Oatmeal, 30
  Baked Apple Brown Rice Pudding, 48
  Baked Oatmeal with Pecans, 39
  Banana Nut Oatmeal, 33
  Blueberries and Cream Oatmeal make-ahead
    packet, 37–38
  Blueberry Baked Oatmeal, 40
  Cinnamon Raisin Oatmeal make-ahead
    packet, 37–38
  Cinnamon Swirl Oatmeal, 35
  Cranberry Oatmeal make-ahead packet, 37–38
  Make-Ahead Oatmeal Packets, 37–38
  Maple Pecan Oatmeal make-ahead packet,
    37–38
  Maple Pecan Oatmeal, 31
  Overnight Green Chile Grits, 48
  Overnight Honey Nut Granola, 43
  Overnight Spiced Granola, 43
  Peach-Raspberry Breakfast Parfait, 52
  Peaches 'n Cream Oatmeal, 34
  Peanut Butter–Chocolate Cream of Wheat, 45
  Protein-Packed Cereal Bars, 49
  Pumpkin Spice Oatmeal, 32
  Raspberry Cereal Bars, 50–51
  Slow Cooker "Cran-ola," 44
  Slow Cooker Raisin Oatmeal, 36
  Tropical Granola, 41
  Vanilla Brown Rice Pudding, 47
breakfast meal planning, 12–15
  the "days of the week" plan, 12–13
  the "eat-at-home" plan, 14–15
  the "grab-and-go" plan, 13–14
breakfast sandwiches. *See* breakfast tacos and
  breakfast sandwiches
breakfast tacos and breakfast sandwiches, 127–36
  Bacon, Avocado, and Cheese Breakfast Taco,
    131
  Bacon, Egg, and Cheese Bagel Melts, 136
  Bean and Cheese Breakfast Tacos, 133
  Ham and Swiss Breakfast Wraps, 132
  Hawaiian Ham-wiches, 135
  Potato, Egg, and Cheese Breakfast Tacos, 127
  Sausage, Egg, and Cheese Breakfast Tacos, 128
  Sausage Eggwiches, 134

Brown Rice and Red Bean Burritos, 181
brownies
    Black Bean Coconut Brownies, 296–97
    Double Chocolate Brownies, 295
burritos
    Brown Rice and Red Bean Burritos, 181
    Spicy Black Bean Burritos, 182
buttermilk
    Buttermilk Biscuits, 102
    Buttermilk Waffles, 86
Butterscotch Muffins, 290

Caesar Tuna Wraps, 180
Cajun Popcorn, 281
California Club Wraps, 179
Caramel Apple Breakfast Casserole, 77
cash instead of plastic, 2
casserole
    Caramel Apple Breakfast Casserole, 77
    Cranberry-Apple Breakfast Casserole, 76
    Egg Tortilla Casserole, 56
    Fiesta Breakfast Casserole, 74
    Sausage, Apple, and Egg Casserole, 72
cereal bars
    Protein-Packed Cereal Bars, 49
    Raspberry Cereal Bars, 50–51
cereals. See breakfast cereals
challenge weeks, 301
cheese
    Bacon, Avocado, and Cheese Breakfast Taco,
        131
    Bacon, Egg, and Cheese Bagel Melts, 136
    Bacon and Egg Quesadillas, 55
    Baked Parmesan Chicken Fingers, 204–5
    Bean and Cheese Breakfast Tacos, 133
    Cheesy Drop Biscuits, 101
    Cheesy Sausage Muffins, 113
    Cream Cheese–Stuffed French Toast, 75
    Grilled Cheese Sandwiches with Creamy
        Tomato Soup, 195–96
    Ham and Cheese Omelet, 79
    Ham and Swiss Breakfast Wraps, 132
    Ham and Swiss Frittata, 68
    Honey Mustard Ham and Cheese Melts, 166
    Mini Sausage Quiches, 62–63
    Parmesan Potato Wedges, 249

Potato, Egg, and Cheese Breakfast Tacos, 127
Sausage, Egg, and Cheese Breakfast Tacos, 128
Spinach and Swiss Omelet, 80
Swiss BLT Melts, 167
Swiss Tuna Melts, 165
Tuna Parmesan Sandwiches, 164
Turkey and Provolone Sandwiches, 168
chicken
    Baked Parmesan Chicken Fingers, 204–5
    Chicken-and-Tomato Bagel Sandwiches, 170
    Chicken Caesar Pasta Salad, 226
    Chicken Caesar Pita, 188
    Chicken Caesar Wraps, 174
    Chicken Pesto Sandwiches, 169
    Chicken Quesadillas, 189
    Chicken Spinach Pesto Pasta Salad, 225
    Chicken with Asparagus Pasta Salad, 223
    Curried Chicken Salad Sandwiches, 160
    Fruity Chicken Salad Sandwiches, 158
    Grilled Chicken and Avocado Wraps, 178
    Mandarin Chicken Salad Sandwiches, 159
    Salsa and Black Bean Chicken, 214
    Sesame Chicken Salad, 231–32
    Thyme Chicken Noodle Soup, 201
    Waldorf Chicken Salad Sandwiches, 161
Chickpea Summer Salad, 254
chili
    Chuckwagon Chili, 210
    Cincinnati-Style Chili, 211
    Oven Chili Fries, 248
    White Bean Chili, 212
chilies
    Fiesta Breakfast Casserole, 74
    Huevos Rancheros, 54
    Overnight Green Chile Grits
    Spicy Sloppy Joes, 213
chocolate
    Chocolate Chip Raspberry Pancakes, 97–98
    Chocolate Chocolate Chip Muffins, 288
    Chocolate-Covered Bananas, 293
    Double Chocolate Brownies, 295
    Peanut Butter–Chocolate Cream of Wheat, 45
    Peanut Butter Chocolate Muffins, 291–92
    Pumpkin Chocolate Chip Muffins, 289
    Pumpkin Chocolate Chip Waffles, 90
chopping (lunch hour), 140–42

Chuckwagon Chili, 210
Cilantro Black Beans and Rice, 217
Cincinnati-Style Chili, 211
cinnamon
    Apple Cinnamon Oatmeal, 30
    Apple Cinnamon Pancakes, 93
    Cinnamon Butter, 99–100
    Cinnamon Butternut Squash Muffins, 120–21
    Cinnamon Raisin Oatmeal make-ahead
        packet, 37–38
    Cinnamon–Sweet Potato Fries, 250
    Cinnamon Swirl Oatmeal, 35
    Drop Biscuits with Cinnamon Butter, 99–100
coconut
    Black Bean Coconut Brownies, 296–97
    Coconut Rice and Beans, 216
    Lemon Coconut Mini Loaves, 284
    Pumpkin Coconut Bread, 285
coffee, 16–17
cookies
    Oatmeal-Cranberry Cookies, 298
    Peanut Butter Walnut No-Bake Cookies,
        294
corn
    Avocado, Corn, and Black Bean Salsa, 255
    Cajun Popcorn, 281
    Corn and Black Bean Quesadillas, 192
    Pizza Popcorn, 283
    Quick Caramel Popcorn, 282
    Succotash Summer Salad, 256
couponing resources, 312–13
coupons
    combined with sale prices, 3
    organizing, 3
    See also strategic couponing
cranberries
    Cranberry-Apple Breakfast Casserole, 76
    Cranberry Oatmeal make-ahead packet,
        37–38
    Cranberry-Raisin Loaf Bread, 105–6
    Cranberry Turkey Salad Sandwiches, 162
    Slow Cooker "Cran-ola," 44
Cream Cheese–Stuffed French Toast, 75
Creamy Garlic and White Bean Dip, 272
Creamy Mango Tropical Popsicles, 280
Crunchy Tuna Sandwiches, 163

cucumber
    Cucumber and Orange Salad, 235
    Cucumber-Dill Sandwiches, 172
    Mint Cucumber Onion Salad, 254
Curried Chicken Salad Sandwiches, 160

Dehydrated Fruits, 267
Deviled Egg Salad Sandwiches, 171
Double Chocolate Brownies, 295
dressing
    Cilantro-Lime Dressing, 239–40
    Yogurt Dressing, 243
Drop Biscuits with Cinnamon Butter, 99–100
Dutch Baby with Berry Syrup, 57–58

egg dishes (frittatas, breakfast casseroles, French
        toast bakes, and more), 54–84
    Bacon, Egg, and Cheese Bagel Melts, 136
    Bacon, Egg, and Tomato Salad, 236–37
    Bacon and Egg Breakfast Pizza, 81–82
    Bacon and Egg Quesadillas, 55
    Bacon and Tomato Omelet, 78
    Bacon-Spinach Frittata, 65–66
    Baked Walnut French Toast, 71
    Berry Breakfast Bread Pudding, 59
    Blueberry Breakfast Bake, 73
    Caramel Apple Breakfast Casserole, 77
    Chorizo Breakfast Tacos, 130
    Cranberry-Apple Breakfast Casserole, 76
    Cream Cheese–Stuffed French Toast, 75
    Deviled Egg Salad Sandwiches, 171
    Dutch Baby with Berry Syrup, 57–58
    Egg in a Nest with Avocado Circle Sandwiches,
        83–84
    Egg Tortilla Casserole, 56
    Fiesta Breakfast Casserole, 74
    Ham and Cheese Omelet, 79
    Ham and Swiss Frittata, 68
    Huevos Rancheros, 54
    Italian Herb Frittata, 67
    Mini Sausage Quiches, 62–63
    Potato, Egg, and Cheese Breakfast Tacos, 127
    Raspberry French Toast, 70
    Salsa Breakfast Tacos, 129
    Sausage, Apple, and Egg Casserole, 72
    Sausage, Egg, and Cheese Breakfast Tacos, 128

Sausage Eggwiches, 134
Spinach and Swiss Omelet, 80
Tomato-Basil Quiche, 60–61
Vanilla Almond French Toast, 69
Zucchini-Tomato Frittata, 64
English muffins
    English Muffin Pizzas, 193
    English Muffins Toppings, 124

Fiesta Breakfast Casserole, 74
$5 Dinner Mom's Recipe for Being Successful
    with Breakfast and Lunch Preparation, 6
freezer
    batch cooking and stocking, 17
    single ingredients, batch cooking for, 20–21
freezer-friendly foods, 21–22
freezing and thawing foods (tips for), 26–28
    containers, 26–27
    freezing, length of time for, 27
    thawing options, 27–28
French toast
    Baked Walnut French Toast, 71
    Blueberry Breakfast Bake, 73
    Cream Cheese–Stuffed French Toast, 75
    Raspberry French Toast, 70
    Vanilla Almond French Toast, 69
frittata
    Bacon-Spinach Frittata, 65–66
    Ham and Swiss Frittata, 68
    Italian Herb Frittata, 67
    Zucchini-Tomato Frittata, 64
Four Bean Salad, 252
Fruit Salad with Yogurt Dressing, 243
Fruit Kebabs with Yogurt Dipping Sauce, 269
Fruity Chicken Salad Sandwiches, 158

Ginger Maple Pancakes, 96
granola
    Overnight Honey Nut Granola, 42
    Overnight Spiced Granola, 43
    Tropical Granola, 41
Grilled Cheese Sandwiches with Creamy Tomato
    Soup, 195–96
Grilled Chicken and Avocado Wraps, 178
grocery list and budget, 300–301
grocery shopping. See strategic grocery shopping

grocery store coupon matchups, 313
Guacamole Veggie Pitas, 187

Half Whole Wheat Pancakes, 91
ham
    Ham and Cheese Omelet, 79
    Ham and Swiss Breakfast Wraps, 132
    Ham and Swiss Frittata, 68
    Hawaiian Ham-wiches, 135
    Honey Mustard Ham and Cheese Melts, 166
Hawaiian Ham-wiches, 135
Homemade Hamburger Buns, 305–6
Homemade Pizza Sauce, 304
Homemade Spaghetti Sauce, 304
Honey Ginger Citrus Salad, 242
Honey Mustard Ham and Cheese Melts, 166
Huevos Rancheros, 54
hummus
    Roasted Garlic Hummus, 271
    Turkey and Hummus Sandwiches, 173

Italian Herb Frittata, 67
Italian Stuffed Shells, 209

kitchen gadgets
    baking essentials, 311
    handy gadgets, 311
    for the stovetop, 311
    small appliances, 310

Lasagna Roll Ups, 207–8
leftovers, 4
loaf bread
    Banana Blueberry Loaf Bread, 107
    Cranberry-Raisin Loaf Bread, 105–6
    Lemon Coconut Mini Loaves, 284
    Pumpkin Coconut Bread, 285
    See also bread
lunch hour (at home), 151–53
    cleanup, 152–53
    summertime, 152
lunch hour (brown bag for work), 146–48
    eating at desk, 146
    forgetting your lunch, 147
    packing for the office, 147–48
    taking a shorter lunch break, 146–47

lunch hour (time-saving tips), 140–43
  batch cooking, chopping and make-ahead
    foods, 140–42
  slow cooker adaptable, 142–43
lunches (at home and on-the-go), 139–56
  brown bag for work, 146–48
  frustrations, 153–56
  meal planning, 145–46
  money-saving tips, 143–45
  pasta salads and garden salads, 220–40
  planning, 300
  sandwiches, wraps, quesadillas, and more,
    158–97
  school and day care, 148–51
  side salads and side dishes for lunch, 242–56
  soups and other hot lunches, 199–218

Macaroni Salad, 220
magic grocery store budget number, 2
make-ahead foods (lunch hour), 140–42
Make-Ahead Oatmeal Packets, 37–38
Mandarin Chicken Salad Sandwiches, 159
mangos
  Creamy Mango Tropical Popsicles, 280
  Mango-Raspberry Smoothies, 274
maple
  Maple Pecan Oatmeal, 31
  Maple Pecan Oatmeal make-ahead packet, 37
  Maple Pecan Pancakes, 94
marketing strategies, avoiding, 2
meal planning. *See* strategic meal planning
meal planning (breakfast), 12–15
  the "days of the week" plan, 12–13
  the "eat-at-home" plan, 14–15
  the "grab-and-go" plan, 13–14
Meatless Shepherd's Pie, 218
melts
  Bacon, Egg, and Cheese Bagel Melts, 136
  Honey Mustard Ham and Cheese Melts, 166
  Swiss BLT Melts, 167
  Swiss Tuna Melts, 165
  See also quesadillas; sandwiches; tacos; wraps
Minestrone Pasta Salad, 221
Mini Sausage Quiches, 62–63
Mint Cucumber Onion Salad, 254
morning people vs. night owls, 10–11

morning routines, 9–18
Muffin Pan Snacks, 268
muffins
  Blackberry Mini Muffins, 286–87
  Blueberry Oat Muffins, 118–19
  Butterscotch Muffins, 290
  Cheesy Sausage Muffins, 113
  Chocolate Chocolate Chip Muffins, 288
  Cinnamon Butternut Squash Muffins,
    120–21
  English Muffins Toppings, 124
  Lemon Blueberry Muffins, 114
  Peanut Butter Chocolate Muffins, 291–92
  Pumpkin Chocolate Chip Muffins, 289
  Pumpkin Nut Muffins, 116–17
  Southwest Sausage Muffins, 112
  Sweet Bran Muffins, 122–23
  Zucchini-Carrot Muffins, 115
  See also bread
Mustard Potato Salad, 244

"never-pay-more-than" prices, 3
nuts
  Baked Oatmeal with Pecans, 39
  Baked Walnut French Toast, 71
  Banana Nut Oatmeal, 33
  Banana Nut Waffles, 88
  Chicken Pesto Sandwiches, 169
  Maple Pecan Oatmeal, 31
  Maple Pecan Oatmeal make-ahead packet,
    37–38
  Maple Pecan Pancakes, 94
  Overnight Honey Nut Granola, 42
  Peanut Butter–Chocolate Cream of Wheat, 45
  Peanut Butter Surprise Sandwiches, 197
  Peanut Butter Walnut No-Bake Cookies,
    294
  Protein-Packed Cereal Bars, 49
  Pumpkin Nut Muffins, 116–17
  Vanilla Almond French Toast, 69
  Waldorf Chicken Salad Sandwiches, 161

oatmeal
  Apple Cinnamon Oatmeal, 30
  Baked Oatmeal with Pecans, 39
  Banana Nut Oatmeal, 33

Blueberries and Cream Oatmeal make-ahead
    packet, 37–38
Blueberry Baked Oatmeal, 40
Blueberry Oat Muffins, 118–19
Cinnamon Raisin Oatmeal make-ahead
    packet, 37–38
Cinnamon Swirl Oatmeal, 35
Cranberry Oatmeal make-ahead packet,
    37–38
Maple Pecan Oatmeal, 31
Maple Pecan Oatmeal make-ahead packet,
    37–38
Oatmeal Pancakes, 92
Peaches 'n Cream Oatmeal, 34
Pumpkin Spice Oatmeal, 32
Slow Cooker Raisin Oatmeal, 36
omelets
    Bacon and Tomato Omelet, 78
    Ham and Cheese Omelet, 79
    Spinach and Swiss Omelet, 80
online resources, 312
    couponing resources, 312–13
    grocery store coupon matchups, 313
    portion sizes and recommended daily food
        requirements, 313
oranges
    Cucumber and Orange Salad, 235
    Mandarin Chicken Salad Sandwiches, 159
Oven Chili Fries, 248
Overnight Green Chile Grits, 48
Overnight Honey Nut Granola, 43
Overnight Spiced Granola, 43

pancakes
    Apple Cinnamon Pancakes, 93
    Chocolate Chip Raspberry Pancakes, 97–98
    Dutch Baby with Berry Syrup, 57–58
    Ginger Maple Pancakes, 96
    Half Whole Wheat Pancakes, 91
    Maple Pecan Pancakes, 94
    Oatmeal Pancakes, 92
    Pumpkin Pancakes, 95
pantry staples list, 303
    backing, 307
    freezer, 307
    herbs and spices, 308

Homemade Hamburger Buns, 305–6
Homemade Pizza Sauce, 304
Homemade Salsa Fresca (Fresh Salsa), 306
Homemade Spaghetti Sauce, 304
other cooking supplies, 309
pantry/cupboard, 308
refrigerator, 307
Pantry Trail Mix, 266
Parmesan Potato Wedges, 249
pasta
    Chicken Caesar Pasta Salad, 226
    Chicken Spinach Pesto Pasta Salad, 225
    Chicken with Asparagus Pasta Salad, 223
    Italian Stuffed Shells, 209
    Lasagna Roll Ups, 207–8
    Macaroni Salad, 220
    Minestrone Pasta Salad, 221
    Spinach Orzo Pasta Salad, 229
    Ranch BLT Pasta Salad, 227
    Southwest Pasta Salad, 222
    Summer Squash Pasta Salad, 224
    Tuna with Lemon and Dill Pasta Salad, 228
peaches
    Peach-Raspberry Breakfast Parfait, 52
    Peach-Strawberry Smoothies, 278
    Peaches 'n Cream Oatmeal, 34
peanut butter
    Peanut Butter–Chocolate Cream of Wheat, 45
    Peanut Butter Chocolate Muffins, 291–92
    Peanut Butter Surprise Sandwiches, 197
    Peanut Butter Walnut No-Bake Cookies,
        294
    Protein-Packed Cereal Bars, 49
pecans
    Baked Oatmeal with Pecans, 39
    Maple Pecan Oatmeal, 31
    Maple Pecan Oatmeal make-ahead packet,
        37–38
    Maple Pecan Pancakes, 94
    Overnight Honey Nut Granola, 42
Piña Colada Popsicles, 279
pineapple
    Fruity Chicken Salad Sandwiches, 158
    Hawaiian Ham-wiches, 135
    Pineapple Coleslaw, 247
    Tropical Granola, 41

pitas
    Chicken Caesar Pita, 188
    Guacamole Veggie Pitas, 187
    Pepperoni Pizza Pitas, 84
    Spaghetti Sauce Pitas, 185
    Tuna Pitas, 186
pizza
    Bacon and Egg Breakfast Pizza, 81–82
    English Muffin Pizzas, 193
    Pepperoni Pizza Pitas, 84
Pizza Popcorn, 283
popcorn
    Cajun Popcorn, 281
    Pizza Popcorn, 283
    Quick Caramel Popcorn, 282
popsicles
    Creamy Mango Tropical Popsicles, 280
    Piña Colada Popsicles, 279
pork
    Bacon and Egg Breakfast Pizza, 81–82
    Bacon and Egg Quesadillas, 55
    Bacon and Tomato Omelet, 78
    Cheesy Sausage Muffins, 113
    Ham and Cheese Omelet, 79
    Ham and Swiss Breakfast Wraps, 132
    Ham and Swiss Frittata, 68
    Hawaiian Ham-wiches, 135
    Honey Mustard Ham and Cheese Melts, 166
    Mini Sausage Quiches, 62–63
    Sausage, Apple, and Egg Casserole, 72
    Sausage, Egg, and Cheese Breakfast Tacos, 128
    Sausage Eggwiches, 134
    Southwest Sausage Muffins, 112
portion sizes and recommended daily food requirements, 313
potatoes
    Cinnamon–Sweet Potato Fries, 250
    Mustard Potato Salad, 244
    Oven Chili Fries, 248
    Parmesan Potato Wedges, 249
    Potato, Egg, and Cheese Breakfast Tacos, 127
    Roasted Red Potato Salad, 245
    Twice-Baked, Fully Loaded Baked Potato Soup, 202–3

prep work, 301
Protein-Packed Cereal Bars, 49
pumpkins
    Pumpkin Applesauce, 270
    Pumpkin Chocolate Chip Muffins, 289
    Pumpkin Chocolate Chip Waffles, 90
    Pumpkin Coconut Bread, 285
    Pumpkin Nut Muffins, 116–17
    Pumpkin Pancakes, 95
    Pumpkin Smoothies, 276
    Pumpkin Spice Oatmeal, 32
    Spiced Pumpkin Waffles, 87

quesadillas
    Bean Quesadillas, 190
    Beef Taco Quesadillas, 191
    Chicken Quesadillas, 189
    Corn and Black Bean Quesadillas, 192
    See also melts; sandwiches; tacos; wraps
quiche
    Mini Sausage Quiches, 62–63
    Tomato-Basil Quiche, 60–61
Quick Caramel Popcorn, 282

raisins
    Broccoli-Raisin Salad, 251
    Cinnamon Raisin Oatmeal make-ahead packet, 37–38
    Cranberry-Raisin Loaf Bread, 105–6
    Slow Cooker Raisin Oatmeal, 36
Ranch BLT Pasta Salad, 227
raspberries
    Chocolate Chip Raspberry Pancakes, 97–98
    Mango-Raspberry Smoothies, 274
    Peach-Raspberry Breakfast Parfait, 52
    Raspberry Cereal Bars, 50–51
    Raspberry French Toast, 70
rice
    Brown Rice and Red Bean Burritos, 181
    Cilantro Black Beans and Rice, 217
    Coconut Rice and Beans, 216
rice pudding
    Baked Apple Brown Rice Pudding, 48
    Vanilla Brown Rice Pudding, 47
Roasted Garlic Hummus, 271
Roasted Red Potato Salad, 245

rolls
    Whole Wheat Cinnamon Rolls with Flaxseed,
       110–11
    See also bread

salads
    Autumn Salad, 238
    Avocado and Tomato Salad with Cilantro-Lime
       Dressing, 239–40
    Bacon, Egg, and Tomato Salad, 236–37
    Cucumber and Orange Salad, 235
    Sesame Chicken Salad, 231–32
    Summer Squash and Lentil Salad, 230
    Taco Salad, 233–34
salads (pasta)
    Chicken Caesar Pasta Salad, 226
    Chicken Spinach Pesto Pasta Salad, 225
    Chicken with Asparagus Pasta Salad, 223
    Macaroni Salad, 220
    Minestrone Pasta Salad, 221
    Ranch BLT Pasta Salad, 227
    Southwest Pasta Salad, 222
    Spinach Orzo Pasta Salad, 229
    Summer Squash Pasta Salad, 224
    Tuna with Lemon and Dill Pasta Salad,
       228
salads (side)
    Broccoli-Raisin Salad, 251
    Chickpea Summer Salad, 253
    Four Bean Salad, 252
    Fruit Salad with Yogurt Dressing, 243
    Honey Ginger Citrus Salad, 242
    Mint Cucumber Onion Salad, 254
    Mustard Potato Salad, 244
    Pineapple Coleslaw, 247
    Roasted Red Potato Salad, 245
    Succotash Summer Salad, 256
    Sweet and Spicy Coleslaw, 246
salsa
    Avocado, Corn, and Black Bean Salsa, 255
    Salsa and Black Bean Chicken, 214
    Homemade Salsa Fresca (Fresh Salsa), 306
sample batch cooking plans (breakfast), 22–25
    one hour prep: plan A, 22–23
    one hour prep: plan B, 23–24
    one hour prep: plan C, 24–25

    while prepping dinner: plan A, 25
    while prepping dinner: plan B, 25–26
sandwiches
    Chicken-and-Tomato Bagel Sandwiches,
       170
    Chicken Pesto Sandwiches, 169
    Crunchy Tuna Sandwiches, 163
    Cucumber-Dill Sandwiches, 172
    Curried Chicken Salad Sandwiches, 160
    Deviled Egg Salad Sandwiches, 171
    Egg in a Nest with Avocado Circle Sandwiches,
       83–84
    Fruity Chicken Salad Sandwiches, 158
    Hawaiian Ham-wiches, 135
    Mandarin Chicken Salad Sandwiches, 159
    Peanut Butter Surprise Sandwiches, 197
    Sausage Eggwiches, 134
    Spicy Sloppy Joes, 213
    Tuna Parmesan Sandwiches, 164
    Turkey and Hummus Sandwiches, 173
    Turkey and Provolone Sandwiches, 168
    Waldorf Chicken Salad Sandwiches, 161
    See also breakfast tacos and breakfast
       sandwiches; burritos; melts; pitas;
       quesadillas; tacos; wraps
sauce
    Homemade Pizza Sauce, 304
    Homemade Spaghetti Sauce, 304
sausages
    Cheesy Sausage Muffins, 113
    Chorizo Breakfast Tacos, 130
    Mini Sausage Quiches, 62–63
    Sausage, Apple, and Egg Casserole, 72
    Sausage, Egg, and Cheese Breakfast Tacos,
       128
    Sausage Eggwiches, 134
    Southwest Sausage Muffins, 112
Sesame Chicken Salad, 231–32
side dishes
    Avocado, Corn, and Black Bean Salsa, 255
    Cinnamon—Sweet Potato Fries, 250
    Oven Chili Fries, 248
    Parmesan Potato Wedges, 249
side salads. *See* salads (side)
single ingredients, batch cooking for freezer,
    20–21

slow cooker
    Slow Cooker "Cran-ola," 44
    Slow Cooker Raisin Oatmeal, 36
smoothies
    Blueberry Smoothies, 275
    Mango-Raspberry Smoothies, 274
    Peach-Strawberry Smoothies, 278
    Pumpkin Smoothies, 276
    Strawberry-Banana Smoothies, 273
    Spinach "Green" Smoothies, 277
snacking
    grazing or scheduled snacks, 260
    meal-planning tips, 261
    planning, 300
    portion control, 262
    sensible snacking, 259–60
    snack habits, changing, 260–61
    snack recipes, 263–64
    snack time presentation, 262–63
    time-and money-saving tips for healthy snacks, 261
snacks
    Cajun Popcorn, 281
    Creamy Mango Tropical Popsicles, 280
    Dehydrated Fruits, 267
    Muffin Pan Snacks, 268
    Pantry Trail Mix, 266
    Piña Colada Popsicles, 279
    Pizza Popcorn, 283
    Quick Caramel Popcorn, 282
soup
    Balsamic French Onion Soup, 199–200
    Creamy Tomato Soup, 195–96
    Thyme Chicken Noodle Soup, 201
    Twice-Baked, Fully Loaded Baked Potato Soup, 202–3
Sour Cream and Chive Drop Biscuits, 103
Southwest Pasta Salad, 222
Southwest Sausage Muffins, 112
Spaghetti Sauce Pitas, 185
Spiced Pumpkin Waffles, 87
Spicy Black Bean Burritos, 182
Spicy Sloppy Joes, 213
spinach
    Bacon-Spinach Frittata, 65–66
    Spinach and Swiss Omelet, 80

Spinach "Green" Smoothies, 277
    Spinach Orzo Pasta Salad, 229
stockpiling, 3
store circulars, look at before entering, 2
strategic couponing
    coupons combined with sale prices, 3
    "never-pay-more-than" prices, 3
    stockpiling, 3
strategic grocery shopping
    cash, use instead of plastic, 2
    magic grocery store budget number, 2
    marketing strategies, avoid, 2
    store circulars, look at before entering, 2
strategic meal planning, 4–6
    batch cooking, 4
    benefits, 4
    leftovers, 4
    phases of meal planning, 4
strawberries
    Peach-Strawberry Smoothies, 278
    Strawberry-Banana Smoothies, 273
Succotash Summer Salad, 256
summer squash
    Summer Squash Pasta Salad, 224
    Summer Squash and Lentil Salad, 230
Sweet and Spicy Coleslaw, 246
Sweet Bran Muffins, 122–23

tacos
    Bacon, Avocado, and Cheese Breakfast Taco, 131
    Bean and Cheese Breakfast Tacos, 133
    Beef and Zucchini Tacos, 215
    Beef Taco Quesadillas, 191
    Chorizo Breakfast Tacos, 130
    Potato, Egg, and Cheese Breakfast Tacos, 127
    Salsa Breakfast Tacos, 129
    Sausage, Egg, and Cheese Breakfast Tacos, 128
    Taco Salad, 233–34
    See also melts; quesadillas; sandwiches; wraps
thawing foods. *See* freezing and thawing foods
Thyme Chicken Noodle Soup, 201
tomatoes
    Avocado and Tomato Salad with Cilantro-Lime Dressing, 239–40
    Bacon, Lettuce, and Tomato Wraps, 177

Bacon and Tomato Omelet, 78
Chicken-and-Tomato Bagel Sandwiches, 170
Creamy Tomato Soup, 195–96
Ranch BLT Pasta Salad, 227
Swiss BLT Melts, 167
Tomato-Basil Quiche, 60–61
Zucchini-Tomato Frittata, 64
tortillas
    Bacon and Egg Quesadillas, 55
    Egg Tortilla Casserole, 56
Tropical Granola, 41
tuna
    Caesar Tuna Wraps, 180
    Crunchy Tuna Sandwiches, 163
    Swiss Tuna Melts, 165
    Tuna Parmesan Sandwiches, 164
    Tuna Pitas, 186
    Tuna with Lemon and Dill Pasta Salad, 228
turkey
    Cranberry Turkey Salad Sandwiches, 162
    Turkey and Hummus Sandwiches, 173
    Turkey and Provolone Sandwiches, 168
Twice-Baked, Fully Loaded Baked Potato Soup, 202–3

Vanilla Almond French Toast, 69
Vanilla Brown Rice Pudding, 47

waffles
    Banana Nut Waffles, 88
    Buttermilk Waffles, 86
    Pumpkin Chocolate Chip Waffles, 90
    Spiced Pumpkin Waffles, 87
    Whole Wheat Apple Waffles, 89

Waldorf Chicken Salad Sandwiches, 161
walnuts
    Baked Walnut French Toast, 71
    Banana Nut Oatmeal, 33
    Banana Nut Waffles, 88
    Peanut Butter Walnut No-Bake Cookies, 294
    Pumpkin Nut Muffins, 116–17
    Waldorf Chicken Salad Sandwiches, 161
weekend breakfasts, 12
White Bean Chili, 212
whole wheat
    Half Whole Wheat Pancakes, 91
    Whole Wheat Apple Waffles, 89
    Whole Wheat Cinnamon Rolls with Flaxseed, 110–11
    Whole Wheat Toasting Bread, 108–9
wraps
    Bacon, Lettuce, and Tomato Wraps, 177
    Balsamic Veggie Wraps, 175
    Black Bean, Pepper, and Onion Wraps, 183
    California Club Wraps, 179
    Caesar Tuna Wraps, 180
    Chicken Caesar Wraps, 174
    Grilled Chicken and Avocado Wraps, 178
    Ham and Swiss Breakfast Wraps, 132
    Pepper Turkey Wraps, 176
    See also melts; quesadillas; sandwiches; tacos

zucchini
    Beef and Zucchini Tacos, 215
    Summer Squash Pasta Salad, 224
    Zucchini-Carrot Muffins, 115
    Zucchini-Tomato Frittata, 64

Learn to be a savvy supermarket shopper...cut your weekly food budget...banish fast food from the dinner table... serve your family meals that are delicious and good for them. Erin Chase, "The $5 Dinner Mom," is here to help.

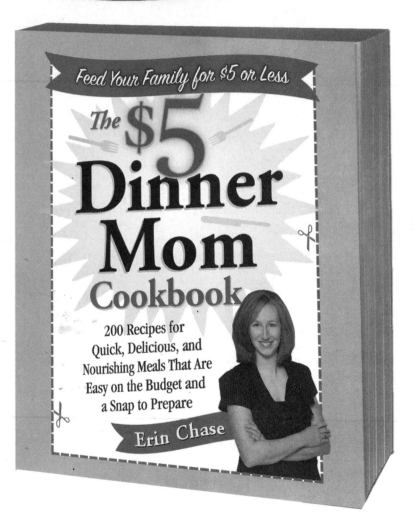

Feed Your Family for $5 or Less

The $5 Dinner Mom Cookbook

200 Recipes for Quick, Delicious, and Nourishing Meals That Are Easy on the Budget and a Snap to Prepare

Erin Chase

"Her recipes are simple, healthy, delicious, and always affordable. She proves that budget cooking does not have to be boring!"
—Stephanie Nelson, author of *The Coupon Mom's Guide to Cutting Your Grocery Bills in Half*

 St. Martin's Griffin   www.stmartins.com